**Unavoidable
Industrial
Restructuring in
Latin America**

Unavoidable Industrial
Restructuring in
Latin America

Fernando Fajnzylber

Duke University Press
Durham and London
1990

To Alicia Barrios

© 1990 Duke University Press
All rights reserved
Printed in the United States of America
on acid-free paper ∞
Library of Congress Cataloging-in-Publication Data
appear on the last page of this book

Contents

Illustrations

Tables

Acknowledgments

The author wishes to express his acknowledgments to the institutions and persons who contributed to this study, particularly the Center for International Studies at Duke University, sponsor of the McWane Lectures, where the first version was presented in February 1987. The content of the study is based on the research and technical assistance activities the author has performed as UNIDO Regional Advisor in Latin America within the framework of the Joint ECLAC / UNIDO Industry and Technology Division. Invaluable documentation support was provided by the ECLAC office in Washington and the ECLAC library in Santiago, Chile. The author also benefited from the suggestions and comments of various colleagues: Oscar Altimir, Antonio Barros de Castro, Colin Bradford, José Casar, Enzo Faletto, Ricardo Ffrench-Davis, Gary Gereffi, David Ibarra, Eduardo Jacobs, François Le Guay, Philippe Lorino, José Mindlin, Herman Muegge, Aníbal Pinto, Gert Rosenthal, Jaime Ross, Alejandro Schejtman, Osvaldo Sunkel, María C. Tavares, Morris Teubal, Alain Tourain, Víctor Tokman, and Roberto Zahler. This work could not have been completed without the technical collaboration, enthusiasm, and efficiency of Regina Postas, and the generous and competent secretarial backing of Elvira Lindstrand, both ECLAC staff members.

The content of the work is the exclusive responsibility of the author and does not necessarily reflect the viewpoints of the institutions and persons mentioned above.

Introduction

Reflections on Latin American development necessarily encounter the question of the applicability of the current analytical categorization of the region. Given the diversity of the situations and the formative processes of the respective nations, a suitable typology would include a number of cases equal to the number of countries. Unfortunately, the central problem is the lack of a ready development theory that would provide a sufficient explanation for recent global socioeconomic transformations, so there would continue to be numerous doubts, even for each of the national cases.

After two centuries of abundant, rigorous study of the origins and consequences of the Industrial Revolution in England, there is still controversy with respect to those themes and the subsequent decline in the relative position of that country within the international context. The diverse interpretations of the remarkable "late industrialization" of Japan are still far from convergence, and the experiences of some Latin American countries do not throw any light on this situation. Argentina, which had a per capita income in 1913 greater than that of France and almost double that of Italy (the latter situation lasting until the end of the 1950s), presently has a per capita income equivalent to one-fifth that of France and somewhat more than one-third that of Italy. Brazil's industrialization has perhaps received the greatest attention from the academic media, both in Latin America and abroad. Nevertheless, there would appear to be four different interpretations of the origins and processes that led to Brazilian industrialization, all based on an agricultural export element:[1]

1. The "adverse impacts" theory
2. The theory that industrialization is guided by the expansion of primary exports

3. The interpretation based on the evolution of capitalism in Brazil
4. The approach that stresses public sector responsibility in the promotion of industrialization.

Governments must act despite this lack of firm theoretical consensus; moreover, they find themselves exposed to intellectual fashions that periodically invade the social sciences. In the face of this double challenge— theoretical precariousness and intellectual fashions—there is at least one remedy which, although not sufficient to confront these intellectual challenges, does tend to lessen some of their unfavorable consequences: that is, to recognize those internal and international realities that persist despite the absence of coherent interpretations.

Accumulated experience in economic development indicates that one of the prominent features of the recognition process is the combination of learning from the lesson of the more advanced societies as well as from the economic and social innovations specific to the deficiencies and potentialities of the less advanced countries. This explains the widely recognized fact that the inroads of transformation vary in terms of content, itinerary, and institutions, thus reflecting this combination of learning and innovation.[2] For industrialization, essential to the development process due to its inclusion of technical progress and increase in productivity, the relevance of the learning-innovation axis acquires greater importance. One of the main features of the industrialization process in Latin America has been the asymmetry between the salient component of imitation, a phase which precedes learning, and the marginal component of socioeconomic innovation.

This study has been built on the basis of the following fact: notwithstanding that Latin American countries have shared and reiterated the relevance of the objectives of growth and equity, their incapacity to simultaneously reach reasonable levels of success in those two goals is evident. This is the "empty box" syndrome to which reference will be made later on.

A previous study[3] posited the need for Latin American countries to modify the pattern of industrialization around which the productive structure of recent decades has rotated. An effort is made here to consider both the prevailing characterization of the industrialization pattern, which must be modified, and the directions, requisites, and features of the policies necessary to overcome the empty box.

Chapter 1 presents the empty box syndrome and attempts to characterize the process of industrialization in Latin America in terms of its contribution to the objectives of growth and equity. The basic common traits of the distinct countries as well as those national specificities that define regional heterogeneity are identified. Moreover, the features that characterize the industrial crisis of the 1980s are presented schematically. Chapter 2 explores the basic trait of the industrialization and development pattern of Latin America, the "black box." This refers to *Latin America's precariousness in terms of creatively absorbing and incorporating technical progress in order to respond to regional deficiencies and potentialities*. Also, the links between technical progress, the industrial sector, and the fragile contribution of macroeconomics are highlighted. Finally, the technological transformations at an international level, as well as their implications for Latin America, are outlined. Chapter 3 proposes an analytical framework for addressing the central relationship that serves as the backbone of this work, the link between the pattern of industrialization and development and the attainment of the objectives of growth and equity.

In the following chapters this analytical framework is contrasted with reality. Chapter 4 presents evidence from the three advanced industrial countries—the United States, Japan, and the Federal Republic of Germany (FRG)—that form and determine the pattern of consumption, production, communications, transportation, and energy currently prevailing at an international level. In chapter 5 attention moves to Europe, where two subregions are distinguished. The first group is composed of the major Western European countries with which Latin America has had important economic, political, and cultural relations in the past; in many cases, these relations still exist, particularly in the southern part of Latin America. The second group is composed of the Nordic countries, where an interesting relationship exists among the availability of natural resources, specialized industrialization oriented toward the international market, and a solid democratic, participative system. Chapter 6 returns to Latin America, using the analytical framework proposed in chapter 3 to compare that region with other countries undergoing recent industrialization whose industrial performance seems more favorable. Specifically, the contrast between Latin America and a group of countries identified as "growth-with-equity industrializing countries"

(GEICs) is emphasized. In conclusion, reflections are made with regard to the goals and actions, in Latin America and in the industrialized North, that could contribute to confront what was defined in the first chapter as the challenge of Latin America: that is, to approach the heretofore "empty box" wherein growth converges with equity.

The optimism with which the Latin American countries embarked on the process of industrialization—in the hope that it would lead to a more dynamic and equitable growth—has given place to disillusionment and perplexity and, in some cases, to a false analysis which questions industrialization as such and not particular regional processes. There is no theory to guide the formulation of strategies and policies geared towards changing the pattern of development and the role of industrialization, and the proposals derived from purely macroeconomic considerations have demonstrated their insufficiency. The dubious nature of the inspirational sources for the implementation of a process of structural change conducive to growth with equity is thus clear.

The aim of this study is to analyze the factors that lie at the root of the peculiar inability of all Latin American countries to achieve growth *and* equity. This is in clear contrast with the experience of many developed and underdeveloped nations, in spite of the wide range of institutional and political arrangements and the diverse availability of resources that can be found in Latin America. Our hope is to contribute to the current intense debate in the region among researchers, economic policy-makers, and politicians who perceive the urgent need to ensure that measures adopted to overcome the profound regional crisis do not reinforce those structural factors that led to stagnation and/or inequity.

1. The Empty Box in Latin America

Industrialization, Growth, and Equity

Under the most varied circumstances, the governments of Latin America, like the rest of the world, uphold growth and equity as the fundamental objectives of development. To what degree have the countries of the region reached one or both of these objectives throughout the course of their development?

If we define the rate of expansion of advanced countries during the last two decades as a criterion of dynamism (annually 2.4 percent of per capita GDP) and accept the relationship between the earnings of the 40 percent of the population with the lowest income and the 10 percent of the population with the highest income as a definition of equity, we find that this relationship in the advanced countries reaches an average of 0.8 percent at the end of the 1970s and the beginning of the 1980s. In other words, 40 percent of the population have earnings equal to 80 percent of the earnings of 10 percent of the population. Supposing that for Latin America we accept as a dividing line between the most equitable and the least equitable countries a relationship similar to this one, but with a value of 0.4 percent, this would mean proposing as an objective a level of "equity" equivalent to half that prevailing in industrialized countries.[1] In crossing these two variables, growth and equity, wherein the dividing line for dynamism is the average growth of advanced countries during the 1965–1984 period and the dividing line for equity is the abovementioned 40–10 relationship, a double-entry matrix is created, where an "empty box" can be found (see table 1.1). This empty box should correspond to those countries that have simultaneously reached a faster growth rate than that of the developed countries *and* achieved

1

Table 1.1 Strategic Goals: Growth-Equity in Latin America (percentages)

$$\text{Equity:} \frac{40\% \text{ lowest incomes}}{10\% \text{ highest incomes}} \text{(since 1970)}$$

	<0.4[b]	≥0.4
GDP per capita average annual growth rate (1965-1986) <2.4[a]	Bolivia Costa Rica Chile El Salvador Peru Guatemala Venezuela Honduras Haiti Nicaragua GDP:21.0[c]	Argentina Uruguay GDP: 13.0[c]
≥2.4	Brazil Panama Colombia Dominican Ecuador Republic Mexico Paraguay GDP: 66.0[c]	

Source: Joint ECLAC/UNIDO Industry and Technology Division, based on data from the World Bank, *World Development Report*, 1987 and 1988, Oxford University Press.
[a]Industrialized countries GDP/per capita growth rate 1965–1974.
[b]Industrialized countries half comparable relation.
[c]GDP regional participation.

a level of equity higher than half the level of equity that prevails in those countries. The empty box poses a key questions that this work will attempt to answer.

Approximately 66 percent of the regional gross domestic product (GDP) is generated in countries that we could call dynamic-disarticulated (Brazil, Mexico, Colombia, Ecuador, Panama, Paraguay, and the Dominican Republic); 13 percent could be found in those countries that we could call articulated but stagnant (Argentina and Uruguay), and the remaining 21 percent would correspond to countries in which the condition of disarticulation and stagnation coexist. The latter category is comprised of some national situations considered to be potentially "explosive," so much so that—vis-à-vis a structural situation of stagnation and social disarticulation reflected in unequal income distribution—it would certainly not be surprising to witness the upsurge of a broad spectrum of alternative proposals invoking society to overcome this unsatisfactory, ongoing reality. Nevertheless, until now, the growth-with-equity box is empty, at least for the group of countries where comparative information is available.

The location of a country in the different boxes is obviously conditioned by a divider. Thus, for example, if the limit of equity were to be moved down slightly, countries such as Costa Rica, Chile, and Venezuela would appear in the upper right-hand box; if the limit of growth were moved up, the number of dynamic countries would be reduced, maintaining the insertion of countries such as Brazil, Mexico, Ecuador, and Colombia. The empty box could be imagined as a space to which only countries that have advanced in their development process could have access. This speculation, however, would be refuted by hard facts when considering countries from other regions with an income and development level in some way comparable to that existing in Latin America.

The comparative study of distinct national cases within and outside the region constitutes the basic approach of this work. Specialists in history would agree that, in order to understand a region such as Latin America, it is indispensable to know about other regions. Although this would seem to be obvious, it has not always been at the center of the methodological approach utilized in addressing the subject of development in the region.[2] In initiating the exploration of the origins of the empty box, it might be interesting to contrast the relative position of Latin America vis-à-vis the international economy in the different areas of economic activity (see table 1.2). This could serve as an initial "clue" to this research.

In terms of economic indicators, the greatest contribution of the region is to that of population. More precisely, there is a tendency toward a consistent decrease in the participation of the region as indicators of activities with growing intellectual aggregate value are approached. In terms of population, the region falls into the 8 percent category. When considering its GDP, it drops to 7 percent. If manufactures are considered, it is reduced to 6 percent. If, within the manufacturing sector, attention is concentrated on capital goods, the presence of the region is drastically reduced to 3 percent. Consideration of the participation of engineers

Table 1.2 Latin America: Fragile World Insertion (percentages)

Participation with respect to the world in: (early 1980s)	
Population	8.0
GDP	7.0
Manufacturing product	6.0
Capital goods	3.0
Engineers and scientifics	2.4
Research and technological development resources	1.8
Manufactured exports[a]	1.8
Scientific authors	1.3

Source: Joint ECLAC/UNIDO Industry and Technology Division, based on data from UNESCO, *Statistical Yearbook,* various years; UNIDO, DATABASE; and United Nations, *Demographic Yearbook 1986* (STA/ESA/STA/SER.R:/16), New York, 1988.
[a]Manufactured exports defined as SITC, Section 5 to 8 less division 68 (nonferrous metals).

and scientists would produce a continued decline to 2.4 percent. Furthermore, if we examine the resources available to engineers and scientists in developing their activities and the exports of manufactured goods, the presence deteriorates even more, reaching 1.8 percent. Finally, with reference to the presence of scientific authors, recognizing the degree of the precariousness in this type of indicator, the Latin American presence is slightly over 1 percent.

A basic feature of the regional development pattern then would be the fact that the aggregation of intellectual value to available human and natural resources has been particularly low, implying that regional development has resulted more from an imitative process than from an evaluation of internal deficiencies and potentialities. The unsuitable adaptation of the development process to the specific deficiencies of regional realities and potentialities will be a recurring topic when making international comparisons. This phenomenon could be summarized by stressing the fundamental features of the Latin American development process — its weak incorporation of technical progress, its feeble contribution of original thought arising from reality — to illuminate the wide range of decisions conveyed by economic and social transformation.

In other words, the empty box would be linked directly to the inability to open the "black box" of technical progress. The black box would also be influenced by the origin of Latin American formations, their institutionality, the cultural context, and a series of structural economic factors whose ties with the sociopolitical element are complex yet undeniable.

Common Traits of the Industrialization Pattern of Latin America

The definition and characterization of the industrialization pattern adopted by Latin American countries are based on four fundamental features that, as will be shown, are shared by all countries of the region:

1. International insertion based almost exclusively on the trade surplus generated in the sectors of natural resources, agriculture, energy, and mining, and a systematic trade deficit in the manufacturing sector (with the exception of a trade surplus generated in the manufacturing sector of Brazil in 1982)

2. An industrial structure conceived and promoted fundamentally with a view to the respective internal markets

3. The aspiration to reproduce the life-style of the advanced countries at the level of both consumption and, to a varied extent, internal production

4. Limited social appreciation of the entrepreneurial function and the precarious leadership of the national public and private business community in the sectors whose dynamism and content define the industrial profile in each of the countries.

International Insertion Through Raw Materials

Empirical evidence has proven that, after more than forty years of industrialization and with an opportune awareness of the tendency toward deterioration in the exchange terms of natural resources—of which, as in the United States, there is an abundant supply vis-à-vis manufactures—all the countries of the region, without exception until 1982, presented a positive trade balance exclusively in either agriculture, energy, or mining, and a significant deficit in the manufacturing sector (see table 1.3). Since 1982, Brazil has been the only country in the region to generate a surplus in the manufacturing sector.

Table 1.3 Latin America: Trade Balance by Sector of Economic Activity, 1985 (Millions of Dollars)

	Total sectors	Agriculture
Total Latin America	34,541	19,372
Petroleum export countries	20,241	− 285
Bolivia	− 17	− 107
Ecuador	1,258	743
Mexico	9,197	− 209
Peru	1,084	224
Venezuela	8,719	− 936
Nonpetroleum export countries	14,300	19,657
Argentina	4,581	5,576
Brazil	11,265	8,567
Colombia	− 559	1,748
Costa Rica	− 159	595
Chile	904	887
El Salvador	− 493	234
Guatemala	− 305	641
Honduras	− 171	549
Nicaragua	− 792	143
Paraguay	− 197	237
Uruguay	233	480

Source: Joint ECLAC/UNIDO Industry and Technology Division, updated from ECLAC's DATA-BASE (BADECEL)

In the case of Brazil there are diverse options with respect to the progressively structural character of the manufacturing surplus. There are those who argue that this is a fragile situation linked to the fall of the internal market (1980–1983), the dynamism of U.S. imports in 1984, and the relative decline in the internal investment rate in the first half of the 1980s. Other opinions maintain that Brazil's tremendous investment effort in the industrial sector during the 1970s had generated conditions for a solid, plentiful manufacturing surplus.[3] The deterioration of the trade balance of the manufacturing sector in 1986, associated with a sharp increase in internal demand, contributed to the viability of this polemic, undoubtedly relevant for the rest of the region. With regard to exchange terms, unfortunately, it has been shown that the fears of the 1940s were completely warranted. The rela-

Manufacturing industry[a]	Energy	Mining	Other sectors
– 13,649	22,593	6,282	– 57
– 11,606	29,566	2,593	– 27
– 538	371	257	—
– 1,346	1,897	– 35	– 1
– 5,092	14,049	455	– 6
– 948	637	1,171	—
– 3,682	12,612	745	– 20
– 2,043	– 6,973	3,689	– 30
– 1,113	151	– 34	1
5,791	– 4,901	1,822	– 14
– 2,271	94	– 114	– 16
– 570	– 165	– 19	—
– 1,523	– 512	2,052	—
– 470	– 253	– 4	—
– 487	– 447	– 12	—
– 520	– 220	21	– 1
– 596	– 339	– 7	—
– 286	– 142	– 6	—
2	– 239	– 10	—

[a]Manufacturing industry includes SITC sections 5 to 8 less division 68 (nonferrous metals).

tive price index for agriculture and manufactures was 168 in 1950 and 81 in 1985 (1979–1981 = 100); in mining the index was 124 in 1950 and fell to 79 in 1985; in the case of oil, whose effects vary according to country, the index was 26 in 1950, 13 in 1970, 107 in 1980, and 101 in 1985.[4]

Though the region denounces these tendencies, changes in the productive structure have failed to neutralize their adverse effects. This responsibility can hardly be delegated abroad. In the mid–1970s some countries of the region, bolstered by the unsatisfactory results of this industrialization pattern, adopted policies that led to an intensification of the manufacturing deficit without substantially modifying the natural resource surplus. International financial liquidity permitted circumstantial regional absorption, but the problem surfaced more dramatically in

Table 1.4 Latin America: Manufacturing Export Coefficient[a]
(percentages)

	1965	1970	1975	1980
Argentina	2.0	7.0	2.9	3.9
Brazil	2.1	2.8	3.0	5.3
Mexico	—	2.5	2.2	2.8
Bolivia	4.8	2.6	3.5	3.2
Colombia	1.4	2.0	4.9	4.9
Chile	1.3	2.2	5.4	6.1
Ecuador	1.8	1.9	5.4	9.8
Paraguay	12.5	9.0	10.6[b]	—
Peru	0.6	0.5	0.5	5.1
Uruguay	3.9[c]	2.3[d]	4.8	7.8
Venezuela	1.2	0.6	0.8	1.0
Costa Rica	3.8	9.7	11.5	12.3
El Salvador	5.0	15.7	17.6	24.3
Guatemala	26.8[c]	18.3[d]	15.8	21.2
Honduras	5.5	10.4[d]	15.3	13.3
Nicaragua	2.6	9.2	8.9	7.6
Dominican Republic	1.8	1.8	7.1	6.7

Source: Joint ECLAC/UNIDO Industry and Technology Division, based on data from UNIDO DATABASE; ECLAC DATABASE.
[a]Manufactured exports as percentage of gross domestic output, manufactured exports defined according to UNCTAD in manufactures and semimanufactures, UNCTAD document TD/B/C.2/3.

1982 when the net flow of financial resources became negative and the decline in the exchange terms was accentuated.[5] The scenario acquires a more serious tone given that the manufacturing deficit is concentrated precisely in the sectors of greatest dynamism and technological content, properties that condition their relevance for the insertion of the countries into international trade: capital goods, chemicals, and automotive industry. The region is in bad shape in those areas that ensure a promising future in international trade.

Industrialization Oriented Toward the Internal Market

Independent of all national specificities, the countries of the region share a basic phenomenon: industrial exports represent a low percentage of

1981	1982	1983	1984	1985
4.5	5.6	4.5	3.8	5.5
6.1	5.0	7.4	17.3	28.4
2.5	3.7	6.3	6.0	7.1
2.1	1.6	—	—	—
5.0	4.5	3.5	3.6	4.6
4.4	5.1	5.4	6.0	6.6
7.4	6.6	2.4	4.4	—
—	—	—	—	—
3.3	3.5	2.5	3.1	—
6.6	7.6	11.3	11.7	10.3
1.3	1.0	0.7	1.9	5.0
18.3	13.5	11.8	—	—
17.0	15.9	13.2	—	—
17.1	16.4	16.5	14.4	—
11.6	10.3	9.4	7.6	—
5.0	2.7	2.7	1.6	—
6.6	3.9	4.9	4.0	—

[b]1974.
[c]1968.
[d]1971.

industrial production and, more importantly, the conception of product technology, process, and manufacturing of the industrial plant has basically been along the lines of supplying the respective internal markets. This common trait is illustrated—with exceptional cases in periods, sectors, and countries—by the export promotion policies initiated in the mid-1970s that failed to solve the crucial dilemma presented by the greater profitability of the internal market (see table 1.4).

Since the late 1970s, investment in exports has had to compete not only with the easily reached and protected domestic market, but also with an even more attractive option, that of placing money on the international financial market at high dollar interest rates. To give an idea of the magnitude of this new phenomenon—which works against productive investment in exports and in the domestic market and which is related, among other factors, to the U.S. deficit—suffice it to say that on the Eurodollar market alone, the volume of trading each year is equivalent to 25 times the volume of international trade in goods and services. Even allowing for some duplication in the recording of these transactions, the orders of magnitude involved show that this is a new phenomenon which is potentially very significant.

Even in the case of Brazil, whose industrial exports represent half of the manufacturing exports of the region and more than 50 percent of its own total exports, the industrial exports coefficient is low and the internal market continues to be the priority objective for the majority of the businesses and sectors. In 1980, the export coefficient as a percentage of production was 5.3 percent with a strict definition of manufactures, and 8.0 percent using a broad definition. This is applied with little variation, to national private, foreign, and state firms. This situation — existing in a country whose GNP is equivalent to that of Sweden, Norway, Denmark, and Finland combined (all of whose production is oriented toward the international market) — is accentuated and takes on a more serious quality in the medium and small countries of the region (export coefficients on the order of 10 percent). Today, the prevailing U.S. scheme (the concentration of production in the internal market) is reproduced in Latin America with the small qualification that even the country with the greatest internal market of the region, Brazil, is one-thirteenth of the economic size of the United States, whereas at the end of World War II, it was approximately one-twenty-fifth. At that time, the United States possessed 6 percent of the world population and generated 40 percent of the world product and 60 percent of world exports.

What is specific about the region, however, does not reside in the application of an import substitution policy, a feature shared with the rest of the world (with the exception of late-eighteenth- and early-nineteenth-century England) but in the economic modality in which this policy is applied. Concretely, this means that import substitution has been an integral element of the industrialization pattern, characterized by a series of elements that support and reinforce each other. Isolating and focusing on any of these components is unprofitable from the viewpoint of the design of different industrialization strategies. However, note should be made of the fact that a region with an hourly manufacturing sector cost that fluctuates between one-seventh and one-twentieth of that prevailing in developed countries, an inferior tax rate, levels of productivity smaller by no more than 50 percent of that existing in developed countries, and access to similar technologies cannot passively accept the prospect of maintaining a level of indiscriminate protectionism. "Successful" international experiences show that a drastic, straightforward opening is not viable, as would be a sectoral, transitory proposition based on the learning of the technological processes which would lead to a solid insertion into the international market.

Consumption Pattern

The aspiration to reproduce the life-styles of the advanced countries and, particularly, of the United States is common not only to all Latin American countries, but also to the overwhelming majority of the world population regardless of development levels, socioeconomic systems, and ethnics. A regional peculiarity is the modality through which this is incorporated into industrial demand and supply, the energy platform, commercialization, communications, and consumer financing. The degree to which the distinct consumer items are filtered down through the income pyramid varies according to the respective unit price. The diffusion of inexpensive goods—beverages, clothing, and some appliances—reaches even the rural sectors. If consumer electronics are considered, the diffusion reaches urban popular sectors, and, in that item that symbolizes this consumption pattern—the automobile—the diffusion reaches middle sectors.

The model life-style has come of age endogenously in a country in which per capita income currently amounts to more than seven times the per capita income of Latin America, and whose economic dimension equals practically five times that of Latin America. To this obvious contrast, the recent predicament can be added that the life-style is so "costly" that internal resources in the United States are insufficient to maintain it. This explains why the United States has recently entered the category of net debtor; the only differential feature is that it has the capability to coin the same currency on which its debt is calculated. In order to attempt a recuperation of its level of international competitiveness and neutralize the imbalance in terms of growth and productivity, it must resort to the measure of eroding the relative level of internal salaries by means of devaluation.

What is fundamental about the case of Latin America, however, is that it has proceeded to transplant the consumer items at a faster pace than the knowledge and institutions necessary for designing, producing, and adopting them to local conditions. The anxiousness to possess these items has been more intense than the passion to incorporate the modernity of knowledge and interpersonal relations utilized in their design.

Accepting the fact that the U.S. life-style forms part of a "collective fantasy," the challenge consists in adapting this circumstance to the simultaneous search for internal socioeconomic integration and a solid insertion in the international economy. The aspiration to reproduce the model life-style in Latin America has become a more important priority than the objectives of integration at a national level and solid international insertion. This is reflected, for example, in the fact that the density of the consumption of certain "expensive" objects (a car, for instance) is significantly greater than in other countries with a later industrialization and a comparable income level. Besides, unlike other countries and regions, local production of those objects has been established through national markets with a high number of small-scale plants that are structurally incompatible, in the majority of the countries, with international market demands. Access to these goods has been facilitated by reproducing the consumer credit mechanisms existing in the countries of origin, with the inevitable consequences on family savings and the availability of funds for investment.

In an advanced country like Japan, where the per capita income is approximately 80 percent and its automobile density 40 percent of that of the United States, consumer credit availability in relation to the GNP amounts to one-seventh that of the United States. Interestingly, Japan is the top foreign supplier of automobiles to the United States. Several of the Nordic countries, with per capita income levels comparable to the United States and with markets, in terms of GNP, superior to the medium countries of Latin America, present a high automobile consumption density, but have not established internal production. South Korea, with a per capita income similar to the largest Latin American countries and a product equivalent to one-third that of Brazil and half that of Mexico, is currently exporting cars to Canada and the United States through national enterprises and has an automobile density equivalent to between one-fifth and one-tenth of that existing in Latin America.

In the area of foodstuffs, a clear neglect can be observed in Brazil and Mexico with regard to the basic areas dedicated to internal market consumption (in the Argentine case, these areas coincide with the principal export products). In the last decade, a considerable increase in agricultural export production can be noted, as well as in the case of Brazil, where the increase in the production of sugarcane has been directed toward substituting that of oil and there has been a drop in the per capita production of cereals. The cereals import coefficient has grown systematically in both countries and reached a level of approximately 20 percent at the beginning of the 1980s. In the cases of Argentina and South Korea, the former due to the generous supply of natural resources and the latter due to the importance of strategies of food self-sufficiency, the subject of basic foodstuffs for internal consumption has been fundamentally resolved (per capita calorie consumption in Argentina is similar to that of the United States and higher than that of Europe and Japan).

In terms of diet content, a clear contrast can be observed between South Korea, which adapts to the internal deficiencies and potentialities, and the Latin American countries, which seek to reproduce the U.S. food pattern in the uppermost part of the income pyramid: a greater ratio of foods of animal origin (especially beef) in Latin America, in contrast to a predominance of grains and fish in South Korea (see table 1.5). Although the calorie and protein content is comparable, the composition varies drastically. In the case of Latin America, the configuration appears by superimposing the diet of the middle and upper urban sectors, whose content more closely resembles that of the United States, and the diet of the peasant and popular sectors, in which the absolute levels and content in meat and milk are notoriously inferior.

An additional contrast between the food regimens under consideration is that of energy efficiency.[6] Losses in efficiency result from the transformation of grains into foods of animal origin. Estimates made for the U.S. food system — the model of imitation — indicate that around

Table 1.5 Latin America and South Korea: Daily Intake

	CONSUMPTION			
	Latin America		South Korea	
	Kg/Year	%	Kg/Year	%
	(1979–81)		(1975)	
Vegetable origin	459.9	76.1	364.4	88.6
Rice	39.7	6.6	126.0	29.8
Wheat	58.1	9.6	40.9	9.7
Corn	37.7	6.2	—	—
Other grains	3.7	0.6	48.6	11.5
Total foodgrains	139.2	23.0	215.5	51.0
Fruit	102.7	17.0	15.2	3.6
Vegetables	37.6	6.2	105.1	24.9
Potatoes	—	—	27.6	8.9
Total fruit and vegetables	140.3	23.2	147.9	37.4
Other vegetable origin	171.4	38.4	—	—
Pulses	9.0	1.5	1.0	0.2
Animal origin	144.8	23.9	48.2	11.3
Beef	16.6	2.7	1.9	0.4
Pork	6.1	1.0	4.7	1.1
Chicken	7.0	1.2	1.9	0.4
Fish and seafood	13.5	2.2	24.9	5.9
Other meats	5.4	0.9	—	—
Total meat and fish	48.6	8.0	33.4	7.8
Milk	87.4	14.5	11.3	2.7
Eggs	6.2	1.0	3.5	0.8
Animal oils and fats	2.6	0.4	—	—
Total	604.7	100.0	412.6	99.9

Source: ECLAC/FAO Division and World Bank.

nine calories of fossil energy are needed per calorie available "in the plate of the consumer."[7] The consumption models of Japan and, even more so, South Korea probably require less than half the amount indicated. In this sense, it is only the great inequality of the patterns of food consumption in Latin America that makes it feasible for the model pattern to be in operation at the top since "in the specific case of South America, twice its total current consumption of crude oil (1980) would have to be used if production pat-

CALORIES				PROTEINS			
Latin America		South Korea		Latin America		South Korea	
Value	%	Value	%	Grams	%	Grams	%
(1979–81)		(1975)		(1979–81)		(1975)	
2,184	83.3	2,282	93.2	39.6	59.2	53	75.7
265	10.1	1,243	50.8	5.3	7.9	23	32.9
400	15.3	408	16.6	11.8	17.7	12	17.1
337	12.8	—	—	8.4	12.6	—	—
26	1.0	472	19.3	0.8	1.1	11	15.7
1,028	39.2	2,123	86.7	26.3	39.3	46	65.7
144	5.5	24	1.0	1.6	2.4	1	1.4
30	1.2	40	1.6	1.3	1.9	3	4.3
—	—	86	3.5	—	—	2	2.9
174	6.7	150	6.1	2.9	4.3	6	8.6
897	34.2	—	—	4.2	6.3	—	—
85	3.2	9	0.4	6.2	9.3	1	1.4
437	16.7	166	6.8	27.0	40.8	17	24.3
97	3.7	9	0.4	6.3	9.5	1	1.4
34	1.3	48	2.0	1.9	2.9	2	2.9
29	1.1	6	0.2	2.1	3.2	1	1.4
24	0.9	68	2.8	3.4	5.1	11	15.7
18	0.7	—	—	2.4	3.7	—	—
202	7.7	131	5.4	16.1	24.4	15	21.5
155	5.9	19	0.8	9.2	13.8	1	1.4
23	0.8	16	0.6	1.7	2.6	1	1.4
57	2.2	—	—	—	—	—	—
2,621	100.0	2,448	100.0	66.6	100.0	70	100.0

terns and consumption modalities were to be generalized such as those of the model that it tends to imitate."[8] In both Japan and South Korea there has been a tendency toward an approximation of the "American life-style" in terms of both vehicles and diet. But the internalization of that tendency in those countries has been tempered by the awareness of the need to proceed cautiously with dynamism, international competitiveness, and the minimal norms of equity, while favoring the process of social integration.

Limited Social Appreciation and Precarious Leadership of the National Business Community

There is empirical evidence that the leadership of the more dynamic industrial sectors—which incorporate technical progress and, as such, define the national productive profile—has not been exercised by national private enterprises (automotive, chemical, capital goods) in the majority of cases. Moreover, in all the major enterprises of each country, the largest national private businesses occupy a discrete third place, behind public and transnational enterprises.[9] An analysis of the presence and weight of small and medium businesses, which by definition are considered to be national private, has revealed it to be notoriously less significant in Latin America than in other developed countries having late industrializations (Italy, Japan, India, and Spain).

The weight and growing attention that small and medium industry receives in the developed countries—in various sectors exposed to international competition—suggest the need to qualify the determinism frequently assigned to the limited size of the internal Latin American markets, a factor often used to justify both the absence of investment opportunities and the need for high, ongoing protection barriers. Additionally, since the mid-1970s, the ostensibly greater dynamism of the small and medium industries in the advanced countries has been confirmed empirically in terms of employment, flexibility, and technological innovation. Finally, analysis of the execution of research and technological development activities indicates that, even in the most developed Latin American countries, the ratio corresponding to the national private sector is conspicuously marginal.[10]

Two facts that are difficult to quantify, but still no less important, can be added to those already mentioned: the entrepreneurial function in Latin America receives little social appreciation and, instead, the subject of property, which is profoundly ideologized, arouses a great deal of public interest. While in the former subjects—consumption pattern, preferential orientation toward the internal market, and international insertion by means of natural resources—a certain similarity to the United States has been maintained, the gap with respect to subject could not be wider. This is, moreover, one of the fundamental features that differentiates the region from those recently industrialized countries that have achieved a successful insertion in international markets.

Social appreciation for and the creativity of the entrepreneurial class, whatever the size of the firm or type of property, constitutes a necessary condition for overcoming this "showcase modernity." The complexity of this topic transcends the sphere of fiscal or monetary trade policy, including the adoption of doctrinary positions imposed by decree. The instruments of economic policy and decree can, undoubtedly, favor or prejudice, but they are not sufficient. This is a cultural, valuational dimension, with respect to which the political debate built on reality, social agreement, the transparency of information flow, mass media, and the educational process performs an indispensable role.

In this aspect there are several basic differences between South Korea and the countries of Latin America. First, a dominant feature in South Korea (even more pronounced than in Japan) is the close tie between the state and a group of national conglomerates with particular incidence in the manufacturing sector and a high degree of diversification. As seen in table 1.6, the ten principal conglomerates generate practically 25 percent of GNP and the forty-six principal conglomerates originate 43 percent of GNP. The national private conglomerates that exist in Latin America do not even near that weight and their organic ties to the state are noticeably more subtle. Second, while the public sector in South Korea has exercised a determinant role in financial mediation, "[t]he financial system . . . at the beginning of the 1980s was largely the product of government initiatives. Except for the 'local banks' and branches of foreign banks, financial institutions were either government-created, government-owned, or government-controlled by virtue of a majority shareholding."[11] In Latin America, the relatively important public development banking sector coexists with a largely private banking sector in short-term financial mediation. In the third place, the relative weight of the branches of transnational corporations (TCs) is significantly less determinant in South Korea than in Latin American countries, where they exercise leadership and concentrate on the internal market. Finally,

Table 1.6 Importance of Different Entrepreneurial Agents

	Argentina	Brazil	Mexico	South Korea
Foreign investment: stock of foreign investment (end of 1970s) (millions of dollars)[a]	5,489 (1983)	13,005	3,868	737
Share of transnational corporations in manufacturing gross output	31 (1972)	44 (1977)	39 (1970)	11 (1975)
Share of transnational corporations in exports of manufactures[a]	>30 (1969)	43 (1969)	34 (1974)	27 (1978)
Public enterprises: share in fixed total investment[b]	20 (1978–80)	23 (1980)	29 (1978)	25 (1974–77)
Contribution of private national conglomerates to GNP (1978):				
10 largest				23.4
46 largest				43.0

State corporations (I)
Private national corporations (II)
Transnational corporations (III)

Percentage structure in total sales (1983)[c]	Argentina			Brazil			Mexico			South Korea		
	I	II	III	I	II	III	I	II	III	I	II	III
10 largest corporations	45.1	7.1	47.8	59.3	11.2	29.5	83.7	14.2	2.1	—	—	—
50 largest corporations	37.1	24.5	38.4	47.4	20.8	31.8	65.9	24.5	9.6	—	—	—

Source: Joint ECLAC/UNIDO Industry and Technology Division.

[a] Centre on Transnational Corporations, *Transnational Corporations in World Development: Third Study*. New York, 1983.

[b] Sachs, *External Debts and Microeconomic Performance in Latin America and East Asia*. Brookings Papers on Economic Activity No. 219, 1985; and K. S. Kim, *Industrial Policy and Industrialization in South Korea*, Kellogg Institute Working Paper No. 39, 1985.

[c] Joint ECLAC/UNIDO Industry and Technology Division, *Industrialización y Desarrollo Tecnológico*, Informe No. 1, Santiago, Chile, September 1985; and ECLAC, *Las Empresas Transnacionales en Argentina*, Estudios e Informes de la CEPAL, No. 56, Santiago, 1986.

the participation of public enterprises in investment would present a higher level in South Korea than in Argentina and Brazil, and would be inferior only to the case of Mexico, which is strongly influenced by the oil sector (PEMEX).

In summary, in South Korea direction for industrialization would come from a strong, planner state organically integrated with a small number of powerful national conglomerates with lower complementary participation of TC branches in localized sectors and with a strong export orientation. In Latin America, a distribution of functions can be observed in which leadership is exercised by TCs in the most dynamic industrial sectors. In terms of infrastructure, the public enterprises carry out the task, confining national private businesses to the industrial activities of lesser dynamism and technological complexity and to the production of services, including financial mediation (see table 1.6).

Reciprocal Relations Among the Basic Features

The four common traits previously mentioned are linked to and support each other. Thus, it would be difficult to understand the transplantation of "showcase modernity" and the systematic orientation toward the internal market without the existence of national entrepreneurial precariousness and vice versa. The convergence of these three factors explains why, after several decades of industrialization, international insertion through natural resources persists. The availability of natural resource sectors, in turn, has an influence on the adopted modality of industrialization. From the standpoint of the formulation of new industrialization strategies, what is of interest is to assume the interdependence of these factors and approach them as a whole. If, for example, attention is concentrated exclusively on the need to open up the internal markets, the immediate effect will be to intensify "showcase modernity," further weaken the fragile entrepreneurial base, and accentuate insertion through natural resources. On the other hand, it would seem to be somewhat arbitrary to reinforce the national entrepreneurial base through the seemingly efficient measure of redistributing the property of already established businesses among different agents (privatization or statization), maintaining constant a consumption pattern

Table 1.7 Growth of Manufacturing Value Added Per Capita
by Economic Grouping and by Developing Region, 1963–1985[a]
(Average annual growth rate percentage)

	1963–1973	1973–1980	1981
Developed market economies	4.6	1.0	– 0.1
Centrally planned economies	8.6	6.1	1.9
Developing countries	5.1	3.5	– 1.9
Africa	4.5	2.7	– 0.2
West Asia	6.2	2.3	– 2.0
South and East Asia	4.6	5.4	3.6
Latin America	5.1	2.8	– 5.1

Source: Joint ECLAC/UNIDO Industry and Technology Division, based on data from UNIDO, *World Industry: A Statistical Review, 1985,* UNIDO/IS.590.
[a]At constant prices, 1975.

incompatible with growth during a period in which net capital inflows disappear and private investments abroad are facilitated.

Regional and international experience suggests that, in order to attain the general development objectives, it is necessary to advance simultaneously toward internal socioeconomic integration and a solid insertion into the international economy. To seek international insertion by way of the partial exclusion of social sectors and regions is illusory, since latent social tensions lead inexorably to uncertainty and, in the final analysis, compromise investment and growth. Alternately, to concentrate attention exclusively on internal integration at the expense of international insertion is infeasible due to both the growing transparency of communication, aspirations, and modes of conduct, and, more importantly, to the reality that raising the standard of living of the population is linked to growth in productivity. As a result, the increase in productivity is associated with the incorporation of technical progress, which requires growth, thereby making international insertion a means of gaining access and a stimulus at the same time.

The industrialization pattern characterized by the convergence of these four elements—showcase modernity, comfortable internal market, preferential international insertion by means of natural resources, and na-

1982	1983[b]	1984[b]	1985[c]	1980–1985
− 2.9	2.4	6.1	2.5	1.6
2.1	3.7	3.5	2.7	2.8
− 2.0	1.0	7.0	3.7	1.5
− 0.9	− 2.0	1.3	2.0	0.1
5.1 ⎫ 1.0 ⎭	8.0	9.6	6.2	7.9[d]
− 3.9	− 5.3	2.6	1.9	− 2.0

[b]Preliminary figures.
[c]Estimates.
[d]1982–1985.

tional entrepreneurial precariousness — reflects the weakness of what has been defined elsewhere as the "endogenous nucleus of technological dynamization" (ENTD).[12] To alter this pattern would necessitate the reinforcement and integration of ENTD and the goods and services subsystems that conform it. The national expressions of this pattern are the outcome of combining these common traits with those specific features of society and the industrial sector itself. The schematic identification of some of those specificities will be covered next.

Differential Features of Industrialization Processes in Latin American Societies

The industrialization pattern whose common traits have been previously identified forms part of societies that also present differences that are equally significant. The peculiarities of the industrialization process — in content, results, challenges for the future, and strategies and policies necessary to confront these challenges — are directly influenced by the interaction between the common traits of the industrialization pattern and the specificity of the features that characterize the respective societies. Attention will be dedicated to some of the dimensions in which the similarities and differences seem to exercise more influence on the results, challenges, and future strategies: type of natural resources, characteristics of the agricultural system, the historical moment in which industrialization was introduced, population dynamic, market size, and predominating political system.

Type of Natural Resource

The type of natural resource utilized by countries to gain insertion into the international economy exerts various well-known influences on the development style including, among others, the level, evolution, and stability of foreign exchange revenue, and the distribution of foreign exchange availability among distinct economic agents, depending upon the type and nature of the business participating in the corresponding activities. The weight and relative economic position of the state with respect to society as a whole and abroad will be directly influenced by the types of natural resources and the business nature of their exploitation. The heterogeneity of productivity will also reflect, to a fair degree, the supply and utilization of natural resources. From these considerations, it can be seen that the backward linkages of the industrial sector—raw materials, inputs, and equipment—and the popular demand for industrial goods will be directly influenced by the type and nature of the natural resource and its particular modality of business management.

In the distinct countries of the region there have been such highly varied situations as mining enclaves under the responsibility of foreign businesses, later transferred to public enterprises and eventually becoming a pivot for public financing in both foreign and national currency; large agricultural ventures in which industrial improvements predominate in modern business exploitations of property belonging to national capital and later assuming a protagonistic function in industrial development; and analogous situations in which business responsibility falls upon companies that interact at an international level. The differential impact of the last two situations on the ties with and the later role of the state, as well as on the development style, are far from being marginal. There are also situations in which agricultural export areas coincide with basic foodstuffs for internal consumption and property, although relatively concentrated, includes a large number of medium and small property owners. In this last situation, structural heterogeneity weakens, income distribution becomes more favorable, and the relative autonomy of the society vis-à-vis the state tends to be reinforced.

An extremely simplified typology of Latin American agriculture would emphasize the distinction between the border cases of Argentina and Uruguay, on one extreme, and the rest of the region, on the other. The first case would be a situation characterized by fertile, highly homogeneous lands with a considerable availability of land per capita, basic export areas that coincide with the internal diet of meats and grains, a strong predominance of medium-to-large commercial businesses, and very little else of importance in the rest of the economy. In the agriculture of the other countries, although in some there are similar subsystems with growing weight, there is a predominance of industrial improvements, unequal land fertility, a strong influence of irrigation, a combination of large modern exploitations with a significant peasant economy, and a growing dependence on imports to supply the increasing components of the internal basic diet (grains). In this case, a strong technological dualism exists within agriculture and between agriculture and the rest of the economy.

The Timing of Industrialization

The historical moment in which the industrialization process is initiated will also exercise a significant influence on its scope and content. Although the "late industrialization" of the region is frequently mentioned, in reality this generic interpretation includes countries in which the onset of the process took place in the second half of the last century: the *Unión Industrial Argentina* (UIA) was founded in 1887 and the *Sociedad de Fomento Fabril* (SOFOFA) in Chile was founded in 1883. The beginning of the process in other Latin American countries would seem to have occurred after World War II, with intermediate situations between World Wars I and II. Moreover, the crisis of the 1930s would have played a definite detonator role in that process.

It could be argued that the later a country initiates industrialization, the more advanced the technological level to which it can aspire will be. This positive aspect is countered, however, by the greatest gap ever to exist between the modalities of the "functioning" of preindustrial society and the demands posed by the introduction of "industrial logic." The longer a preindustrial society delays, the greater the remnants and latent social tensions.

The fact that the modernization of health will be faster than industrial development, with the consequent effects on population dynamics, is an additional factor. The population flow from the peasant "tedium" to the urban "neon lights" in Latin America reaches unprecedented rates in the process of industrialization. In the past, those excluded from progress also found themselves excluded from information and political participation. This situation was surmounted with the appearance of the transistor, which incorporated both urban marginality and the majority of the peasantry into the collective aspiration for modernity, symbolized by determined consumer items and life-styles. The social tensions generated in preindustrial society are reinforced in the initial phases of industrialization with the incorporation of those formerly excluded into the shared environment of the collective fantasy of benefiting from modernity, even though that may mean merely the fragile modality of physical contact with certain objects.

There is no trustworthy, comparative empirical background data available to evaluate the weight of the industrial sector in the economy of Latin America in the second half of the nineteenth century. From the sources available, however, it would appear that Argentina, Brazil, Chile, Mexico, and Cuba probably arrived at World War I with some degree of industrial development, linked primarily to textiles, clothing, mills, shoes, and some areas of metallic instruments. The crisis of the 1930s and World War II set off industrialization in Colombia, Peru, Costa Rica, and Bolivia. The process of industrialization began after World War II in Venezuela, Paraguay, Honduras, Guatemala, Panama, Ecuador, Nicaragua, the Dominican Republic, Haiti, and other Caribbean countries. This is a tentative chronology that has the principal objective of stressing the wide spectrum of situations attributed to "late industrialization": from countries with more than a century of industrialization to others in which industrial history does not exceed three decades.

The Size of the National Economy

The economic dimension of the countries is obviously a differential factor in the industrialization process, fundamentally because the minimum plant sizes in determined sectors — basically in those of intermediate inputs of widespread use (cement, iron, and steel producing, petrochemicals, the automotive sector, and some areas of mass-produced capital goods) — reach dimensions that are hardly compatible with the internal market sizes of some countries. Additionally, certain areas of infrastructure (transport, energy, communications) require high fixed amounts of investment that would be easily accessible in countries of greater economic size. In general terms, what can be affirmed is that the smaller the size of a country, the higher the degree of industrial specialization and the more distinctive its configuration in reference to the sectoral structure.

When these considerations are contrasted with the existing productive structure of the region, it is evident that this has not been a fundamental criterion in the design of industrial strategies and policies. In many countries, due to considerations of another nature hardly justifiable from an economic or technological standpoint, industrial sectors have been developed whose minimum scales are incompatible with the size of the country (iron and steel manufacturing, automotive), while compatible sectors have not been developed. An example of this would be certain businesses of nonmass-produced capital goods. Moreover, the degree of excessive pulverization of the productive structure and the consequent high margin of unemployed capability constitutes a long-lasting feature present in various sectors and numerous countries of the region, a situation that was made viable economically through elevated, indiscriminate protection barriers which required the preservation of that "artificial climate."

In the case of the Central American Common Market, integration partially neutralized the small size of the national markets, and in the Andean Group the same principle was attempted and somewhat achieved. In general terms, it seems possible to affirm that the limiting effects originating in the small internal markets have been enhanced by internal policies and, at the same time, the neutralization of that limiting factor by means of integration has received, in practice, insufficient attention.

Political Systems

At the level of constitutional texts, there is a relative similarity within the region, and between it and the European liberal doctrine of the past century. What is not coherent, however, is the fact that only a very small ratio of the Latin American population has experienced a continuous system of representative democracy. Since the beginning of the 1980s, a majority of the regional population has succeeded in attaining that advanced mode of political existence. The relative absence of representative democracy as a structural fact in the political history of Latin America probably has some incidence in the explanation of the insufficent development of the regional integration process which, in the light of the international and regional experience, is favored by the establishment of democratic regimes. The most significant recent advance is the agreement between Argentina and Brazil, whose content has been qualitatively innovational with respect to the regional integration experience.[13]

The Latin American Industrial Crisis of the 1980s

Relative Magnitude of the Industrial Crisis

Due to predominantly external factors and the convergence of internal factors of a structural and political economy nature, since 1980 the Latin American economy has been experiencing a crisis that affects the industrial sector with particular intensity. With an emphasis on the restriction of foreign exchange, the productive sector, with greater import content, little export capacity, and a large trade deficit, has been affected more drastically than economic activity as a whole. Demand is affected more than proportionately by the fall in national income. In terms of supply, the restriction of foreign exchange hinders access to inputs, parts, and equipment due to higher prices. With few national and sectoral exceptions, the lack of experience and the nature of the productive plant impedes it from compensating for the decline in the internal market due to exports, to which can be added the increase in the interest rate and the overindebtedness inherited at the end of the 1970s.

In comparison to the rest of the world (see table 1.7) the drop in the per capita manufactures product is more pronounced in Latin America than in the developed countries with either market or planned economies, and in the rest of the developing regions.[14] In the developed economies, the decline is concentrated in the 1980–1982 period and during none of those years does it reach 3 percent (– 2.4 percent in 1980, – 0.1 percent in 1981 and – 2.9 percent in 1982). In Latin America, the drop observed in the 1981–1983 period reaches magnitudes of or higher than 4 percent (5.1 percent in 1981, 3.9 percent in 1982 and 5.3 percent in 1983). In Africa, the fall, which also corresponds to the 1981–1983 period, is less than 2 percent annually, and in Asia the per capita manufactures product not only did not suffer negative rates, but, since 1983, has been attaining rates higher than 6 percent annually (in 1983 in Latin America the decline in the per capita manufactures product is 5.3 percent and in Asia the growth is 8 percent). In the countries with planned economies, the growth has been maintained at smaller, but positive, rates than in the past (1.9 percent in 1981, 2.1 percent in 1982, and 3.7 percent in 1983).

The per capita manufactures product in Latin America in 1985 reached an index of 89 (1980 = 100) and a per capita GDP of 93 (1980 = 100). The industrial recovery of 1984 and 1985 (2.6 percent and 1.9 percent for the per capita manufactures product) was insufficient for a recuperation of the 1980 levels. In no country of the region with available comparative information did the per capita manufactures product in 1985 exceed that of 1980, regardless of the outstanding differences in the distinct national cases. If an abstraction is made of the growth in population and attention is centered on the level of the manufactures product, Colombia, Ecuador, and Venezuela would be on one extreme, where the manufactures product of 1985 exceeds that of 1980 by 8 percent and, on the other, Bolivia, where the manufactures product equals 61 percent of that reached in 1980 (53 percent in terms of per capita manufactures product).

Explanatory Factors and the Evolution of the Industrial Crisis

Among the multiple factors that have an incidence in the explanation of the distinct behaviors found in Latin American industrial sectors during the 1980s, the following stand out: degree of industrialization and integration of the industrial apparatus; volume and sectoral assignment of investments and industrial growth during the preceding decade; nature and intensity of the external negative impact (exchange terms, degree of indebtedness, capital flow, incidence of interest rate, and evolution of export quantum); and the macroeconomic and sectoral internal policies adopted by the different countries during the crisis. The conjunction of the diversity of structural factors, external impact, and internal policies generated the broad variation in behavior that the industrial sector underwent during the 1980–1985 period.

The generic description of a decline during the 1980–1983 period, with a recuperation during 1984–1985 of the per capita manufactures product, is highly influenced by the evolution encountered in Brazil, whose contribution to the manufactures product is around one-third of the regional product. This profile of a sustained decline until 1983 and a recuperation during the following years can be observed in that country, but that is not so for the majority of the other countries in the region. There are some in which the drop has been maintained since 1980 (Bolivia, Guatemala, Honduras, and Panama); others in which, after the initial decline until 1982–1984, there are no clear signs of recuperation in the following years (Argentina and Uruguay); still others in which the initial decline is slight or even nonexistent, but appears later (1982–1983 in Mexico and Ecuador). In Mexico, an explicit program for the "defense of the productive plant" was implemented which weakened and deferred the impact of the adjustment. Another category would be those countries in which the industrial recession did not reach great proportions at any time (Colombia, Venezuela, and Paraguay). In these countries, the lowest level of the manufactures product is 96 for Colombia in 1982, 98 for Venezuela in 1981 and 97 for Paraguay in 1983; the per capita manufactures product was 91 for Colombia and Venezuela in 1983 and 88 for Paraguay in 1985.

Brazil merits special treatment for various reasons. It is the only country of the region that, for the first time, achieved during that period a trade surplus in the manufacturing sector representing 50 percent of total manufacturing exports of Latin America. It also presents the greatest degree of relative development of the capital goods sector. Its procyclical nature explains, on the one hand, the more rapid decline of the industrial sector during the 1980–1983 period, which lasted until 1986. In 1984, when the world economy was strongly stimulated by an increase in U.S. imports (27 percent), Brazilian exports to that country increased by 54 percent, while those of all of Latin America rose by only 7 percent, and even exceeded the exports of Southeast Asia to the United States, which increased by 34 percent during that year. This result reflects Brazil's sustained investment effort during three decades and, particularly, the endeavor made during the second half of the 1970s, which is estimated to have contributed to the increase in the foreign exchange balance of the industrial sector equalling $3 billion in 1981–1982, $5 billion in 1983 and $7 billion in 1984.[15]

It is interesting to observe that in those countries having the greatest industrial dynamism during the former decade (Brazil, Mexico, Venezuela, Colombia, Ecuador, Costa Rica, Panama, Paraguay, and the Dominican Republic), aside from the degree of industrialization and the size of the internal market, the performance in terms of dynamism in the 1980s is more favorable than in those countries where the erosion of industrial dynamism had been manifested during the 1970s (Argentina, Chile, Uruguay, and Peru). In the latter group, the external crisis overlaps with preexisting internal factors.

Modifications in the Sectoral Profile

The diversity in behavior with regard to the dynamism of the industrial sector is also projected onto the sectoral profile. Considering the entire region during the period prior to the crisis, the most dynamic sectors include transport materials, chemicals, and capital goods, and the least dynamic include textiles, clothing, and leather. This profile, however similar to that of the advanced countries, corresponds principally to that of the most industrially advanced countries of the region. In a country such as Colombia, for example, whose satisfactory economic performance had been previously outstanding, the food sector appears among the most dynamic in the period prior to the crisis; the same occurs in those countries with a lesser degree of industrialization.

From the standpoint of the changes which occurred in the sectoral profile, three major developments stand out during the period 1980–1983. First, the transport equipment and capital goods sectors moved into the category of less dynamic sectors, an understandable shift given their role in the investment process and the complementary impact of the rise in interest rates and the fall in GDP. Second, the industrial chemicals sector (ISIC 351) remained dynamic both before and during the crisis, an indication of the widespread use of this type of goods in overall production activities (agriculture, mining, construction, nondurable consumer goods). Third, the food sector, whose growth is associated with basic survival needs, became highly dynamic in 1980 in such different countries as Brazil, Mexico, Chile, the Dominican Republic, and Venezuela.

The most dynamic sectors in the entire region during the crisis period were foodstuffs and two sectors of intermediate inputs, the chemical industry and iron and steel manufacturing (the significant, growing exports of Brazil have an incidence in the case of the latter). Despite the still fragmentary nature of the information available, during the recuperation period observed in some countries around 1984 and 1985 there is evidence that the productive profile existing before the crisis was recovered, with a marked recuperation of dynamism on the part of the automotive sector and, in some of the countries (Brazil in particular), the capital goods sector. In the majority of Latin American countries, however, there is still no evidence of an industrial recuperation process. It would be premature to evaluate the eventual modification of the productive profile, even though it seems possible to affirm that certain sectors — such as the automobile industry, and some areas of intermediate inputs of widespread use, such as petrochemicals and iron and steel manufacturing — must undergo deep-seated processes of rationalization besides the general process of industrial restructuring.

Effects on Scientific and Technological Research Activities

Perhaps the most revealing characteristic of the industrial peculiarity of Latin America is related to the fact that, in notorious contrast to what occurs in advanced countries, spending on technological research and development (R&D), strongly associated with the public budget, has undergone a systematic decline, even in Brazil. This tendency has been quantified for Argentina, Brazil, Mexico, Chile, Peru, and Venezuela.[16] This decline reveals the fragile social and political appreciation of R&D in the region, and reflects the very weak link that exists between these activities and the industrial production preferably oriented toward the internal market. In those countries where international insertion depends on the industrial sector, the idea would be inconceivable that resources allotted to scientific and technological research be sacrificed for reasons of budgetary austerity.

General Characterization of the Current Situation

The current situation of the industrial sector of Latin America can be described by the following features, none of which are particularly stimulating: relatively high margins of unemployed capability in numerous countries and various sectors, the precarious financial situation of the businesses associated with the decline of the internal market, overindebtedness, high interest rates, and (in various countries) an impact on imports and foreign debt service produced by successive devaluations. The drastic decline in the investment rate (in several countries hardly sufficient for replacement) has increased the age of the industrial complex precisely at a time when the acceleration of technological change in the capital goods sector on an international level increased the degree of technical obsolescence. In addition, Latin America has recently witnessed the weakening and, in some cases, the dismantling of design groups in manufacturing businesses and engineering firms, and the deterioration in the level of job qualifications in that part of industrial labor displaced to other activities due to unemployment.

Besides the obvious restriction of investment funds, attention in the public sector has been placed on short-term problem management, resulting in an inevitable disregard for the strategic evaluation necessary for a minimal business orientation. Additionally, although the drastic decline in public sector wages and the restriction in personnel have contributed to eliminating activities that were not strictly necessary, these factors have weakened public support for certain decisive sectors such as technological R&D. This combination of unfavorable factors has probbly had a tremendous impact on smaller businesses having more fragile political ties with governmental entities. Indeed, in some countries of the region, the solvency of part or all of the system of financial mediation has been seriously compromised.

Consequently, this is not a situation of specific problems in determined agents or sectors, but one affecting the functioning of the entire "industrial system" integrated by productive, financial, public and private technological agents, and the existing consensus regarding industrialization policies. Although there are countries in the region where this characterization would be perceived as "apocalyptic," there are others where it would be catalogued as "euphemistic." What is of interest is the fact that the challenge of reactivating the business level, reorienting productive activity, enhancing the industry–natural resource and industry-service articulation, designing strategies and policies, and strengthening the diverse public and private institutions that have an impact on the functioning of the industrial productive sector must be confronted simultaneously.

2. The Black Box
of Technical Progress

Technical Progress and Manufactures

The innovation and technological development effort is not distributed homogeneously throughout production activity. This effort is concentrated chiefly in the manufacturing sector, representing between one-fourth and one-third of the GDP in most of the industrialized countries and consuming a quota that, in the majority of the cases, exceeds 90 percent of all resources allocated to R&D (see table 2.1). In other words, the manufacturing sector possesses a density of effort and technological content that equals three to four times the average density of economic activity. This basic fact explains the greater dynamism exhibited by the demand for these products over natural resources and, combined with other factors, influences the evolution of exchange terms between the manufacturing sector and distinct natural resource sectors.

The deterioration in the relative prices of natural resources, along with the renowned evolution of the oil sector, is very clear (see figure 2.1). Later it will be seen that the unfavorable evolution in the exchange terms of natural resources (normally associated with developing countries) actually appears to be favorable for some developed countries and unfavorable for others. In the North there are countries with a relative position similar to those of the South, while, in the South, the insertion of some countries resembles that formally prevailing in the countries of the North.

Returning to the subject of sectoral concentration of the technical effort in given production activities, it is interesting to note that within the manufacturing sector there are certain branches in which the technological effort is concentrated (see table 2.2). In other words, not all the

Table 2.1 Production and R&D Expenditure Distribution by Major Economic Activities, 1979

	Agri-culture	Mining	Manu-facturing	Infra-structure	Other Services
United States					
Industrial Production	3.8	3.6	28.5	16.2	44.7
R&D Expenditure	—	—	96.4	3.6	—
Japan					
Industrial Production	5.1	0.7	33.7	20.5	40.0
R&D Expenditure	0.2	0.3	91.8	7.6	—
West Germany					
Industrial Production	3.3	1.3	44.6	17.9	32.9
R&D Expenditure	—	2.3	92.2	2.0	1.5
France					
Industrial Production	5.9	0.9	34.5	17.9	40.7
R&D Expenditure	0.6	0.7	93.0	4.0	1.7
United Kingdom					
Industrial Production	3.1	3.7	33.6	21.0	38.6
R&D Expenditure	—	1.7	90.4	7.0	0.9
Italy					
Industrial Production	8.2	—	36.4	21.2	55.4
R&D Expenditure	0.0	0.6	81.4	6.7	18.0
Canada					
Industrial Production	5.6	6.5	27.0	21.5	60.9
R&D Expenditure	—	9.4	78.2	—	12.4
Netherlands					
Industrial Production	5.7	0.2	34.3	20.2	59.0
R&D Expenditure	0.7	2.4	90.1	—	6.8
Sweden					
Industrial Production	5.0	0.7	34.1	22.3	60.2
R&D Expenditure	1.6	0.5	91.8	5.0	6.1
Switzerland					
Industrial Production	—	—	—	—	—
R&D Expenditure	0.0	—	99.4	0.0	0.6
Australia					
Industrial Production	7.1	5.7	22.3	17.4	64.9
R&D Expenditure	—	4.0	64.3	14.4	31.7
Belgium					
Industrial Production	3.0	0.6	33.0	23.4	63.4
R&D Expenditure	0.7	0.3	87.4	2.1	11.6

(Table 2.1 continued)

	Agri-culture	Mining	Manu-facturing	Infra-structure	Other Services
Austria					
Industrial Production	6.0	0.7	37.4	21.9	34.0
R&D Expenditure	0.4	0.9	92.3	1.3	5.1
Norway					
Industrial Production	6.3	11.3	22.0	27.1	33.3
R&D Expenditure	1.0	5.8	79.1	11.0	3.1
Denmark					
Industrial Production	7.0	0.2	26.6	25.2	41.0
R&D Expenditure	0.5	—	78.6	2.2	18.7
Yugoslavia					
Industrial Production	—	—	32.5	—	—
R&D Expenditure	—	—	—	—	—
Finland					
Industrial Production	11.2	0.6	34.4	23.0	30.9
R&D Expenditure	1.0	1.6	90.5	4.4	2.5

Source: Joint ECLAC/UNIDO Industry and Technology Division, *Industrialización y Desarrollo Tecnológico, No. 1:* "Ciencia y tecnología en la OCDE, posición relativa de América Latina," Santiago, September 1985.

industrial branches are equally intensive in terms of knowledge and technological endeavor. In fact, chemical products and engineering products principally receive a minimum of 80 percent of the ongoing research effort under circumstances in which their weight in total production activity is less than 40 percent. Engineering products should be understood here as metalmechanics—capital goods, transport equipment (mainly cars), and household appliances, all of which correspond to the U.S. pattern spread throughout the rest of the world after World War II. Consequently, the "technological density" of these branches is double that of the entire manufacturing sector and six times that of all production activity combined.

These sectors exhibit at least three additional important characteristics. In the first place, they have undergone the greatest growth during the postwar period in many types of countries with differing levels of development. Moreover, they evidence the greatest dynamism in international

Figure 2.1 Weighted Indexes of Commodity Prices: 1950–2000*

(Constant U.S. dollars, 1985 = 100)

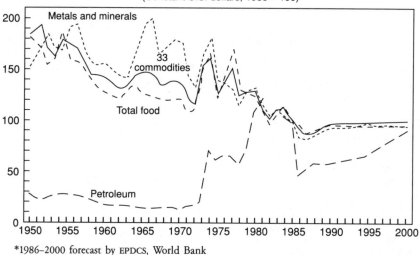

*1986–2000 forecast by EPDCS, World Bank

trade; that is, these sectors absorb a growing percentage of industrial production and international trade and, furthermore, are the sectors where the internalization process of production has also been the most dynamic. Figure 2.2 shows the sectoral evolution of the industrial sector for the principal industrialized regions during the period 1970–1987.[1] The graph shows that the electric equipment sector, whose primary dynamic component is the electronic subsector, demonstrates a high degree of dynamism in all four regions. If Japan, where the transformation of the production sector has been initiated by the electronic subsector, were to be excluded, the sectors of plastics, industrial chemicals, and electrical machinery, would become the axes of the industrial transformation in the United States and Western and Eastern Europe.

Consequently, in international economics and independently of the socioeconomic system, the sectoral content of technical change has been marked by two clear axes common to the various types of countries. On the one hand, the axis of the chemical sector, stimulated by the relative decline of oil prices between 1950 and 1973 (notwithstanding the 1973 and 1979 shocks) continues to present a high degree of dynamism, although lower than in the past. The result of this phenomenon has

Figure 2.2 Industrial Structural Change: North America, Western Europe, Eastern Europe, and Japan, 1970–1987

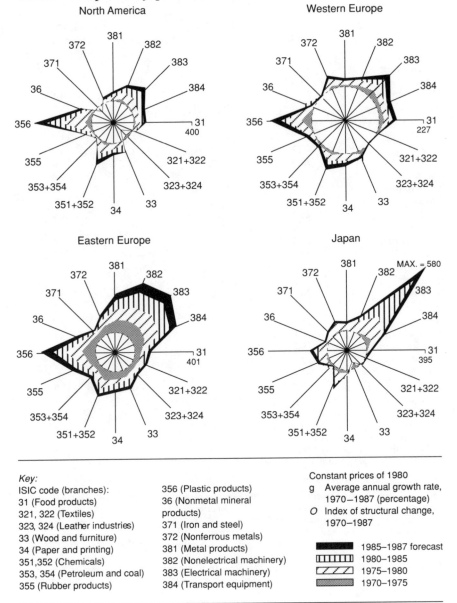

Key:
ISIC code (branches):
31 (Food products)
321, 322 (Textiles)
323, 324 (Leather industries)
33 (Wood and furniture)
34 (Paper and printing)
351,352 (Chemicals)
353, 354 (Petroleum and coal)
355 (Rubber products)

356 (Plastic products)
36 (Nonmetal mineral products)
371 (Iron and steel)
372 (Nonferrous metals)
381 (Metal products)
382 (Nonelectrical machinery)
383 (Electrical machinery)
384 (Transport equipment)

Constant prices of 1980
g Average annual growth rate, 1970–1987 (percentage)
O Index of structural change, 1970–1987

1985–1987 forecast
1980–1985
1975–1980
1970–1975

Sources: United Nations Industrial Statistics, estimates and forecasts by UNIDO / IS / GLO.

Table 2.2 Comparative Structure of BERD[a] by Industry Group,[b] 1981 (BERD = 100)

	Electrical	Chemical	Aerospace	Other transport
United States	20.2	13.9	22.6	10.8
Japan	24.5	18.1	0.0	17.2
West Germany	23.9	23.1	6.2	14.1
France	24.7	18.8	17.5	11.8
United Kingdom	31.1	16.1	20.1	5.0
Italy	14.9	23.2	9.1	14.4
Canada	22.5	18.0	12.3	2.4
Spain	16.3	22.8	37.6	19.6
Australia	10.9	15.6	—	9.4
Netherlands	—	34.2	—	—
Turkey	—	—	—	—
Sweden	23.1	9.8	—	21.9
Belgium	25.1	34.0	0.4	2.5
Switzerland	24.7	48.5	—	0.6
Austria	22.8	12.2	—	9.3
Yugoslavia	—	—	—	—
Denmark	11.8	18.1	—	3.3
Norway	20.1	9.4	—	5.1
Greece	5.9	20.3	8.0	5.8
Finland	20.9	16.1	0.2	3.0
Portugal	16.8	22.8	0.0	7.9
New Zealand	9.4	11.2	0.2	4.2
Ireland	22.6	17.2	0.2	3.3
Iceland	31.8	13.0	—	—
Total OECD[b]	22.0	17.0	15.0	11.5

Source: OECD/STIIU data bank, December 1985.
[a]BERD = R&D performed in the business enterprise sector.
[b]Partly estimated by OECD, except for the Netherlands.
[c]The sum of the indicated industry groups may be less than 100 percent, the difference representing R&D in agriculture and mining.

Detailed composition of industry groups

Electrical group: Electrical machinery, electronic equipment, and components (computers excluded)
Chemical group: Chemicals, drugs, petroleum refineries
Aerospace: Aerospace (missiles included)
Other transport: Motor vehicles, ships, other transport
Basic metals: Ferrous metals, nonferrous metals, fabricated metals products
Machinery group: Instruments, office machinery and computers, machinery n.e.c.
Chemical-linked group: Food, drink, and tobacco; textiles and clothing; rubber and plastics
Other manufacturing group: Stone, clay, and glass; paper and printing; wood, cork, and furniture;
    other manufacturing

Basic metals	Machinery	Chemical-linked	Other manu-facturing	Services	BERD^c
2.9	20.2	3.1	3.1	4.1	100.0
8.3	13.3	7.2	4.2	6.6	100.0
4.5	16.1	3.2	1.9	2.4	100.0
3.3	9.2	5.3	2.1	5.8	100.0
2.4	12.0	4.7	2.1	4.8	100.0
2.5	10.0	3.9	4.2	16.5	100.0
6.0	7.3	3.9	5.1	12.2	100.0
6.9	5.5	7.2	5.1	14.1	100.0
10.0	5.8	5.8	3.9	32.0	100.0
—	—	7.2	0.7	7.5	100.0
—	—	—	—	—	—
7.1	14.7	3.5	6.4	11.1	100.0
8.1	5.9	6.3	5.0	12.2	100.0
4.8	16.0	2.6	0.8	2.0	100.0
8.9	23.8	9.3	5.4	7.2	100.0
—	—	—	—	—	—
2.0	22.9	8.6	13.7	19.5	100.0
11.4	15.2	4.6	4.3	11.2	100.0
12.4	0.9	4.6	11.6	30.6	100.0
8.2	24.6	7.8	12.0	5.7	100.0
2.9	3.3	3.9	4.2	29.0	100.0
5.8	3.3	24.0	5.0	34.4	100.0
6.0	8.1	26.6	5.8	8.5	100.0
27.3	1.3	8.4	7.1	0.1	100.0
4.0	17.0	4.0	3.0	5.5	100.0

Services group: Utilities, construction, transport and storage, communications, commerce engineering services, other services been an increasing substitution of natural products by synthetic ones. On the other hand are those sectors that comprise "engineering products" and whose key features are a high degree of technical progress conducive to a diffusion of the productivity increases throughout the entire productive sector and a foothold vis-à-vis growing shortages, increased cost, and the heightened unification and political clout of the labor sector. The intensification of international competition associated with the spread of progress and industrialization to new regions and countries reinforces the need for technical progress and the expansion of the capital goods sector.

The explanation for the productivity increases requires the analytical identification and isolation of those sectors that have more responsibility for technical progress. To neglect this role, peculiar to given sectors, would result in the sterilization of the analytical potential for explaining technical progress and the increase in productivity, which is one of the chief factors in the growth and transformation of an economy.

The main source of inspiration for economic policies — Macroeconomics — is, in fact, based on the assumption that sectoral disaggregation serves no purpose in achieving the analytical goals pursued. These goals involve the definition of short-term macroeconomic equilibria among variables which result from adding up the effect produced in the different sectors by the various agents participating in economic activity. Macroeconomics is concerned with defining to what extent it will be possible to achieve equilibria among product, consumption, and investment, and to balance public accounts and short-term external accounts.

In explaining this indifference with respect to technical progress, some authors emphasize the influence of the trauma produced by resource underutilization inherited from the crisis of the 1930s:

> Perhaps on no topic does hindsight make the state of economic thinking in the late 1940s seem as archaic as in the area of productivity and economic growth. Productivity growth was not viewed primarily as the wellspring of economic progress, but rather as a source of unemployment. The lack of attention to productivity and long-term economic growth reflected the obsession with the possibility of underutilized resources and the doubt that the economy could remain along a full-employment path.[2]

Others link it with an essential trait of the neoclassical conceptual framework:

The neoclassical tradition in economics, beginning in the late nineteenth century, turned away from the classical concern with long-term economic growth prospects and concentrated instead on examining the implications of maximizing a static behavior in a static framework. A main concern, which has dominated this tradition up to the present day, is to analyze how a market economy generates forces bringing about a return to equilibrium after some force has disturbed that equilibrium. Considerable attention has been devoted to analyzing the conditions determining the stability and the efficiency of the equilibrium state to which the economic system gravitated. However, neoclassical economics consists largely of a comparison of successive equilibrium states and does not incorporate an analysis of the adjustment process per se. Technological change, when it is considered at all, is usually treated as some exogenous, once-and-for-all, cost-reducing process innovation to which the economy subsequently adjusts.[3]

Some of today's most renowned economists recognize that the contribution of macroeconomics is particularly precarious in the sphere of growth and the increase in productivity. Among other factors, this is because it overlooks the breakdown of the sector, which would isolate those factors that have more responsibility in this process: "Admittedly, growth theory is still at the frontier of economics, and the experts are not all agreed on the mechanisms of past and future paths of development."[4] The need to overcome this insufficiency is expressed in the convergence of viewpoints with respect to the need for an analytical breakdown of the sector with the goal of opening up the "black box" of technical progress.[5]

Technical Progress and Macroeconomics

Productivity growth has witnessed a deterioration in dynamism since the mid-1960s. From World War II until that time, productivity in all of the industrialized countries grew at a minimal rate of 3 percent. Since that time and until the mid-1970s and today, productivity in the United States has remained at very low levels and has recuperated only slightly in other industrialized countries. Concern about this subject has been widespread and has reached the highest levels of debate among in-

Table 2.3 Macroeconomic Similarities and Structural Differences
(percentage of GNP)

	Public consumption	Private consumption	Gross domestic investment
Lower middle-income economies[a]	13	71	19
Upper middle-income economies[a]	14	65	22
Industrial market economies[b]	17	62	21
Panama	19	64	18
United Kingdom	22	61	17
Costa Rica	16	61	25
France	17	64	19

Source: World Bank, *World Development Report 1986,* Tables 5, 26, and 27.
[a]Middle-income developing countries with 1984 GNP per capita of $401 or more.
[b]Members of OECD (excluding Greece, Portugal, and Turkey) included among middle-income developing countries.

dustrialized countries. "The sharp decline in economic growth in industrialized countries presents a problem comparable in scientific interest and social importance to the problem of mass unemployment in the Great Depression of the 1930s. Conventional methods of economic analysis have been tried and found to be inadequate. Clearly, a new framework will be required for economic understanding."[6] Even in the summit meetings of industrialized countries held during the 1980s, the subject of productivity and technical progress came to occupy a prominent position.

Table 2.3 shows a macroeconomic contrast of the situation of distinct countries with differing levels of development: lower middle income, corresponding to an approximate range of between $500 and $1,500 per capita; upper middle income, between $1,500 and $5,000; and industrial market economies, which are, in general, higher than $5,000 to $6,000 and reach $16,000 per capita (1984). From the standpoint of macroeconomic indicators, the profile of these three groups of countries does not appear to be radically different. There are two possible traits, however, that would differentiate the three groups of countries. The first refers to the increase in the gravitation of the public sector in line with

Gross domestic savings	Export of goods and nonfactor services	Total current revenue central gov't.	Total current expenditure central gov't.	Overall central gov't. Surplus/Deficit
16	21	21.0	24.0	− 5.0
26	26	24.0	27.0	− 6.0
21	18	27.0	30.0	− 6.0
17	36	30.2	40.4	− 12.1
17	29	37.6	41.4	− 5.0
24	34	24.3	26.4	− 2.2
19	25	42.7	44.8	− 3.6

the development level and per capita income increases. The second refers to the fact that the degree of opening, measured by total exports with respect to GDP, appears lower in the most industrialized countries. Paradoxically, these two differences contradict the current growth recommendation to developing countries to shrink the public function and increase the degree of opening.

This noteworthy similarity seems still clearer in the process of comparing developing and developed countries, wherein the differences from the macroeconomic profile are practically imperceptible. In contrasting the cases of Panama and the United Kingdom, the level of differences seems notoriously more discrete than what would be assumed a priori given the nature of the countries being compared. The same occurs with the cases of Costa Rica and France. If there were no differentiation as to which country had which figures, even an informed observer could make the mistake of attributing the figures of one country to another. What does this mean? It would mean that, from the viewpoint of macroeconomic analysis, the differences among structurally dissimilar countries are irrelevant with respect to their analytical conclusion, which is equated with short-term macroeconomic equilibriums.

To make an analogy (which as such is both limited and frail), this would be equivalent to a physiologist proposing the weight of each of the distinct organs of the human body as a measure of the arithmetical sum of the weight of the distinct organs, thus negating the specific role that each performs. Its equivalence in the sphere of economics would be to deny that determined productive sectors present the peculiar property of being privileged recipients of technical progress, and thereby deny recognition of one of the determinant factors explaining the growth and socioeconomic transformation of the countries. An even more prosaic analogy could be illustrated by the automobile mechanics specialist who affirms knowledge of everything there is to know about the functioning of an automobile except for the engine. The recognition of this limitation constitutes a significant advancement that is becoming increasingly more visible.[7]

Consequently, we are faced with a crucial methodological problem, the countries of Latin America that present the particularity of the empty box in terms of growth and equity. Their chief feature would be their fragile capacity to absorb, process, and develop technical progress, a phenomenon that would mark the development pattern characterized by four common elements — international insertion by means of natural resources, industrialization oriented toward the internal market, the precariousness of the national industrial business class and a critical reproduction of the consumption pattern of the developed countries.

In a period when industrialized countries are making a systematic effort to resolve the problem of accelerating the incorporation of technical progress, they discover that the theoretical framework that serves as a reference for economic policy design negates the subject that is the main feature of the development problem. Hence, the need arises to formulate an analytical scheme that, without having general interpretative pretensions, permits a systematization or organization of thought regarding the links between the industrialization pattern and development and, consequently, the achievement of these two key objectives. An outline of this analytical framework will be formulated and described in the following chapter, and later will be submitted to the test of reality by contrasting distinct national situations. Before approaching that topic, however, it would be interesting to portray the industrial technological transformations at an international level and their implications for Latin America.

Fundamental Tendencies of the Transformations

Erosion of dynamism. During the 1950s and 1960s, when the profiles of the industrialization of Latin America were defined, the international economy was characterized by the existence of a "virtuous circle" between economic growth and the increase in productivity which induced a rapid internationalization of trade and industrial production. From the standpoint of the consumption, production, and energy pattern, the basic technological referent originated in the United States, a country which in 1950 generated 60 percent of the world manufactures product. Europe, Japan, and the developing countries, along with their specificities,[8] were inserted in this wave of growth through which markets were expanded, technical knowledge was spread, and overseas investments of corporations were enhanced.

Since the end of the 1960s and the beginning of the 1970s, a deterioration in both productivity and economic growth has been evident. The circle has reversed, wherein a movement of financial resources whose dynamics tends to gain its independence from real economics combines with the recycling of oil resources after the shocks of 1973 and 1979 and the U.S. deficit to contribute to the step of floating exchange rates.[9]

The crisis of productivity and the specificities of the United States, Europe, and Japan. In real economics, attention is centered on the decline in the growth rate of productivity[10] and its effects on inflation, the decline in investment, the difficulty in overcoming socioeconomic rigidities, and the erosion in the competitiveness of the United States and Europe with respect to Japan and the newly industrialized countries (NICs). In explaining this phenomenon, a wider range of factors is explored, among which are included technical progress, the savings-investment relationship, business management, job qualifications, and, in recent years, "quality of the product and production process," which would have an impact on the efficiency of both the manufacturing process and the use of inputs.

There are notorious differences in the challenges faced by the United States, Japan, and Europe. In the first case, a problem of competitiveness is sharpened, primarily affecting the products of less technological content (clothing, shoes, textiles), but currently enveloping areas of medium technological content (iron and steel manufacturing, automobiles, naval industry) and areas of high technological content (computers, semiconductors, and telecommunications equipment). Growth in productivity is slow; however, the ability to generate employment is relatively high. Fifteen million jobs in the last decade have been the outcome, but this has been restricted to activities (predominantly in the service industry) whose average salary levels are lower than those of the preceding period (between 1973 and 1980 the productivity of the manufacturing sector rose at a rate of 2.1 percent and the work hours at a rate of 1.2 percent annually). In Europe, the central topic is unemployment, while the growth in productivity reaches high levels in Germany, Italy, and France (5 percent annually), and low levels in England (2 percent annually). In the last sixteen years, there have been practically no new jobs in Europe, and employment in the industrial sector has dropped to an approximate annual rate of 2 percent.

For different reasons (lack of competitiveness and unemployment) protectionist stands in the United States and Europe have been reinforced, leading Japan, whose principal markets are precisely the United States and Europe, to foresee the need for a change in its growth pattern and to direct a greater percentage to its internal market.

Central role of technological change. From the end of the last decade until the present, industrialized countries have come to accept the idea that technological change performs an essential function in the structural change perceived necessary because of the impact of this process on the patterns of consumption, production, communications, transportation, and energy. In the recent summit meeting in Tokyo, this idea was reaffirmed in the first paragraph of the document covering the conclusions in the area of economics: "We stress the need to implement effective structural adjustment policies in all countries across the whole range of economic activities to promote growth, employment, and the integration of domestic economies into the world economy. Such policies include technological innovation, adaptation of industrial structure, and expansion of trade and foreign direct investment."[11]

Unlike what happens often in Latin America, this proposal reflects on the empirical evidence that science and technology spending of the advanced countries since the end of the 1970s has been undergoing a sustained growth in relation to GDP, gross fixed capital formation, and, regardless of austerity policies, total public spending.[12] Resources are being concentrated with growing emphasis in the manufacturing and "high-tech" sectors (consumer and industrial electronics, computers and semiconductors, scientific and pharamaceutical instruments) whose dynamism at the level of production and international trade, has split away from the slow growth of the rest of productive activity.[13]

Erosion of the comparative advantage based on natural resources. The effects of the process of technological intensification on the utilization of both natural resources and the work force have been accentuated with respect to past tendencies. At the beginning of 1986, prices of raw materials, excluding oil, were on a comparable level to those of the Great Depression of the 1930s. A study recently elaborated by the International Monetary Fund (IMF) estimated that the raw materials content of a product unit has been declining systematically at an annual rate of 1.25 percent. This implies that the quantity of raw materials necessary for a unit of industrial production would be approximately 40 percent of that required at the beginning of the century. This tendency would appear to have accelerated in recent years. In 1984, Japan utilized 60 percent of the raw materials needed for an equivalent industrial production in 1973.[14] In 1977, U.S. plastics production reached the same levels as steel production and currently equals the combined production of steel, aluminum, and copper. In the last ten years, U.S. energy consumption per product unit has dropped 25 percent and that of oil, 33 percent.

Exchange rate terms projections for the rest of the decade would reflect a continuity of this tendency with the corresponding consequences for those countries whose insertion into the world economy relies upon natural resources, among which can be included the United States since 1982 (net exporter exclusively in agriculture, with a deficit in industry, energy, and mining). The principal favored countries would be those whose insertion in the international market is based on a surplus in their manufacturing sector.

Erosion of the comparative advantage based on cheap labor. In reference to the impact of technical progress on employment, there is a wide range of projections that vary in magnitude, but not in the direction in which they point, that is, toward a reduction in labor needed to achieve similar levels of future production. In Japan and in large U.S. corporations, estimates have prognosticated a duplication in the production during the next fifteen to twenty years, with a reduction in employment of between 25 and 40 percent. Sectors that were labor intensive are rapidly increasing their capital intensity (textiles, clothing, electronic assembly). High-tech sectors (semiconductors and fine chemicals) with a labor content smaller than that of a completely robotized automobile plant are being developed. In combination with a general process of automation in the distinct productive sectors, this leads to the erosion of the comparative advantage based on the availability of cheap labor.

Institutional modifications. Some important modifications being produced in the institutional sphere affect Latin America's access to technological progress. These modifications are linked to a move that is being made from a technological pattern characterized by high standardized production scales and low, decreasing energy costs to a flexible system based on the integration of small productive modules with a greater emphasis on scientific knowledge and supported by the drastic decline in the costs of information processing, transmittal, and organization. Distinct expressions of this would be: advanced technology sectors (microelectronics and genetic engineering), cooperative R&D schemes among firms from different countries in the same sector (automobile), the upsurge of joint ventures for high-tech areas among industries of different sectors (robots in automotive companies, computers, machine tools, and electronics), cooperative research programs between businesses from different countries and the respective governments (European programme, EUREKA), and the fading of the boundaries between industry and services in the specific area of information technologies (displacement of telecommunications firms toward the computer field and vice versa).[15]

Industrial restructuring in developed countries. Developed countries have a concern for integrating structural changes into their production structures so as to recuperate or consolidate their respective international insertions, but they do so from radically different perspectives and traditions. For Japan, the structural adjustment in the industrial sector constitutes the basic feature that would describe historically its industrialization process, successive displacement of resources toward the sectors in which greater dynamism in the international markets is foreseen, with an emphasis on those activities benefiting from technical progress.

A similar concern, although with different institutional modalities, has been evidenced in the case of the Federal Republic of Germany (FRG) and, in the case of France, in given sectors linked to the purchasing power of the public sector. On the other hand, U.S. industrial restructuring implies a conceptual and institutional innovation in treating the structural change as an ex post reflex of a series of successive adjustments produced by the market. In this conception, the legitimate instruments of structural adjustment are macroeconomic variables. The devaluation of 30 percent in the last two years, however, implemented as a means of attenuating the tremendous trade deficit, would seem insufficient, according to recent estimates, and consequently forbodes the reemergence of protectionist pressures as opposed to the formulation of positive structural adjustment policies.[16]

Regardless of the differences mentioned, developed countries share basic traits that give specificity to the topic of industrial restructuring in that context. These countries could be defined as having economically and socially articulated societies — relative equity in income distribution, extensive educational coverage, relatively low productivity differentials between sectors and businesses, and varied modalities of participation and social and political representation. Their consumption pattern and production are generated endogenously, and they have an international insertion in which, aside from the degree of competitiveness, they have achieved high levels of specialization in the commerce of manufactured goods. Consequently, industrial restructuring would be oriented toward a limited shared objective: to increase or consolidate international competitiveness within the framework of internally integrated societies.

In sum, the industrialized countries envelop themselves in a process of industrial restructuring. A salient factor in this process is that the country that served as a reference in terms of consumption, production and technological pattern, the United States, has lost competitiveness in the manufacturing sector, and, consequently, has been transformed into a net debtor. It currently absorbs resources generated by countries having surpluses, principally Japan and Germany, plus the resources originating from economic and extraeconomic motivations, including the service of the debt and the "capital drain" from the less developed countries.

The official norm stresses the need for industrial restructuring based on an analytical framework in which macroeconomic dimensions are preferred in order to adapt to technological change and maintain international competitiveness. In practice, however, an analysis of the policies adopted by countries belonging to the Organization for Economic Co-operation and Development (OECD) would show that they include diverse elements of interventionism at a sectoral and even microeconomic level:[17] priorities are defined in given sectors (winners); R&D subsidies are channeled to certain activities; nontariff barriers are erected in specific areas; the purchasing power of the public sector is explicitly used as a promotional tool; a wide range of fiscal incentives are granted; and businesses suffering a financial pinch are saved.

Leading European businesses in advanced technology sectors demand five to seven years of protection from their governments, in addition to those guaranteed by the legislation of industrial property, to ensure the survival of these "budding industries." In the United States, businesses in the iron and steel production sector request twenty-five years of protection to revitalize their activities. In Japan the purchases of automated equipment by small and medium industries are subsidized.

The gap between the recommendation of neutral, uniform policies based on "real prices" and their implementation in the countries where the recommendations originated is even greater when considering the two fundamental traits of those societies: economical and social integration and insertion in the international economy mainly through the manufacturing sector. Both of these could be portrayed as solid arguments in favor of neutral, uniform policies based on "real prices."

Final Reflections:
Implications for Latin America

Less favorable external framework than in the past. Latin America faces an international framework that is ostensibly less propitious and more complex than that in which the previous phase of the industrialization process was inserted. This occurs simultaneously in various areas: dynamism of the world economy; financial flows; transition in the technological pattern; homogenization in the cultural pattern with a high degree of diffusion and transparency of communications; and, finally, the preeminence of a school of economic thought that, while not even reflecting the practice of economic policy in advanced societies, could hardly impart the specificities of Latin American reality.

"Less draw effect." Aside from whatever the economic growth rate would be in developed countries, certain indicators reveal that the "draw effect" on the Latin American economy would be less than in the past due to protectionist tendencies, the consequences of technical change on the demand of natural resources, the decline of competitiveness in labor-intensive sectors and the disappearance of financial flows that enabled an import growth superior to that of exports. Additionally, the growth rate in developed countries would appear to be less than in past decades.

Financial restriction. At a financial level excluding the debt, advanced countries need to channel investment funds into their own economies for reasons linked to internal processes of industrial restructuring and to the intensification of international competition. The regional attempt to serve the interests of the debt — approximately 4 percent of GDP, 25 percent of investment, and almost double net investment — contributes to an intensification of the deterioration in exchange terms as a result of the overexpansion of raw materials exports. It also accentuates the preexisting features of socioeconomic disarticulation — an increase in unemployment, regressive income distribution, the elimination of subsidies to less favored sectors, an increase in tariffs in public services, and a decline in real wages — and limits the possibilities of growth.

Erosion of dynamism and socioeconomic disarticulation. From 1980 to the present, the countries of the region have lost their precarious socioeconomic articulation and dynamism. A growing number of countries would present the double-faceted feature of stagnation and socioeconomic disarticulation; very few could be situated in the category of dynamic but socioeconomically disarticulated or in the category of relatively articulated but stagnant, and none would fulfill the double condition that in some period in their history the majority of the advanced societies have observed, socioeconomic articulated and dynamic. The high degree of urbanization achieved by the distinct countries of the region and the widespread diffusion of mass media have homogenized aspirations but not real access to the goods and services that characterize modern societies.

The adoption and diffusion of this Latin American "urban collective fantasy" contributes to explaining the willingness to serve the interests of the foreign debt as a necessary evil in order to avoid the risk of losing

Figure 2.3 Latin America and the Caribbean:
Net Inflow of Capital and Net Transfer of Resources

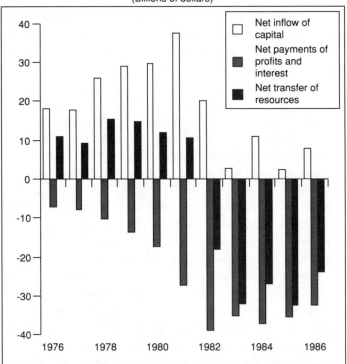

Source: ECLAC, on the basis of data from the International Monetary Fund.
Preliminary overview of the Latin American Economy 1988, December, 1988.

membership in the conglomerate of modern societies (see figure 2.3).[18]
Aside from the likelihood of this hypothesis, what is evident is that Latin
America faces serious obstacles in attaining the two objectives shared
by the different regional governments: growth and socioeconomic integration. Although Latin Americans may have access to the use of modern
objects, without growth and integration they are far from consolidating
modern social relations.

3. The Analytical Framework: From Black Box to Empty Box

At this point, an attempt will be made to identify the chief factors that link the pattern of industrialization and development with the achievement of the objectives of growth and equity. In light of the diverse historical experiences of development, the fragile theoretical base available, and intuition, attention will be centered on some aspects that surface as important explanatory factors. Moreover, these aspects satisfy the conditions of quantification and international comparability. Identification will be made of other elements which cannot undergo a systematic comparative quantitative analysis, but which, from the standpoint of reflection, seem important to incorporate. A hypothesis will be formulated about the type of linkage that would exist between the origin of social formation and the type of leadership that predominates in the distinct societies and the corresponding implications in the economic sphere.

The principal factors to be explored and quantified are: the natural resource base, the structure of the industrial system, its international competitiveness, and the pattern of consumption and investment. It is worthwhile to establish the linkages between these factors and the objectives of growth and equity. Some hypotheses will be formulated about the relations of causality that will explain why both objectives have been reached in diverse countries. Furthermore, the factors that have and would continue to have an impact on the process not being reproduced in Latin America will be individualized. Understanding these factors is vital for designing the specific policies that can contribute to the achievement of the goals of raising the standard of living of the population and, simultaneously, correcting the inequalities.

The purpose of this analytical scheme is basically to organize and systematize reflection in order to enchance an understanding of the linkages that have been produced in existing industrial systems. This does not mean that this scheme can explain the evolution in a given country during a given period, but rather that an attempt is made to extract by means of contrasts useful indications with respect to the type of relations of causality that contribute to the convergence of growth and equity in each case. The attempt to enhance an understanding of the configuration of the virtuous circles is coupled with the risk of not only idealizing historical experiences, whose inevitable "vicious" component is minimized, but also implicitly suggesting the existence of factors that could appear to be prerequisites. In the "backward countries," however, the prerequisites that are lacking will probably be replaced by other factors. It could be that many of the conditions that in the advanced countries could be considered prerequisites are the outcome of the very process of industrialization in Latin America.

Therefore, it could be said that, in the backward countries, a large part of the "preparation" tends to coincide with the industrial boom phase, and that this mixture of periods has been the true precondition of rapid industrialization. Diverse situations in particular periods and countries (that will not be clearly explained by this scheme) could be imagined. Nevertheless, because they deviate from the previously described dynamic, they tend to illustrate additional factors that are not included in this scheme which would be necessary to add when advancing to the normative phase. To the extent that the evaluation or relevance of the scheme is backed by facts, this phase must include the identification of transformations and the design of policy instruments that could have an impact on the economic, social, or political sphere in order to modify previous behavior and induce a directional change desirable according to the analytic framework. As in every comparative analysis, there is a possibility of sacrificing certain national specificities for the sake of introducing the principal explanatory features by means of contrast.

The reasoning is developed in two phases. In the first, the relations of causality on which the interpretation is based are suggested. In the second, the policies that can favor or disrupt the convergence of the development process and the objectives of growth and equity are identified.

An attempt to obtain empirical verification for some of the former propositions will be made in later chapters. Others, principally those that refer to the interrelations among economic, social, political, and cultural aspects are mentioned simply as suggestions for future research in fields other than economics or in interdisciplinary projects. The fact that they cannot be the object of immediate verification does not bar their importance in considering the options confronting Latin American industrialization; the magnitude of the crisis and its complexity is so immense that the possibility of resolving the challenge of the empty box in the partial, limited sphere of economics must be discarded.

Both in the general formulation developed in this chapter and in the subsequent empirical verification, reference is made to the contrast between international insertion through the rise in competitiveness of the industrial sector, technical progress incorporation, and what is called "rentist" insertion. The first one is based more on the deliberate and systematic absorption of technical progress by the production process (with corresponding rise in productivity) than on the maintenance of low real wages. In this respect, proper account must be taken of the need for learning and disseminating internationally available know-how, a possibility which has not been sufficiently exploited by the region in the past. What is needed is to progress from the "transitory rents" derived from natural resources to "continuing rents" offered by the absorption of technical change by productive activities. The easy option based on "rent" would be that which supports itself by the profit of privileges or monopoly on certain scarce natural resources (an idea derived from classical economics) or from the privilege of exercising hegemonic positions at a political, military, economic, or cultural level. "Rent is a venerable concept in economics. Defined as return in excess of resource owner opportunity cost, economic rent has played a prominent role in the history of economic analysis."[1] This definition is an extension of the classical idea and is applied in chapter 4 to the peculiar situation of the United States, whose money, language, and way of life has served as a planetary reference during several decades and has allowed it to partially offset the negative consequences of the persistent erosion of its industrial competitivity. With the generic notion of rent an attempt is made to seize all national situations where the permanent incorporation of technical progress in goods or adjusting services is not perceived as a requisite to maintain or even to raise the population's level of living.

Basic Elements and Relations: Equity, Austerity, Growth, and Competitiveness

The elements and relations of causality to be explored appear in figure 3.1. Two stages in the approach are distinguished: in the first, attention is centered on those factors that constitute the central nucleus of the analysis: agriculture transformation-equity-pattern of consumption/investment-growth and competitiveness of the industrial system. Later, the influence that such factors as the natural resource endowment, demographic tendencies, availability of a national industrial entrepreneurial class, scientific and technological knowledge, foreign direct investment, international financial investments, and the reference consumption pattern at the international level exercise over this central nucleus will be discussed.

The influence that public policies can exercise in the functioning of this system is approached in the following section, which is based on the analysis of the previously mentioned relations. Next, the relations that are explored in the analysis and shown in the diagram will be discussed sequentially (the enumeration of the paragraphs corresponds to the arrows in figure 3.1).

1. The Transformation of the Agrarian Structure and Income Distribution

The starting point of the analysis resides in the transformation of the agrarian structure. This may seem strange, since the principal focus of concern is the industrial sector, the incorporation of technological progress, and international insertion, but the structural transformation of the agricultural sector has performed a determinant role in distinct experiences of industrialization.[2] It is a well-known fact that the modalities adopted by that transformation, as well as the social processes in which it is inserted, have been highly varied in historical experience.[3]

The element of convergence, however, would reside in the fact that the transformation has performed a crucial function in the process of the incorporation of the peasantry into modern society, in the modification of agriculture-industry relations, and has specifically influenced the increase in the levels of equity. Structural transformation of agriculture

Figure 3.1 Growth, Equity, and Patterns of Industrialization

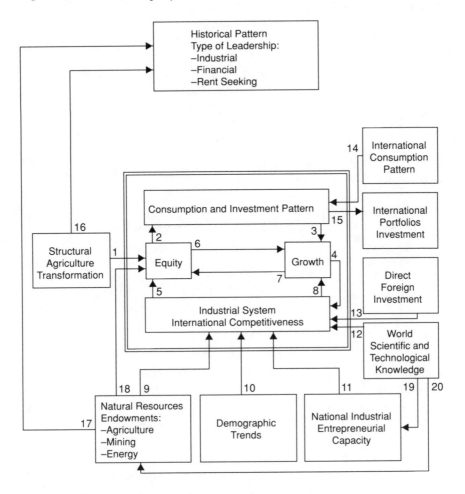

has significantly influenced the patterns of income distribution (entitlements), and therefore the patterns of demand, with which the distinct societies confronted the gestation phase of their industrial structures. In other words, the origin of inequity and even certain behavior patterns of the leading elites — crucial determinants of the paths followed in the processes of development in general and industrialization in particular — seem to be closely linked to the characteristics of the processes of formation and transformation of their agrarian structures.

Figure 3.2 Income Distribution (Upper 20%): ABRAMEX and Selected Developed Countries

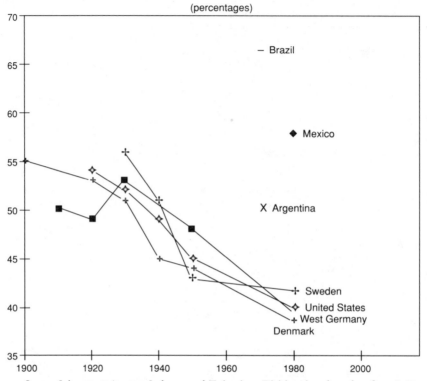

Source: Joint ECLAC / UNIDO Industry and Technology Division, based on data from S. Kuznets, *Modern Economic Growth: Rate, Structure and Spread* (New Haven: Yale University Press, 1966) and World Bank, *World Bank Development Report 1986* (Washington, D.C., 1986).

In the specific case of Latin America, a crucial feature of differentiation with respect to developed countries, and also certain countries of late industrialization from other regions, is found precisely in the "pathology" of inequity. Even those countries that present more favorable profiles in the region — Argentina and Uruguay, which have agricultural structures with relatively more "modern" traits and less differentials of productivity, both within the agricultural sector and between agriculture and industry — currently show patterns of income distribution comparable to that observed in developed countries of the 1940s (see figures 3.2,

Figure 3.3 Income Distribution (Lower 60%): ABRAMEX and Selected Developed Countries

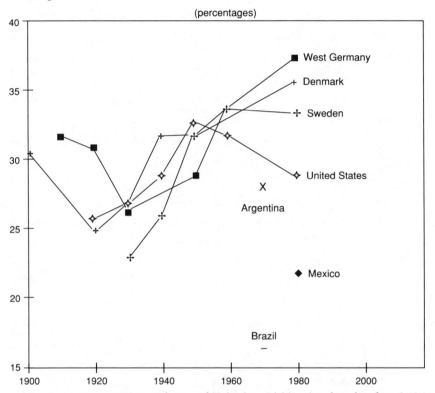

Source: Joint ECLAC / UNIDO Industry and Technology Division, based on data from S. Kuznets, *Modern Economic Growth: Rate, Structure and Spread* (New Haven: Yale University Press, 1966) and World Bank, *World Bank Development Report 1986* (Washington, D.C., 1986).

3.3, and 3.4). The rest of the Latin American countries, where a strong heterogeneity of intersectoral and intrasectorial productivity is perceptible, present an income distribution that apparently has no precedent in the history of developed countries, at least for the time period for which reliable information is available.

In Latin America, 89 percent of the economic activity (GDP) is originated in countries whose level of equity is less than half that prevailing in developed countries. Diverse studies carried out at an international level,[4] as well as the experience of Latin America,[5] affirm the hypothesis

Figure 3.4 Income Distribution (Lower 60%/Upper 20%): ABRAMEX and Selected Developed Countries

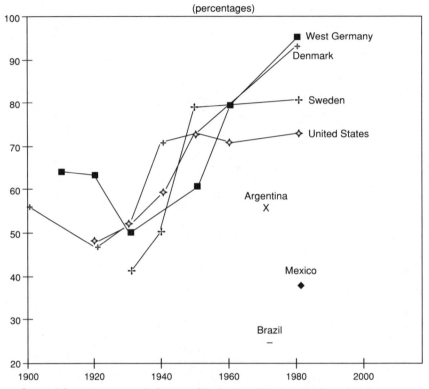

Source: Joint ECLAC / UNIDO Industry and Technology Division, based on data from S. Kuznets, *Modern Economic Growth: Rate, Structure and Spread* (New Haven: Yale University Press, 1966) and World Bank, *World Bank Development Report 1986* (Washington, D.C., 1986).

that there would exist a clear relationship of causality between structural transformation of agriculture and the improvement of income distribution. As will be seen further on, the latter performs an important role in the configuration of the productive system and, consequently, in the capacity for the absorption and generation of technological progress and international insertion.

2. Income Distribution and the Consumption / Investment Pattern

Equity and its impact on social articulation generate a relatively more austere consumption pattern than that prevailing in situations of acute concentration of income, since it inhibits the highest income sectors from reproducing to a caricatural degree a consumption pattern from more advanced societies.[6] In addition to the fact that a more austere consumption pattern frees resources for investment, the hypothesis could propose that a certain relationship would exist between the degree of exuberance "of the consumption pattern" and the level of the capital/output ratio (unverifiable empirically).[7] Productivity of investment would be higher in those societies in which the consumption pattern is relatively austere, this being a consumption pattern with a smaller percentage of durable consumption and less use of energy and foreign exchange. In those countries, the capital/output ratio would tend to be lower than other countries where an attempt is made to reproduce the reference consumption pattern. Those countries would be characterized by a high density of durable consumption and energy consumption, and a physical infrastructure of communications and transportation capable of supporting a reality with an abundance of capital, a low population density, and a large territorial expanse.

3. Consumption / Investment Pattern and Growth

Greater austerity in the consumption pattern and the consequent increased productivity of investment directly favors growth. It assumes the existence of adequate institutional mechanisms for the channeling of savings to investment. In the first industrialization (England), in which a large quantity of small and medium owners accumulated capital, the Weberian hypothesis of "ascetism" encounters clear confirmation. In the lately developing countries, however, that process acquires different institutional modalities; major special "agents" appear, possessing a completely distinct capacity for channeling and generating means of investment, even through external or internal credit. These agents, historically appearing in "latecomers," replace the initially fragmented accumulation with *Crédit Mobilier* style banks (France), then mixed banks (Germany), and, finally, a certain type of recent substitution related to the degree of backwardness, the state.[8]

In Latin America, the state performs a significant role in the transformation of savings into investment. How does it do it? With what distortions? On the basis of what social coalitions? With what stability? These questions, undoubtedly, merit additional research, but apparently they are not resolved by the administrative decision of transferring that responsibility to the private sector. Distinct economic policy instruments[9] will exercise an influence on the channeling of savings into investment and on external linkages with regard to the reproduction of international consumption patterns and the possibility of savings flows overseas, both in terms of financial investments and the payment of interests and utilities. What is interesting here, however, is the linkage — in our judgment, crucial — between the degree of *austerity* of the consumption pattern, the role of the investment agents, dynamism, and the trend of "transparency" accentuated during the last decade between the national and international processes of the conversion of savings into investment. (In the 1980s, Japan, Germany, and, paradoxically, Latin America save more than they invest, while the United States invests more than it saves.)

4. Growth and International Competitiveness

Growth enables the incorporation of new generations of equipment and products, and thus contributes to increasing productivity and reinforces international competitiveness. The broadening of the internal market in a growing range of goods and services associated with growth and favored by equity and austerity constitutes the irreplaceable basis for industrial-technological learning, a necessary condition for international insertion. This virtuous circle between growth and competitiveness, in which the requisites of equity, austerity, and technological learning are often omitted, constitutes one of the central axes of the successful experiences of industrialization.

Due to the insufficiencies within the confines of equity, austerity, and the "frivolous" character of protectionism, both growth and competitiveness in Latin America have tended to be spasmodic, a condition which does not correspond to the cyclical nature that growth demonstrates in industrialized societies. In this case an upward trend of incorporation of technical progress would be indicated; what is periodically evidenced gility of some of the aforementioned links required for the functioning of the virtuous circle.

5. Competitiveness and Equity

In a social context in which a minimal threshold of equity (agrarian transformation) has been overcome, an internationally competitive industrial system favors equity by (at least) the following means: a relatively broad distribution of property associated with the creation of small and medium enterprises, the diffusion of labor qualifications, a more rapid growth of employment associated with the dynamism of the international market, a surge in productivity and wages, the diffusion of the educational system on the widest and most integrated social base (as an essential requisite for sustaining international competitiveness), and, finally, the diffusion of industrial logic by both formal and informal means to the whole of society. This will make society more receptive to absorbing technological progress, a factor that, in turn, will favor the increase in productivity, and the diffusion of the fruits of technical progress in a more equitable form to society.

These achievements, however, are not necessarily found in those cases where competitiveness is attained at the expense of wages. The resources generated in the initial phase, instead of being geared toward the incorporation of technical progress by way of investment, are displaced to consumption or overseas. This could be described as "bogus or ephemeral" competitiveness, which should not be theoretically or historically confused with that described above.

6. Equity and Growth

The fact that a society exhibits a higher degree of equity favors a social disposition toward an endeavor to undertake long-term options that foster growth. In the distinct social strata, the perception of belonging and social integration tend to encourage participation in a collective effort to partially defer the consumption that leads to growth. Hence, equity facilitates growth: directly by inducing a consumption pattern compatible with a high and more efficient investment rate; indirectly by creating a social climate compatible with the effort of the "building of the future," an effort which necessarily requires legitimacy on the part of the elite and the system in order to ensure the willingness of society to undertake the actions and decisions conducive to the proposition of growth.

7. Growth and Equity

Growth, in turn, tends to make social functioning flexible and attenuate the eventual lags in distribution, making them more bearable than in those situations in which stagnation predominates. This does not mean that growth per se leads to equity, a topic systematically refuted in the Latin American experience and in other regions. Nevertheless, with the existence of a process of growth and a competitive industrial pattern, the gap in equity does not lead to the same kind of social conflicts found elsewhere, since there is a perception that the future situation will be more favorable than the present one. In sum, equity would support growth and growth would support equity as long as a more austere pattern of consumption/investment and a competitive industrial system coexist.

8. Competitiveness and Growth

The competitiveness of the industrial sector, which confronts a more dynamic demand than the rest of the productive sectors, contributes positively to growth. Experience shows that the international trade of manufactures is expanding at a higher rate than world trade. This difference is increased for those areas having a greater content of technological innovation, which in the last four decades has been localized in the metalmechanics industry and chemicals. At more disaggregate levels, the leading areas at the level of international trade and technical progress are being modified and, consequently, the capacity of the countries to be inserted solidly in international markets is firmly conditioned by their ability and possibility to accompany those international technological trends.

As that aptitude is developing, the feedback effect on growth is accentuated through the modification of relative prices, the surge in productivity, and the widening of the internal market. The affirmation that competitiveness reinforces growth acquires greater effectiveness when productivity is manifested in areas with more technological content and when businesses and support technological infrastructure form part of the reservoir of the country in question. This does not exclude the potential contribution of areas of little technological content of those that originated in foreign companies. However, it stresses the relevance of the relationship among *productive sectors, enterprises*, and *types of markets*, in which it is vital to dig deeper in order to understand the process of technological innovation. The fact that conventional macroeconomics ignores this linkage (sectors-businesses-markets) inhibits its capacity to capture the central nucleus of the dynamic of technical progress.

9. The Natural Resource Base and the Competitiveness of the Industrial System

The natural resource base exerts a considerable influence on the configuration of the industrial system of the respective countries, particularly in reference to the urgency and moment of the system's need to attain international competitiveness. In countries with a generous base of natural resources, the legitimacy of the system—which assumes a capacity to satisfy basic needs—can draw for a longer period of time on the advantages derived from their resource base;[10] in countries that lack an abundant resource base, that legitimization demands the generation through an internationally competitive industrial sector of the foreign exchange necessary to obtain the resources that permit the growing satisfaction of the basic needs of their populations.

The smaller the resource base and the greater the willingness to penetrate the markets of developed countries and sectors with high, growing technological content through national enterprises, the more demanding this strategy will be. A strategy of this type is the only option for countries with a shortage of natural resources which have chosen to sustain a development pattern that will ensure both growth and equity. In this sense, more than one alternative among many, this is a survival strategy for the very existence of industrial society.

10. The Population Dynamic and the Industrial System

Although it is undeniable that the population dynamic has an impact on the evolution of the industrial system, the essence of its effects is not exempt from the ambiguities of generalization. Greater population growth in the context of a favorable endowment of natural resources can permit the dynamism of the industrial sector to be sustained for long periods of time, even if concentrated in the internal market. In other cases, it can serve as a brake: a high population growth rate leads to hyperurbanization, with the consequent requirements of investment in the physical infrastructure, increase in the capital/product ratio, and the absorption of an important part of the population growth in low productivity activities; these, in turn, lead to the accentuation of inequity that has a negative impact on the process of long-term growth.

The ambiguity of the impact of population growth on economic dynamism is exemplified by the fact that of the possible combinations between the growth rates of the population and economic growth, the only one that is absent in Latin America is that in which low rates of the first and high rates of the latter coincide. Stagnation of the population can accelerate the exhaustion of the growth phase with a low rate of increase in productivity, but rapid population growth without sufficient accumulation and/or market leads inexorably to the erosion of dynamism.

11. The National Entrepreneurial Class and the Industrial System

The availability of the national entrepreneurial base will unquestionably be a determinant factor in the construction of an internationally competitive industrial system. This is not a key requirement in supplying the internal market and, in fact, the leadership of the most dynamic sectors can be displaced to foreign firms, whose behavior will become assimilated without difficulty into the market conditions. In order to penetrate international markets, however, the requisite absorption of technical progress and innovation must be accomplished through the addition of intellectual value to natural resources or to the available unskilled labor force so as to stay solidly inserted in a lasting manner. The existence of the national entrepreneurial base in a wide range of possibilities and linkages with foreign investment will be determinant.

Transnational corporations (TCs) can contribute to dynamizing exports in determined periods and sectors in those countries with a large internal market or persistently low wages. The solidity of international presence is determined, however, by the existence and development of national enterprises capable of competing, alone or associated with foreign investment, with the corporations that actually supply international markets. The subject of entrepreneurial capacity is necessarily linked to that of the existence of the worker, technician, and professional sectors, and their respective union organizations. The nature of the relations within the business sectors influences the sociopolitical institutional configuration, the evolution of productivity, and the absorption of technical progress.

12. Access to Scientific-Technological Knowledge and the Industrial System

Access to the reservoir of available technological knowledge at the international level undoubtedly reinforces the possibility of consolidating internationally competitive industrial systems. This access naturally tends to reinforce the national entrepreneurial base and vice versa. The existence of the national entrepreneurial base constitutes a determinant factor for the absorption of this knowledge. The limited success attained by scientific-technological development institutions diffused in the 1970s throughout Latin America with limited resources is partially attributable to the limitations of those the public and private industrial entrepreneurial bases that performed the leading role in the task of absorbing, applying, and demanding this type of knowledge. The reciprocal linkage between policies of "frivolous" protectionism and entrepreneurial fragility is still not clear. Moreover, the scientific-technological reservoir influences both the available supply of natural resources (techniques of prospecting and exploitation) and their demand.

13. Foreign Investment and the Industrial System

The presence of international enterprises with direct investment in the industrial sector is a circumstantial factor that can either reinforce or weaken national entrepreneurial capacity, but it is not the sole determinant of the competitiveness of the respective industrial system. In those countries where the industrial system is conceived primarily for supplying the internal market, this direct foreign investment will tend to assimilate the behavior of the national sector. Thus, the export coefficient of foreign companies in Latin America does not differ from national businesses, whereas in other countries with a pronounced dedication to international insertion they present a coefficient even higher than that of the national enterprises. In some countries, their presence is accepted to the extent that their export coefficient is notoriously higher than that of national firms. Thus, access to the international market, which they tend to favor, is required in exchange for access to the internal market (see table 1.6 in chapter 1).

Except in specific cases in which geographical location or the availability of cheap labor enhance a country's attraction as a platform for exports, in general terms the key purpose of the expansion of foreign enterprises is to cover new markets. Consequently, their primary interest is to supply the respective internal market. It would be illusory, therefore, to expect that the mere incorporation of foreign investment would resolve the problem of the international competitiveness of the respective industrial system.

14. The Cosmic Consumption Pattern

In the 1970s, communications advances and the increasingly more fluid flow of people and ideas resulted in a high degree of transparency in the predominant consumption pattern at the world level. This factor must necessarily be incorporated as a fact of reality considering the consumption patterns of each country. It would be unwise to ignore the existence of a "cosmic consumption pattern" that constitutes a reference pattern which conquers the "collective fantasy," including the rural zones. (Diverse national experiences confirm this, including some of a continental size.) The differences among the countries does not lie so much in the fact that some choose this consumption pattern and others opt for another which apparently does not exist, but rather in the rate and methods by which the unique and dominant reference pattern is internalized in each society. In the case of Latin America, this reproduction, this absorption of modernity through the cosmic consumption pattern, has been carried out with minimal concern for the internal requirements of socioeconomic integration and the creation of conditions for a solid international insertion, and with middle income levels highly inferior to those prevailing at the time of the absorption by the societies in which those models originated. The universal nature of that consumption pattern is expressed even in the growing penetration by determined, symbolic goods and services of the markets of the planned economy countries. These countries are willing to pay royalties through the exportation of local products or in hard money in order to permit their populations access to certain goods that could hardly be justified for objective reasons. They constitute a reflection of the recognition that in the "collective fantasy" of those countries, the cosmic consumption pattern exported by the United States had attained a level of incorporation that is politically difficult to ignore.

15. Financial Resource Flow Overseas

Since the end of the 1970s and during the expansion of the 1980s, the possibility of investing financial resources abroad could be added to the cosmic consumption pattern through expedient, rapid modalities that are difficult to control and regulate. Agents that possess the national financial resources currently have the option of investing them rapidly with high degrees of security in hard money at satisfactory interest rates. The possibility of generating internal resources for investment does not guarantee that their investment necessarily take place in the country itself.

Pressure from developed countries to liberalize the financial markets of developing countries results in the developing countries having to face not only the problem of the definition of options for the investment in and generation of their own available internal resources, but also the option of investing in hard money overseas in a preferred, expedient manner due to the progress in communications and computers. Information technologies have had an undeniable, though dubious, impact as a means of absorbing liquid financial resources. Obviously, that is not the origin of capital drain, but simply a technical means that favors it.

16. The Transformation of the Agrarian Structure
and the Type of Leadership

Specialists in the subject of agriculture, backed by economic history, assert that its structural transformation significantly influences the modification of leaderships and, consequently, the evolution of respective social formations.[11] In the specific case of Latin America, the concrete expression of the insufficiencies in the structural transformation of agriculture would be the unequal income distribution and a certain component of "rentism" incorporated into the respective national leaderships.

The formation of the citizenry free men with rights and duties with respect to the state, has a strong impact on the type of leadership and equity since it favors the organization of demands in that direction. It implies transition from the relationship of personal dependence (bonds of slavery) to the relationship of citizen. In those situations in which political change does not transform the agrarian social structure, a mechanism of a sort of *gotopardesco* domination surfaces through which traditional sectors develop the flexibility to "absorb" and deform the processes of modernization.[12]

> When we consider the implications of recent analytical advances in the context of historical experience, we find, however, that it is hard to avoid the conclusion that it has been a great advantage to a country to be able to enter the period of modern agricultural growth with a unimodal, small-scale, predominantly owner-operator agrarian structure. The political costs of improving land tenure arrangements are very high even under the most favorable of circumstances. When agriculture was organized along bimodal lines, such as the traditional *minifundio-hacienda* system that characterized much Latin American agriculture, the political costs often permitted nothing more than marginal adjustments toward more efficient land tenure arrangements.[13]

The insufficiencies of the structural transformation of Latin American agriculture lead to a productive structure that specialists have labelled bimodal[14] (with the exception of Argentina and Uruguay), and is composed of a small entrepreneurial sector (20–25 percent of the productive units) concentrated on the major part of arable land and a still more significant percentage of irrigated land. It probably generates around 60 percent of commercialized production. A vast "peasant" sector is located on the other extreme of the scale, where a high percentage of productive units is concentrated on a small percentage of irrigated surface area and production. The entities defined as *minifundio* represent 71 percent of the units and 5 percent of the surface area.[15] Between these two limits, entrepreneurial and peasant, there is a sector that, in approximate terms, could be assimilated by the European middle peasantry, whose weight varies according to country and is normally concentrated in certain regions and commercial areas with high unit value.[16]

This productive structure arrived after a process in which agriculture underwent considerable transformation. In various countries of the region, agrarian reforms have been executed that projected changes in property structure, but whose later evolution has been regressive due to the rigidity of the social structure. "There appear to be relatively few areas, however, where the land reforms have been accompanied by the policies needed to sustain productivity growth in the small-scale peasant sector. And there are even fewer areas where the Latin American reforms have succeeded in resolving the problems of equity in the agrarian structure."[17]

The other structural change that cannot be ignored is the emergence of a modern agricultural sector whose contribution to export growth and production has been significant. However, a negative effect associated with the modality of the adopted technological modernization would have surfaced. This modernization would have contributed to

a) widening the income gap between large land exploitations that are modernized and small ones that cannot do so; b) reducing work demand of the large exploitations, directly affecting the minifundists that need waged employment as a complement to obtain a livable income; and c) increasing the profitability of the land and its value along with it, making even more remote the possibility of the peasantry, which has no land or has an insufficient amount, being able to gain access to it.[18]

17. The Natural Resource Base and the Type of Leadership

In those societies in which the possession of a generous base of natural resources creates situations of high concentration of property in either the private or the public sector, the emergent leadership is upheld by the use of revenue associated with those natural resources. Hence, stratified societies and patrimonialist states are formed. All rentism, independently of its specific nature, is based on a politically constituted "privilege" or monopoly.

This constellation normally will be associated with given origins of the respective social formations. That certain rentist elements predominate in leadership does not bar associate or subordinate the coexistence of representative sectors of industrial activity. What must be stressed here, however, is that such leadership is reflected in a certain perception of reality and can have an influence on the functioning of the whole society. Accepting the existence of a certain mimicry within society, that is, a diffusion and reproduction of the values passed down by the leadership to society, it would seem that this perception of the world could penetrate and spread to various spheres of the public sector, the private sector, and distinct institutions that participate in its functioning — political parties, armed forces, unions and syndicates, professional organizations, bureaucracy.

The practical expression of this diffusion of rentist values — parochialism, shortsightedness, risk-taking aversion, and the predominance of the personal use of the function performed to the detriment of the institutional roles — at various levels and behaviors goes beyond the sphere of this work, but is a subject that merits additional research, particularly in the case of Latin America, where it has a greater relevance than it has been given. The process of urbanization, industrialization, and institutional modernization perhaps leads to underestimating the relevance of what could be called a latent rentist mentality.

Overcoming the stratified relationship calls for a redefinition of political and civil society, with the state as a former ambit, and the market the natural sphere of the latter. Consequently, the analysis of the nature of the relationship between state and market in the distinct countries, as well as the degree of consolidation and the institutional expressions of both, are a crucial topic, not only in order to enhance our understanding of their functioning, but also for the design of the policies that can exert a true influence on their transformation.

18. The Natural Resource Base and Income Distribution

The natural resource base, whose property in some cases is concentrated in a small percentage of the population or in others is centralized in the public enterprise, tends to have a negative impact on income distribution. Should this refer to private, national, or foreign businesses, it results in a concentration of property in a very small percentage of the population. In the case of public enterprises, rentism could be reproduced within those public enterprises, converting them into veritable bureaucratic fiefdoms which keep a considerable share of the rent generated in the form of notably higher wages and benefits than in the rest of productive activity. The transfer of the property of big enterprises, either to the private sector or to the public sector, would not modify this basic fact, which is linked more to the existence of a patrimonialist mentality than a particular form of property.

The Role of Policies

This section is dedicated to revealing, very tentatively and schematically, the influence that distinct economic policy instruments can exert on the manner of functioning characterized in the former section. In the following chapters, where the various configurations adopted by this system in countries that differ in terms of development level and economic system will be explored, some illustrations concerning the use of specific policy instruments will be provided.

If one accepts the assumptions that the aspiration of growth with equity is shared and knowledge about the nature and pertinence of distinct policy instruments is well known throughout the world, one must necessarily conclude that structural factors have an impact on the explanation of the distinct configurations observed in reality. Some of these factors will be unalterable — size, resource availability, geographic location — while others will reflect the ongoing process of economic, social, political, and cultural transformation. If the application of the "adequate economic policies" — about whose content there are certainly distinct approaches — were a sufficient condition to attain simultaneous growth and equity, we would assuredly be facing a world with more homogeneity and less poverty than what "truly exists," where the conflicts and the various, scarcely moldable "passions and interests" are clearly reflected.[19]

With these limitations in mind and conscious of some degree of repe-

Figure 3.5 The Role of Policy

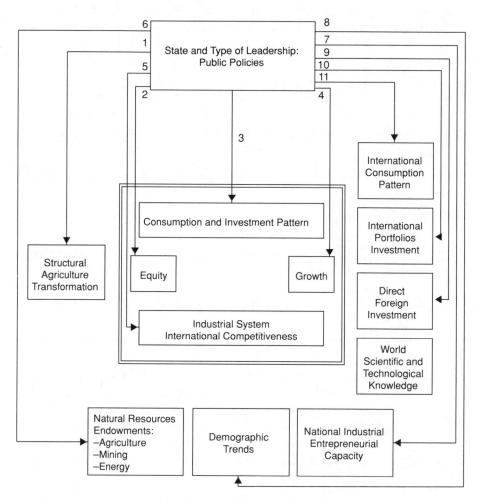

tition regarding the aforementioned, reference will be made to the possible influence that policy instruments can have on each of the elements incorporated into the system described (see figure 3.5, which uses the same graph/text enumeration scheme used in figure 3.1).

1. Structural Transformation of Agriculture

In developed countries, the emergence of industrialization was preceded and then accompanied by profound transformations in the agrarian structure which favored the diffusion and homogenization of the increases in productivity and contributed to the widening of markets in both agriculture and industry. Examples include the Puritan Revolution, the French Revolution, the Meiji Restoration, the U.S. Civil War, and the agrarian reform of Japan and Korea at the request of the United States with the documented effects on productivity and income distribution.[20] The forms of the social organization of agricultural production that preceded the process of the confirmation of their industrial structures were of particular relevance, in the sense that the presence or lack of presence of "unimodal agrarian structures" had a decisive impact on the internalization or not, respectively, of the dynamizing effects of the demand for input and consumer goods of agriculture to budding industry.

Additionally, the possibility of production to scale of consumer goods and simple means of production in the first phases of industrialization firmly depended on the existence of a relative degree of homogeneity in the type and size of the agricultural production units. This also enabled the progressive assimilation, adaptation, and generalization of technological patterns adjusted to the scales and forms of the productive unit organization with normally distributed characteristics.[21]

Although hardly reducible to a mathematical model, it would be impossible not to recognize the principal action in the management and implications of these transformation processes, that of "passions" and "interests." This does not preclude repeating the recommendations designed to attempt a reduction of the contrasts between country and city and between agriculture and industry, which assumes, among other measures:

> 1. Stimulation of the production of inputs and means of production for the agricultural sector (fertilizers, pesticides, plastics for farm use, implements, and, in some cases, machinery) and the growing industrial processing of raw materials of agricultural origin
> 2. Promotion of the ruralization of agroindustry and other industrial branches, with a view to making the former a nucleus for the creation

of superior forms of productive organization for small and medium-sized farmers and turning the latter into a mechanism of absorbing the underemployment and seasonal unemployment typical of this sector (as the experience of many developed countries shows, the combination of partial employment in agriculture with local industrial employment has been a major factor in reducing differences in income and living standards between the country and city)

3. Stimulation of the development of para-agricultural services to permit large-scale access to technical assistance, the mechanization of some tasks, and experimentation with alternative forms of soil management and analysis

4. Increase, or, if resources do not permit this, reallocation of public investment in the agricultural production infrastructure (transport, storage, refrigeration, etc.) and rural social infrastructure (schools, polyclinics, etc.) so that, completing the measures mentioned earlier, it will help to retain the rural population and thus avoid its migration to the cities and the consequent increase in urban poverty.[22]

In this area, Latin America has an "item pending" that significantly explains the high degree of inequity prevailing in the majority of the region and has an impact on the consumption patterns, the productive structure, and the modality of international insertion.

2. Equity

A wide range of factors influence income distribution.[23] They are both structural and emanate from public policies. Figure 3.5 depicts the transformation of the agrarian structure, the level of competitiveness of the industrial sector, and the growth rate. Distributive and redistributive public policies can undoubtedly exert a significant influence with the necessary political volition: fiscal policy, from the standpoint of income, expenditures, wage policy, employment policy (in urban, marginal, and rural sectors), policies intended to favor social organizations (unions, parties, cooperatives, associations), health and education services, training programs, the establishment of collective equipment for popular housing, social welfare systems, support for urban and rural small industry.

The differences existing in the realm of equity in the distinct developed countries (United States and Japan, for example) or developing countries (South Korea and Latin America) can hardly be explained by gaps in the knowledge of respective public policies. The existence in certain countries of some degree of rentist leadership negatively influences equity, both directly in terms of concentration of property and generally by way of institutional and economic policies that tend to consolidate a distribution scheme of the benefits of progress coherent or maximally compatible with the original distribution of power. A drastic opening of the internal market can question or rationalize the rentist industrial scheme, but if unmodified or, worse, concentrated, the consequent industrial regression will lead to an accentuation of insertion by means of natural resources and/or development of commercial and financial mediation.

3. Consumption and Investment Pattern

Just as income distribution exerts an important influence on the consumption pattern, a varied spectrum of economic policy instruments have a direct impact on the consumption pattern as well: tax systems, credit policies, social security schemes, and costs of capital appreciably contribute to explaining the respective differences in the consumption and investment patterns.[24] The presence of sectors of a rentist mentality in the exercise of the public function influences consumption and investment patterns in the following direction: the rentist elite aspires to and succeeds in reproducing the life-style of developed countries independently of the private and social costs, not only in the sphere of direct consumption but also in terms of spreading values and physical investment options congruent with the hypothetical, promised reproduction of that life-style throughout the rest of society. In that way, the reference pattern is spread down through the income pyramid, reaching depths that depend on the unit value of the respective goods and services. From the moment in which the possibilities of extensive growth by way of adding labor from the country or capital resources from abroad have been exhausted, this can contribute to eroding the growth potential.

The reproduction of the consumption pattern of developed countries does not exclude the possibility of coexistence with growth as rural labor is available and resources in the form of foreign exchange (through natural resource exports and foreign indebtedness) are accessible. What is interesting to emphasize is the fact that, having exhausted the possibilities of foreign indebtedness and with the survival of the social consensuses becoming increasingly more expensive and politically more fragile in situations of a high degree of exclusion, the growth process will tend to be questioned. This was perhaps the situation that some countries of Latin America experienced in different modalities at the beginning of the 1970s and lasting until the end of the decade due to the fluid access to foreign indebtedness. In recent years, the net transfer of resources to overseas reached 4 percent of GDP. A return to the situation of net recipient of resources is not evident, at least in the coming years.

4. Growth

As one of the chief objectives of development, a wide range of factors have an impact on the achievement of this goal.[25] In the characterization utilized here, the consumption and investment pattern, the level of equity, the competitiveness of the industrial sector, and the series of policies and orientations that emanate from national leaders — macroeconomic policy, financing of the public sector, institutional mechanisms for savings, financial mediation system, financial flows to and from overseas — are stressed. It is evident, however, that, in relation to both growth and equity, the peculiarities of the respective historical development processes exert a significant influence.

For example, in the case of countries where there is a component of rentist leadership, that leadership does not seem to be obsessed with growth nor with the projects of building for the future. Its interest lies rather in the maintenance of the status quo, which is particularly favorable to it. This is reflected not only in terms of values or more or less diffuse attitudes, but also in terms of "signals" and specific economic policies that tend to discourage a true socioeconomic transformation. In more general terms, the reflection on reality, its deficiencies and potentialities, in the eyes of this type of leadership seems almost by definition to be subversive because it questions the survival of a state of things which, being anachronous, is particularly pleasant and comfortable for those who embody it. This does not bar the possibility that socioeconomic transformations inevitably take place, and are even absorbed to the extent that they do not question essence. Such transformations, however, often merely contribute to externally legitimizing internal government action and, in that manner, have political and financial support.

5. Competitiveness of the Industrial Sector

Other factors[26] come into play in relation to this element, such as the growth rate, natural resource availability, the existence of a national entrepreneurial base, access to the world technological reservoir, the form of the presence of foreign investment, and a series of exhaustively inventoried and analyzed policy instruments: aggregate demand, exchange policy, interest rate, tariff trade policy, export promotion, credit policies, institutional mechanisms for the financing of medium-term investment, and technological, training, and external commercialization infrastructure, to name a few. It is highly probable, however, that in the explanation of the various modalities of international insertion of the European countries, the United States, and Japan, the incidence of the application of different policies may perhaps be less than the group of aforementioned structural factors.

In the case of Latin America, for example, the presence of a leadership with a certain rentist component may have an impact on the peculiar configuration of the industrial system. It is possible that the fact that industrialization is concentrated in the internal market of Latin America and consequently generates a "rent" for the industrial sector constitutes an expression of the diffusion of the rentist mentality of the traditional sectors to the new, emerging industrial sector. In fact, an industrialization lasting for various decades (in some countries almost a century) and concentrated primarily in the internal market is transformed gradually into a source of rent transfer from consumers to the productive industrial sector. Consequently, rentist behavior is generalized within the private industrial sector and the public bureaucratic apparatus that regulates and administrates the concessions to the productive sector which embodies the modernization of society. To this can be added the fact that in the majority of the countries of the region this "rentist industrialization" coexists with a traditional agrarian structure which inhibits the development of dynamic linkages between both sectors. As E. Faletto has stated, "the industrial revolution created its own demand or market, transforming the social structure. Latin American bureaucracy, which attempts to resolve the 1930 crisis, adapts the economy to society and does not revolutionize the society for a new economy."[27]

6. Natural Resource Policies

The application of scientific and technological knowledge to prospecting, extraction, and processing has taken hold with greater intensity in countries exhibiting two simultaneous conditions: the shortage of natural resources and the existence of an advanced scientific technological infrastructure.[28] This appreciation is applicable to both renewable and nonrenewable resources, as well as to the programmed effort to develop substitutes for scarce, strategic natural resources. The application of genetic engineering, the development of composite materials, and the application of the information technologies to the prospecting of resources have acquired particular heights in the last decade in the industrialized countries that seek, on the one hand, a growing degree of autonomy in their supplies and, on the other, the development of materials and products which fulfill precise, stable specifications. The growing knowledge about elemental particles in chemistry, physics, and biology, combined with the perfecting of electronic instruments and equipment, favor the transition to a period in which the "sciences of materials" take on a significant role. To the former factors can be added economic motivations coming from growing energy costs and the intensification of international competition, both of which stimulate businesses and governments of the industrialized countries to boost efficiency in the use of natural resources.

In this context, the challenge for the developing countries and, in particular, Latin America of systematically approaching the design and application of integral policies for renewable and nonrenewable natural resources assumes a certain amount of urgency and, possibly, a dramatic element unthinkable a decade ago. In order to approach this challenge, it is necessary to overcome or neutralize some of the aforementioned obstacles — the structural transformation of agriculture, the development of the scientific technological infrastructure, the thrust of competitiveness of the industrial sector, the establishment of financing mechanisms for long-term investments, and the overcoming of the rentist mentality that was supported precisely by the abundance of natural resources.

7. The National Industrial Entrepreneurial Class

The principal protagonist of the process of the incorporation of technical progress is the private and public entrepreneurial agent, without whom the policies and institutions of scientific and technological research would become "motors running in vacuum."[29] The weight and development of this leading actor is firmly conditioned by the historical development process of the distinct countries and by the changing national and international economic context. The growing weight, for example, of financial mediation with respect to productive activity, a trend that was accentuated during the last decade, erodes the dynamism and creativity of the productive enterprises, even in countries that formerly exercised leadership in the industrial sphere (for example, England at the end of the last century and the United States in the 1970s and 1980s).

In the case of Latin America, the component of rentist leadership largely tends to discourage directly and indirectly the emergence of the innovative industrial entrepreneur as a leading factor. In contrast to societies dominated by an industrial leadership associated with a complete shortage of natural resources, the legitimization of that leadership assumes the strengthening and diffusion of the national industrial entrepreneurial spirit. On the other hand, from the viewpoint of rentist leadership, the indiscriminate presence of foreign affiliate companies seems perfectly acceptable. What is more, it can even become a factor of consolidation of its respective internal forces.

Local rentist leadership does not perceive the need to reinforce a national industrial base, a necessary condition for undertaking a sustained process of technological incorporation and, consequently, of solid penetration into international markets. Rentist leadership is inclined toward the development of businesses and national groups in sectors of nontradable goods and services such as public works, which has a captive market of national public and private investment. This explains why some of the principal modern national entrepreneurial groups in the majority of Latin American countries have their origin and center of gravity in that sector. The same occurs with financial and commercial mediation, where the presence of traditional sectors alongside emerging entrepreneurial sectors is also found.

Although the results require a certain period of maturity, the public policies to foment private and public entrepreneurial development can perform an important role, particularly in reference to the increase in public enterprise efficiency and the fomenting of small and medium enterprise, a subject that acquires growing relevance in the transition period to a technological pattern that favors the reduction of minimum plant scales, increases flexibility, and generally enhances the technical viability of decentralization.

8. Population Dynamics

This subject is theoretically difficult, imperfectly elucidated, and in some countries politically delicate. However, during this period in which the distance between aspirations and possibilities increases, due to the economic context, the general trend would seem to point in the direction of policies destined to favor birth control. With the exception of the United States, where population growth continues to be relatively high, the problem does not exist in the rest of the industrialized countries, where, endogenously, it has been cut back to its minimum expression. In the developing countries and, in particular, in Latin America, the population growth rate has been reduced and institutions and policies have converged on this issue.

9. Direct Foreign Investment

In the industrial sector, this subject emerged in the 1950s and 1960s with the international expansion of U.S. corporations to which European firms were added in the 1960s and 1970s and Japanese in the 1970s and 1980s.[30] The investment flow and the trade flow have been principally centered among the developed countries, but in the 1960s and 1970s growth in direct investment in Latin America and in the larger and more dynamic countries, Brazil and Mexico, reached significant rates and was coupled with the dynamism of the region in that period. Foreign investment acquired relevance during the 1970s and was converted into an important topic on the international agenda. During the 1980s, direct investment of a marked procyclical nature curtailed its interest in the region, intensifying the concentration of the flows among developed countries and primarily toward the United States, a country in which Japanese and European investments converge with a return of the U.S. businesses. At present the subject of foreign investment in the United States happens to contain comparable elements of debate to those existing in Latin America in the 1960s and 1970s, particularly the erosion of sovereignty and self-determination in high-tech sectors. Curiously, present Latin American policy is particularly inclined toward foreign investment, but with meager results, due to the fact that the current market of interest to those companies is the one that defines their capacity for expansion and survival, the markets of the developed countries.

10. International Financial Flows

The possibility of instantaneously displacing large flows of financial resources raises serious doubts as to the autonomy of governments in economic policy design.[31] This statement is applicable to both industrialized countries and developing nations with the considerable difference that in the case of the latter, particularly Latin America, the flows are systematically negative. This is an obstacle that questions the essence of growth in and the productive reorientation of Latin America regardless of the problem of the foreign debt. As long as the international financial system is not reorganized (as with the crisis of the 1930s) and the national financial systems are adjusted to confront this challenge, it would be difficult to imagine national policies that could effectively neutralize the fact that internal saving leads to foreign investment, generally of a financial type.

11. Consumption Pattern

The need for public policies to regulate the process of the absorption of "modern consumption" in order to foster internal socioeconomic articulation and increase the competitiveness of the national industrial system is unquestionable.[32] The appropriate instruments vary according to the national case, but generally those with the greatest impact seem to be tariffs, the regulation of consumer financing, taxes, and an extra-economic factor related to the degree of social consciousness of the need to access modernity and which can be considered to be an ongoing, legitimate motivation compatible with growth and equity. The contribution that the mass media can provide in this task is determinant, whether in converging with or inhibiting this purpose. Ultimately, the modernity of the relations among people must be made compatible with legitimacy is, no more nor less than the physical contact between people and modern goods and services.

4. The United States, Japan, and West Germany: Winners or Losers?

The United States, Japan, and the Federal Republic of Germany (West Germany) possess a population that is approximately 9 percent of the world population and equivalent to that of Latin America. Nevertheless, nearly one-half the resources allocated at a world level and almost three-fourths allocated by OECD countries to R&D is concentrated in them. The availability of per capita R&D funds in these countries equals around five times the world average.

In terms of economic activity, they generate approximately 40 percent of the economic and industrial world activity, that is, a level of productivity equalling four times the world average. The main interest in contrasting the situation of these countries and evaluating them as a whole is based on the fact that their behavior forms the profile and principal features of the world industrial system. Independently of current trade tensions, the relations among these three countries condition the type of product, process, manufacturing modalities, type of institutional agreements, and accessibility that the rest of the countries may have to the future evolution of knowledge in the distinct industrial sectors. To achieve an understanding of the industrial dynamic of these three countries would contribute to the predesign of the frame of reference in which the action of the rest of countries, particularly Latin America, is inserted.

Some very important differences can be noted between the United States, at one extreme, and Japan and Germany, at the other (see table 4.1). The very high density of scientific production in the United States in relation to its population and to the other two countries is striking. The ratio of density of scientific authors to its population is seven times the world average, whereas in Germany, it is four times, and in Japan, two times. Regardless of and in open contrast to this solid scientific pro-

Table 4.1 International Insertion of Latin America, the United States, Japan, and West Germany (percentage of world total early 1980s)

	Latin America	United States	Japan	West Germany
Population	8.0	5.0	2.5	1.3
Gross domestic product	7.0	27.0	9.4	5.8
Manufacturing product	6.0	18.0	11.7	9.4
Capital goods	3.0	14.7	11.1	9.6
Engineers and scientists in R&D	2.4	17.4	12.8	3.4
Research and technological development resources	1.8	30.1	10.2	6.7
Manufactured exports[a]	1.8	12.1	14.2	13.3
Scientific authorship	1.3	42.6	4.9	5.4

Source: Joint ECLAC/UNIDO Industry and Technology Division, based on data from the United Nations, UNIDO, UNESCO, and the National Science Foundation.
[a]Manufactured exports defined as SITC sections 5 to 8 less division 68 (nonferrous metals).

duction base, the relative weight of Japan and Germany in the industrial environment is overwhelmingly higher than that of the United States. On a whole, the manufacturing production of Japan and Germany already surpasses the United States by almost 20 percent, although in terms of population the United States shows a 20 percent advantage. In other words, Japan and Germany own a particular talent for transforming knowledge into industrial production and the United States exhibits a relative lack of proportion between the base of available knowledge and the relatively meager weight of industrial production.

According to the former analysis, this phenomenon is linked to the fact that while in the United States a huge quantity of resources is channeled toward defense and space-oriented activity, in Japan and Germany this element is essentially nonexistent as a consequence of the dispositions imposed as an outcome of the Second World War. Moreover, the same figures substantiate a Japanese peculiarity wherein the ratio between the density of engineers and scientists in Japan and its population is practically five times the world average, while being a little more than triple in the United States and slightly less than triple in the Federal Republic of Germany.

An analysis of the comparison of the industrial situation of these three countries will be developed according to the scheme described in the last chapter. First, international insertion will be analyzed in accordance with distinct subsectors of activity and their incidence in the functioning of the industrial sector. Second, the industrial configuration and the international competitiveness of each will be analyzed. Third, attention will be centered on the comsumption and investment pattern of the three countries. Fourth, the linkages that exist between, on the one hand, the industrial configuration, international competitiveness, and the consumption pattern and, on the other, the achievements of these countries in terms of growth and equity. Finally, reference will be made to the distinct policy instruments that in one way or another influence the previously identified linkages; the contrast between the two cases that appear as polar situations, the United States and Japan, will be stressed in this comparison.

The Crucial Importance of Natural Resources

One of the chief differences that mark the insertion of these countries in international trade is the clear contrast between, on the one hand, Japan and West Germany, whose structural deficit in all natural resources reflects their fragile base in those sectors and, on the other hand, the situation of the United States, which, at least in the agricultural sector, presents a large and, until the 1980s, flourishing surplus (see table 4.2). The only method available to Japan and West Germany for acquiring the natural resources they lack is through a solid insertion in the manufacturing trade. On the other hand, due to its generous resource endowment and its continental size, the United States envisions international trade as a strictly complementary and marginal element. Furthermore, concern for prioritizing sectors is apparently irrelevant for a continental economy such as that of the United States. The U.S. perception, enhanced by a state of global economic predominance for the past forty years, maintains that local production is geared toward the internal market and that the situation in distinct sectors may vary throughout time ("intersec-

Table 4.2   United States, West Germany, and Japan: Trade Balance by Sector of Economic Activity, 1970–1987 (Millions of dollars)

	1970	1975	1981	1982
Agriculture:				
United States	631	12,069	25,344	19,728
Japan	– 5,292	– 13,931	– 24,929	– 23,508
West Germany	– 5,774	– 10,145	– 13,441	– 12,852
Manufacturing industry:[a]				
United States	4,154	21,196	13,369	– 3,942
Japan	13,180	42,393	119,152	107,197
West Germany	14,424	39,338	62,317	68,174
Energy:				
United States	– 1,480	– 21,922	– 73,974	– 54,665
Japan	– 3,858	– 25,432	– 72,091	– 65,306
West Germany	– 1,616	– 10,286	– 32,723	– 29,694
Mining:				
United States	– 863	– 1,295	– 5,183	– 3,426
Japan	– 3,698	– 5,734	– 11,223	– 10,388
West Germany	– 2,343	– 2,662	– 3,835	– 3,651
Other sectors:				
United States	196	640	758	– 280
Japan	105	594	– 2,168	– 1,095
West Germany	– 318	– 431	– 176	– 712
Total:				
United States	2,638	10,688	– 39,686	– 42,585
Japan	437	– 2,110	8,741	6,900
West Germany	4,375	15,814	12,142	21,092

Source: Joint ECLAC/UNIDO Industry and Technology Division, based on data from UN, *International Trade Statistics Yearbook,* various years, and UN, *Commodity Trade Statistics,* various years.

toral neutrality"). The nation on the whole, however, would occupy a position of almost absolute invulnerability, at least until the end of the 1970s. There are diverse indicators in the economic, academic, and political spheres that confirm this perception, centered chiefly on the internal problematique.[1]

With regard to the energy sector, the 1973 oil shock was felt strongly by all three countries. Specifically, between 1975 and 1981, the U.S. fuel bill increased by $52 billion, the Japanese fuel bill rose by $47 billion, and the West German bill increased by $23 billion. The difference lies in the subsequent impact. In Japan and West Germany, this increase

1983	1984	1985	1986	1987
16,518	13,307	3,659	− 320	3,813
− 23,301	− 25,776	− 24,214	− 27,892	− 34,787
− 12,868	− 15,568	12,644	− 15,266	− 17,579
− 28,925	− 82,377	− 107,566	− 138,626	− 146,010
113,403	131,689	137,550	162,311	167,254
59,013	60,235	68,131	89,902	105,152
− 50,349	− 53,814	− 45,759	− 31,652	− 39,014
− 58,636	− 59,989	− 55,319	− 36,565	− 38,779
− 26,694	− 25,545	− 26,212	− 17,971	− 18,044
− 5,298	− 6,424	1,302	− 6,087	− 5,440
− 10,055	− 10,554	− 9,663	− 8,657	− 10,962
− 3,231	− 571	− 3,319	− 3,331	− 2,835
− 1,268	188	− 245	− 3,961	7,963
− 877	− 1,758	− 1,992	− 6,454	− 3,020
375	171	− 484	775	− 650
− 69,322	− 129,120	− 148,609	− 180,646	− 178,638
20,534	33,611	46,362	82,743	79,706
16,595	18,722	25,472	52,559	66,044

[a]Manufacturing industry includes SITC sections 5 to 8 less division 68 (nonferrous metals).

was offset by increases in the manufacturing sector surplus. In the United States, the sharpening of the energy deficit was reinforced by a marked erosion in the manufacturing sector surplus equalling approximately $8 billion between 1975 and 1981. In Japan, the $47 billion increase in the energy deficit was offset and even surmounted by an additional surplus of $77 billion in the manufacturing sector. In West Germany, the $23 billion surplus in the manufacturing sector compensated almost exactly for the growing energy deficit.

The energy problem can hardly be blamed for the deterioration of the competitiveness of the U.S. manufacturing sector. The same energy impact was felt by all three countries, but the manufacturing sector's capacity to react was conspicuously more favorable in Japan and West Germany, where the trends of competitiveness and productivity generated a support base with the flexibility necessary to react to the energy crisis.

The subsequent evolution of the manufacturing sector would diverge radically from 1975 onward in the United States, on the one hand, and Japan and Germany, on the other. Around 1984, while the combined surplus of the manufacturing sector of Japan and West Germany neared $192 billion, the United States was already suffering the bitter taste of a deficit amounting to $82 billion. The first two countries would be the most important sources of manufacturing surplus at a world level; the United States would be the country where the manufacturing deficit had reached its greatest expression.

It is interesting to contrast this radically asymmetrical situation with that prevailing at the beginning of the 1970s, when the three countries possessed a relatively modest surplus, greater in Japan and West Germany than in the United States but comparable in size. Nevertheless, in fifteen years the relative position of these three countries has been radically modified. Ironically, the United States, whose productive pattern served as a reference for the postwar period and generated 60 percent of industrial production at the end of the Second World War, presented the largest deficit in the industrial sector vis-à-vis the two countries that were in a state of destruction by the end of the Second World War.

The international insertion of the United States since 1982 has been similar to that of the majority of the Latin American countries: it is based on an agricultural sector which maintains an appreciable surplus while all other productive sectors, chiefly manufacturing, present a deficit. Hence, the evolution of exchange terms takes on relevance for this nation. In maintaining the trend toward a decline in the exchange terms of the agricultural sector vis-à-vis the industrial sector, even if the quantities of agricultural and industrial products exported and imported were to remain constant, the United States would confront a growing deterioration associated with this decline. This concern, which until recently was considered to be almost a part of Latin American folklore, is relevant for the economic evolution of the nation that leads the world economy.

What Does It Mean to be Competitive?

Figure 4.1 shows the similarity in the configuration of the structural change produced in the three countries in the industrial sector between 1970 and 1987 (estimated for the last two years).[2] In all three cases, the subsectors exhibiting the greatest dynamism are electrical equipment, plastics, and basic chemicals. The main differences are found between the United States and West Germany, where the profile contains common basic elements, and Japan, whose leadership since the 1970s in the electrical machinery sector and, particularly, the electronics industry, is the pivot for the change in its productive structure. Japan placed less emphasis on the oil industry than the rest of the industrialized countries and, particularly, the United States and West Germany.

The axes of dynamism for all three countries coincide with the sectors having a greater content of technical progress than those manifested earlier. In both cases, the axes of dynamism involve the substitution of natural resources with synthetic ones, growing automation associated with the diffusion of the electronics industry in the capital goods industry, and the diffusion and saturation of the consumption pattern of transportation equipment and appliances.

The prior indications correspond to the modifications that the industrial productive structure undergoes, but what is important here is the international competitiveness of the respective productive structures. There is a high degree of consensus with regard to the existence of a solid linkage among competitiveness, the incorporation of technical progress, industrial dynamism, and productivity increase. There is absolute agreement with respect to the decisive importance of competitiveness in a transitional period between technological patterns in determining the relative location of countries in the future international economy. Previously, it was illustrated and schematically detailed to what degree this effort, conducted by developed countries to reinforce their respective competitive positions in the industrial sector, has attained a priority standing, comparable to subjects of political interest. In the past, this situation only had been present in war contingencies.

The importance of Europe's distinct regional programs of scientific and technical cooperation in reinforcing competitiveness confirms this general trend. Consensus regarding how to measure and boost com-

Figure 4.1 Industrial Structural Change: United States, Japan, and West Germany, 1970–1987

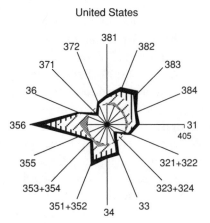

United States

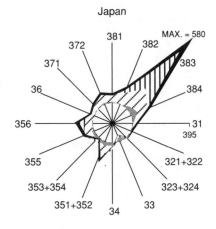

Japan

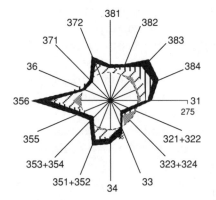

West Germany

(Index of value added: 1970=100)
Key:
ISIC code (branches):
31 (Food products)
321, 322 (Textiles)
323, 324 (Leather industries)
33 (Wood and furniture)
34 (Paper and printing)
351,352 (Chemicals)
353, 354 (Petroleum and coal)
355 (Rubber products)
356 (Plastic products)
36 (Nonmetal mineral products)
371 (Iron and steel)
372 (Nonferrous metals)
381 (Metal products)
382 (Nonelectrical machinery)
383 (Electrical machinery)
384 (Transport equipment)

 1970–1975
1975–1980
1980–1985
1985–1987 forecast

Source: UNIDO.

petitiveness, however, is less evident. There is agreement that the erosion of productivity since the 1960s has serious potential consequences, but consensus on the reason for this erosion and measures necessary to correct and invert this trend has been much smaller.

Seven alternative indicators of international competitiveness have been established for these three countries (see table 4.3). Perhaps the most interesting conclusion of their analysis is that in all seven indicators, the relative ranking of the countries does not vary: Japan is first, West Germany is second, and the United States is third.

In terms of the first indicator, the R&D effort for civilian purposes is significantly higher in Japan and West Germany than in the United States. This condition has been mentioned in many studies as a possible factor explaining the differing rates of competitiveness of the three countries. The next indicator refers to the dynamism experienced by industrial exports in the three countries during the last two decades. The distance between Japan and the other two countries is highly noticeable. The third indicator is related to exports with a higher technological content ("engineering products") as compared to total exported manufactures. Again, there is a significant difference between Japan and the other two countries. The fourth indicator measures the evolution of the relative weight of national exports within world exports between 1963 and 1986. While the weight in Japan is five times greater and remains almost constant in West Germany, the weight in the United States had dropped by 1986 to 61 percent of what it had been twenty years earlier.

The fifth indicator refers more specifically to the competitiveness of engineering products and measures the relationship between exports and imports of those goods for the same year. In 1963, U.S. engineering exports were nearly quadruple that of imports, a ratio that was reduced to almost a quarter in 1986. The United States exports and imports an equivalent amount of engineering products. Engineering exports were double that of imports in Japan in 1963, placing it behind the United States and West Germany for that year; currently, exports equal more than ten times the corresponding imports. The West German ratio, similar to that of the United States in 1963, has been reduced, but a significant surplus level is still maintained.

In terms of productivity growth, the three countries have undergone a substantial reduction between the 1965–1973 period and the 1975–1981

Table 4.3 United States, West Germany, and Japan: Different Indicators of International Competitiveness. (percentages)

	United States	Japan	West Germany
Civilian R&D/GNP			
(1985)[a]	1.9	2.6	2.5
	(3)	(1)	(2)
Growth of manufactured exports			
(1965–1986)[b]	11.1	16.9	9.3
	(3)	(1)	(2)
Engineering exports/Total manufactured exports			
(1986)[c]	48.0	64.0	48.0
	(2)	(1)	(2)
Engineering exports/ World engineering exports			
(1986/1963)[c]	61.0	515.0	90.0
	(3)	(1)	(2)
Engineering exports/ engineering imports			
1986[c]	64.0	1,317.0	246.0
1963	408.0	266.0	399.0
	(3)	(1)	(2)
Productivity growth in manufacturing[d]			
1965–1973	2.8	11.0	4.2
1975–1981	1.7	8.7	3.2
1980–1986	3.7	5.4	3.3
	(3)	(1)	(2)
Manufactured exports/ Manufactured imports			
(1984–1986)[b]	0.5	5.1	1.7
	(3)	(1)	(2)

Source: Joint ECLAC/UNIDO Industry and Technology Division, based on data from:
[a]National Science Foundation, *International Science and Technology Data Update 1986,* NSF 86-307 (Washington, D.C., 1986), 6.
[b]World Bank, *World Development Report 1988* New York, 1988.
[c]United Nations, *Bulletin of Statistics on World Trade in Engineering Products, 1986,* GE 88-30950 (Geneva, 1988).
[d]OECD, *Productivity in Industry* (Paris, 1986); OECD, *Evolution récente des politiques industrielles,* DSTI/IND/88.14 (Paris, 1988).

period. The most drastic slump is evident in the country having the smallest rate during the previous period, the United States. The decline is somewhat less for West Germany and markedly lower for Japan. The growth rate in both periods, however, supports the established hierarchy, Japan first, West Germany second, and the United States third. The growth rate of productivity between 1975–1981 in West Germany is almost double that of the United States, while Japan's growth rate is more than double that of West Germany.

The final indicator utilized in international comparisons with the regions entails the evolution of the ratio of exports to imports of manufactured goods taking an average for the 1984–1986 period. Japanese exports of manufactured goods are five times greater than imports, West German exports almost twice that of imports, and U.S. exports are one-half that of imports. Consequently, both in the level and evolution of competitiveness, the ranking again places Japan first, with a relatively significant distance from the other two countries, and West Germany in an intermediate position, but generally closer to the United States than to Japan.

A more detailed examination will be made of the evolution of the competitiveness of these countries in high-tech areas such as engineering products. The abrupt jump of the dollar early in the 1980s and its drastic drop in 1985 and 1986 has drawn attention to the conjunctural evolution of U.S. competitiveness. Consideration of a longer period (1965–1984) provides a view of general trends and the additional effects of the "exchange disorder" of the 1980s. Figure 4.2 depicts the relative weight of engineering exports for each country. Japan's upward trend, the relative stability of West Germany with a slight decline from 1980 to 1984, and the sustained erosion of the U.S. share of the world market in these goods (weakened since 1980 despite the rise of the dollar) are clearly visible. Both at the beginning and the end of the period, these three countries manifested a total world share slightly higher than 40 percent. In view of the fact that these goods contribute to the formation of the international industrial/technological profile, the figure demonstrates that a significant part of the technical effort used in the production of the goods which delineate the incorporation of technical progress into the productive sector is concentrated in these three countries.

The international competitiveness of engineering goods can be mea-

Figure 4.2 Engineering Products: World Market Share
of the United States, West Germany, and Japan, 1965–1984.

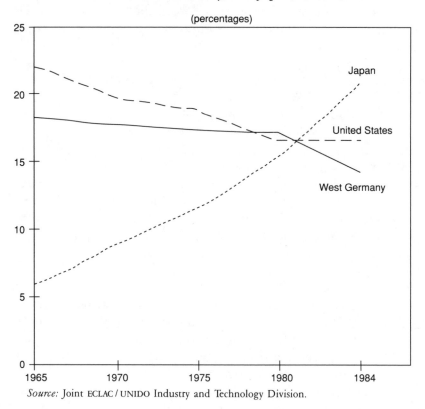

Source: Joint ECLAC / UNIDO Industry and Technology Division.

sured by the export/import ratio depicted in figure 4.3. Japan's participation in the world market rose significantly and rapidly during the 1965–1970 period, and its competitiveness remained constant at a very high level. This was a period when Japan rapidly increased capital goods exports, boosted its imports, and quickly absorbed capital goods technology from other countries. In the 1970s its contribution to the supply of capital goods exports continued an upward swing, and it achieved competitiveness in a wide range of goods. Imports were no longer connected with the growth of exports and the index continued

Figure 4.3 Engineering Products: International Competitiveness (x/m) of the United States, West Germany, and Japan, 1965–1984.

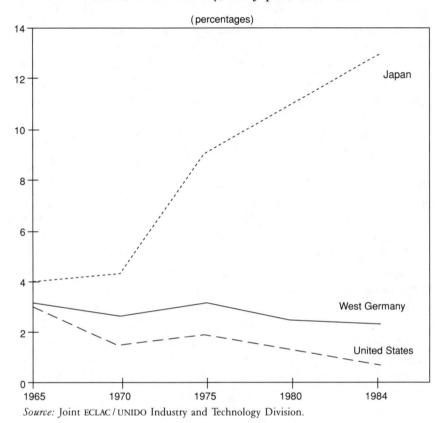

Source: Joint ECLAC / UNIDO Industry and Technology Division.

to grow significantly until reaching an export level in 1984 equivalent to 14 times that of imports.

Japan is almost self-sufficient; its imports of capital goods technology are practically marginal compared to capital goods exports. This does not exclude the fact that Japan continues to be a net importer in the technological balance of payments, clearly reflecting its option for the acquisition of nonincorporated technology and, additionally, the fact that international industrial leadership is exercised by national enterprises.[3]

The West German export/import ratio is maintained at a very high level, greater than two. West Germany exports capital goods in a wide range of areas and at a much higher ratio than it imports. This peculiarity, shared with Japan, in a broad spectrum of capital goods permitted West Germany to incorporate technological progress in electronics and spread it to the entire productive apparatus where these goods were used, both production and service sectors. This broad, competitive capital goods base partially explains the ability of West Germany to compensate (even more so than Japan) for the surge in the oil bill with a significant upswing in the net capital goods balance, which is a determinant factor in the increase in the manufacturing sector surplus.

In the United States, competitiveness underwent a sustained erosion between 1965 and 1970, long before the first oil shock occurred. Then, after a stage of relative stability between 1970 and 1975, it underwent a systematic decline prior to the second oil shock and, obviously, before the rapid rise of the dollar. This would partially explain why, with the rapid plunge of the dollar in March 1985, the United States could hardly innovate in the short run with respect to an erosion trend that had begun twenty years earlier.

During the 1965–1984 period in both the United States and West Germany, macroeconomic policies were applied which varied in terms of sign, intensity, instruments, and international context. These differences in the scope of macroeconomic policies, applied in distinct governments and differing international contexts, would not seem to exercise a determinant influence on that evolution. Macroeconomic and sectoral policies, microeconomic aspects of management, institutional factors such as the educational system, the availability of natural resources, and the size of the internal market — all these factors influence international competitiveness in such a way that it is perfectly understandable why given upward trends in the erosion of competitiveness coexist with alternating and inconsistent macroeconomic policies. This should not be strange since macroeconomics does not rank those sectors incorporating technical progress as a core topic of concern. Thus, while it still exercises considerable influence on the dynamism of aggregate demand, macroeconomics can hardly have a particular influence on those sectors providing the base for the variation of productivity and competitiveness.[4]

Those areas in which each of the countries presents a high degree

Table 4.4 United States, West Germany, and Japan: Specialization in Engineering Products, 1984 (Percentages)

Countries	World share total engineering products	SITC (Rev. 2)[a]	Item	World share (each item)
West Germany	14.8	718.7	Nuclear reactors	44.0
		726	Printing bookbinding machinery	33.0
		725	Paper and pulp machinery	27.0
Japan	21.9	763	Gramophone sound recorder	82.6
		751.21	Calculating machines	76.0
		763.88	Dictating machines	72.9
United States	17.3	714.8	Gas turbines, n.e.s.	66.0
		792	Aircraft	44.6
		759	Machinery parts and accessories for office and automatic data processing machines	40.1

Source: Joint ECLAC/UNIDO Industry and Technology Division, based on data from UN *Bulletin on World Trade in Engineering Products,* E/F/R 88.11.E.14 (New York, 1986).
[a]UN Standard International Trade Classification, Rev. 2, E.75.XVII.6 (New York, 1975).

of specialization are identified in table 4.4. This summary would include those areas whose share of the world market is noticeably higher than their share of the total supply of engineering products, areas that have reached a level of relative excellence vis-à-vis other areas in which they participate in world supply. In Japan in 1977, these areas basically correspond to consumer goods which are different from those subject to a greater degree of specialization.[5] In other words, over a period of seven years, the category of most highly specialized products has changed radically in Japan, and at least the first two of these are products which have a very high growth rate. In West Germany and the United States there is greater stability with respect to specialized goods, which are mostly capital goods for specific purposes. The growth rate of world demand for these products is usually lower than it is for widely used capital or durable consumer goods having a high technology content. In those categories in which Japan has attained a high degree of specialization it has succeeded in attaining a very high share of the world market. This is particularly interesting in view of the recent trends in exchange rates, since in those categories in which Japan has a virtual monopoly of the world's exportable supply, it will take some time for variations in the exchange rate to be reflected in changes in the distribution of the supply among countries.

The cases mentioned here are a particular expression of a more general phenomenon characterized by the fact that Japan's achievement of a significant quota of the world market in a wide range of areas has made it relatively immune, at least in the short run, to the evolution of exchange rates. An export/import ratio of 14:1 in engineering products means that its internal market is virtually closed to those goods, independently of absolute comparative advantages, nontariff barriers, and institutional mechanisms that would inhibit their importation percentage of the world market.

The Strong Erosion of U.S. Industrial Competitiveness

Attention will now be concentrated on the specific case of the United States, which has degenerated from a position of almost absolute domination of the manufacturing sector forty years ago to high deficit levels in those products.[6] Because this has become a topic of economic and political concern, the equilibria and possibilities of economic policy coordination of developed countries and, for that matter, international economic stability are affected.

In analyzing U.S. manufactures trade in the 1980s amid this erosion trend, its relative position in accordance with different trade partners should be distinguished. Table 4.5 shows situations salient to the relative position of the United States: first, those countries providing a solid trade advantage in manufactured products during the first part of the decade; second, those with which there is a systematic, flourishing deficit situation, but where U.S. imports chiefly originate from foreign businesses; and third, a deficit situation provoked by intrafirm commerce through the displacement of U.S. companies overseas with the goal of seeking advantages or neutralizing disadvantages associated with labor costs or special institutional agreements. A good example of this is the case of Canada, particularly in the automobile sector. The asymmetry existing between those cases in which intrafirm commerce produces a surplus (Mexico and England, for example), which does not cause much debate, and the cases

Table 4.5 United States: Trade Balance in Manufactures by Country, 1980–1986 (Millions of dollars)

	1980	1983	1984	1985	1986[a]
World	11,326	– 46,181	– 98,081	– 119,347	– 152,420
Canada	– 517	– 6,897	– 11,308	– 12,054	– 18,050
Western Europe	10,296	– 3,035	– 17,848	– 27,398	– 36,600
United Kingdom	3,720	1,240	982	– 898	– 3,850
West Germany	– 3,505	– 5,288	– 8,984	– 11,968	– 17,200
France	1,103	– 542	– 2,602	– 3,904	– 4,000
Italy	– 540	– 2,750	– 4,993	– 6,515	– 8,150
Latin America	12,869	– 3,450	– 5,153	– 1,558	500
Mexico	2,642	425	1,049	2,262	1,450
Brazil	789	– 2,416	– 5,005	– 4,426	– 3,350
Venezuela	520	– 1,237	– 1,444	– 1,128	– 1,100
Argentina	1,751	57	– 68	– 342	– 200
Other countries	1,451	– 279	315	2,076	3,710
Japan	– 19,386	– 28,235	– 43,709	– 54,987	– 64,700
Taiwan	– 4,284	– 8,922	– 12,584	– 14,309	– 16,200
South Korea	– 1,697	– 3,736	– 5,799	– 6,355	– 8,850
Near East	8,846	9,052	6,332	4,363	2,900
Africa	3,495	2,300	382	613	– 820

Source: Joint ECLAC/UNIDO Industry and Technology Division, based on U.S. Department of Commerce, *U.S. Industrial Outlook 1987* (Washington, D.C., 1987).
[a]Estimates based on first seven months data.

involving a deficit (Taiwan, Canada), which is the center of ongoing polemics, is striking.

At the beginning of the 1980s, the United States possessed a significant surplus with Western Europe and particularly the United Kingdom, Latin America (chiefly Mexico), and the Near East, which, financed by the oil surplus, had turned into a significant manufactures importer. The surplus with each of these regions reached approximately $10 billion. During that same period, the countries with which there already existed a significant deficit were West Germany and Italy in Europe and Japan and South Korea in Asia. In Canada and Taiwan, which fall into the third category of countries where the deficit has a solid component of intrafirm commerce involving U.S. companies, the deficit had already begun to take on meaningful dimensions, particularly in the case of Taiwan.

Between 1980 and 1985, the United States witnessed a deterioration in its manufactures trade balance from an $11 billion surplus in 1980 to a $152 billion deficit in 1986. The rise of the dollar had a strong impact in that dramatically negative evolution, at least during the 1983–1984 period, but differential behaviors were manifested in accordance with the distinct type of country. The only countries with which the United States maintained a surplus until 1985, regardless of whether it decreased, are the United Kingdom, Mexico, medium and small Latin American countries, the Near East, and Africa. In 1985, the United States experienced a deficit with all the rest of the countries under consideration. The most outstanding contribution to the erosion of the U.S. manufacturing surplus came from Europe, $35 billion; Japan, $34 billion; Latin American, $14 billion, a fall related to the precarious financial situation of the region; and South Korea and Taiwan combined, approximately $14 billion. In Western Europe, West Germany and Italy together represented a $13 billion loss for the United States. In Latin America, the country responsible for the largest portion of the U.S. commercial downfall was Brazil, where the deterioration was almost $13 billion.

The countries and regions with which the United States has a manufactures surplus are characterized by their current and future precarious economic situation, thereby making a favorable change in the U.S. trade balance unlikely. These countries possess an import growth rate that will hardly increase significantly during the next few years and several of them, particularly Mexico, the Near Eastern countries and Africa, tend to base their currency on the evolution of the dollar, whose plunge does not improve the relative position of the United States. In countries with which the United States maintains a growing sustained structural deficit, the modification of exchange parity could be influential due to long-term sustained evolutions; however, respective national institutional factors concerning the organization of the productive system, the functioning of enterprises, the educational system, and the ability to convert scientific knowledge into productive efficiency would limit the effect of the modification of exchange parity.

Distinguishing the different types of countries and products with which this trade deficit exists would be helpful in understanding the U.S. global economic situation. Tables 4.6 and 4.7 provide this analysis by individualizing the "smokestack" or traditional capital intensive in-

Table 4.6 United States: Trade Balance in Products of Smokestack
Industries, Net Exports by Country, 1980–1985 (Millions of dollars)

	1980	1983	1984	1985[a]
World	− 21,445	− 38,891	− 55,791	− 63,759
Canada	− 1,760	− 6,151	− 10,452	− 8,641
Western Europe	− 6,239	− 10,935	− 15,047	− 18,906
United Kingdom	− 675	− 1,550	− 1,081	− 1,678
West Germany	− 5,128	− 5,170	− 7,260	− 9,364
France	− 925	− 1,485	− 1,984	− 2,140
Italy	− 475	− 666	− 1,035	− 1,150
Latin America	3,734	− 1,996	− 2,668	− 2,144
Mexico	2,480	− 634	− 532	− 487
Brazil	− 229	− 934	− 1,659	− 1,592
Venezuela	823	303	323	338
Argentina	282	− 47	− 89	− 84
Other countries	378	− 684	− 710	− 321
Japan	− 17,238	− 19,697	− 25,413	− 31,373
Taiwan	− 325	− 658	− 952	− 1,217
South Korea	− 493	− 898	− 1,288	− 1,410
Near East	− 1,984	2,032	1,428	963
Africa	− 927	− 526	− 943	− 667

Source: Joint ECLAC/UNIDO Industry and Technology Division, based on U.S. Department of
Commerce, *U.S. Industrial Outlook 1986* (Washington, D.C., 1986).
[a]Estimates based on first seven months data.

dustrial sectors such as iron and steel manufacturing and the automobile
industry, and high-tech sectors such as electronics, pharmaceuticals, and
special plastics. The panorama varies according to the type of product.
Until 1980, or before the rise of the dollar, the United States possessed
a surplus in smokestack industries with Latin America (excluding Brazil)
and the Near East; it maintained a deficit with all other countries and
regions. By 1985, that surplus had plummeted to include only Venezuela
and the Near East, and in both cases it had eroded considerably. This
was undoubtedly linked to the growing economic fragility of the oil-
producing countries during the 1980s.

With regard to high-tech products, table 4.7 indicates a similar situation, but presents fundamentally different magnitudes and absolute
values. In 1980, the United States presented a deficit in high-tech products exclusively with Japan and Taiwan and a surplus with the rest of

Table 4.7 United States: Trade Balance in Products of High-Tech Industries by Country, 1980–1985 (Millions of dollars)

	1980	1983	1984	1985[a]
World	25,889	17,708	6,589	6,717
Canada	3,225	3,662	3,758	3,772
Western Europe	13,264	13,725	14,449	12,769
United Kingdom	2,748	3,245	3,194	3,415
West Germany	2,067	1,714	1,845	2,370
France	1,675	1,609	1,047	331
Italy	922	613	685	1,011
Latin America	5,606	2,686	2,637	3,154
Mexico	1,381	129	332	485
Brazil	986	559	275	489
Venezuela	820	494	542	601
Argentina	754	343	311	291
Other countries	1,665	1,160	1,177	1,291
Japan	− 2,567	− 7,269	− 14,078	− 16,125
Taiwan	− 565	− 1,475	− 2,496	− 2,712
South Korea	85	− 176	− 782	− 585
Near East	1,980	2,858	2,450	2,496
Africa	1,490	1,659	1,604	1,176

Source: Joint ECLAC/UNIDO Industry and Technology Division, based on U.S. Department of Commerce, *U.S. Industrial Outlook 1986* (Washington, D.C., 1986).
[a]Estimates based on first seven months data.

the world. By 1985 the only change in this situation was that South Korea had joined Japan and Taiwan. The chief sources of U.S. high-tech surplus were Canada, England, and Latin America. In 1985, with an $11 billion deficit in the combined manufacturing sector with West Germany, the U.S. high-tech surplus with that country increased to slightly over $2 billion.

Nearly half of the deficit increase between 1980 and 1985 was based on a third type of product: nondurable consumer products that rely on a high degree of labor intensity. Although this evolution presents differential features according to product, in all product types—smokestack, high-tech, and, above all, traditional nondurable consumer products—there is a significant deficit during the decade. Although showing a surplus until 1985, the relative position of the United States in high-tech products had eroded by almost $20 billion during those five years. Preliminary studies for 1986 indicate a high-tech deficit for the United States for the first time. These studies also reveal that the computer and aeronautics sectors (the latter increasingly threatened by European industry) constitute the principal sources of surplus in this area.[7]

The factors that would explain the decline of U.S. competitiveness, the instruments that played a part in that decline, the differences in the interpretation of its origins, and possible solutions to the situation will be approached at the end of this chapter. First, however, the differences in the consumption patterns of these three countries will be discussed.

Is the United States Living Beyond Its Means?

In order to contrast the role performed by consumption and investment in each country, a group of indicators has been established to evaluate the relative weight of consumption and investment at both macro- and microeconomic levels; such an analysis would reflect the implicit relative importance of the "present" with respect to the "future" in each country.[8] The indicators signal a clear order, showing that consumption would have the greatest relative weight in the United States, with Japan at the other extreme and West Germany in an intermediate position. This ranking is perpetuated without exception for all chosen indicators (see table 4.8).

At the macroeconomic level, U.S. consumption stands at 84 percent, Japan's at 69 percent, and West Germany's at 77 percent. This is reflected in the complement that savings with respect to GDP represents in each country. If attention is directed to the percentage of disposable income allocated to savings, the difference is more conspicuous. In Japan this percentage amounts to 22.5 percent, almost double that of West Germany (13 percent) which, in turn, is more than double that of the United States (5.2 percent). Without entering into the debate on the causality of the investment/savings ratio, the investment rate in Japan is 28 percent; in West Germany, 20 percent; and in the United States, 19 percent.

The differences in investment rates are less than the differences in available savings because a part of these savings in Japan and West Germany has served to enable a higher investment rate in the United States

Table 4.8 United States, West Germany, and Japan:
Pattern of Consumption, Different Indicators (percentages)

	United States	Japan	West Germany
Savings/GDP (1984–1985–1986)[a]	16	31	24
	(1)	(3)	(2)
Saving/disposable income (1984)	5.2	22.5	12.8
	(1)	(3)	(2)
Gross Fixed Capital Formation/GDP (1985)[d]	19	28	20
	(1)	(3)	(2)
Automobiles/1000 persons (1985)[b]	552	270	428
	(1)	(3)	(2)
Person/room dwelling space (1980)[c]	0.5	1.0	0.7
	(1)	(3)	(2)
Dwellings with fix bath/shower (1979)[c]	95.2	65.6	81.8
	(1)	(3)	(2)
Energy consumption per capita (1986) (Kg of oil equivalent)[a]	7,193	3,186	4,464
	(1)	(3)	(2)
Daily calories/needs (1983)	137	113	130
	(1)	(3)	(2)
Animal proteins: grams inhabitant per day (1984)[d]	73	46	69
	(1)	(3)	(2)
Telephones: number/1000 inhabitants (1985)[b]	760	555	621
	(1)	(3)	(2)

Source: Joint ECLAC/UNIDO Industry and Technology Division, based on data from:
[a]World Bank, *World Development Report 1988,* New York, June 1988.
[b]U.S. Bureau of the Census, *Statistical Abstract of the United States: 1988,* 108th ed. (Washington, D.C., 1988).
[c]President's Commission on Industrial Competitiveness, *Global Competition: The New Reality* (Washington, D.C., 1985), Vols. I and II.
[d]OECD, *The OECD Observer,* no. 145, April/May 1987.

than what internal savings would have warranted. Resources in the form of both net resource transfers and capital drain from other countries — particularly Latin America — can be added to those of Japan and West Germany. Since 1985 the United States has been converted into a net debtor.

Let us turn our attention now to that product which, more than any other, symbolizes the U.S. consumption pattern and has become a source of global inspiration and reference — the automobile. Its relevance does not merely pertain to the weight that its acquisition implies for the family budget, but also to the configuration of the physical infrastructure, the energy platform of the style of transportation and communication, and, to some degree, the life-style.[9] Despite the fact that the three countries exhibit a similar level of per capita income (comparison that has become particularly fragile due to the mobility of exchange rates), the differences in the density of vehicles are particularly radical. In the United States there is practically one vehicle for every two inhabitants; in West Germany, one for every three inhabitants; and in Japan, a ratio of one vehicle for slightly less than five inhabitants. Moreover, both Japan and West Germany are important net exporters of automobiles, supplying the international market and, more importantly, the U.S. market (28 percent in 1986).[10]

Concentrating exclusively on this indicator could neutralize its comparative relevance with respect to other references, such as population density, physical space, and availability of community services. In all these comparisons, however, greater "austerity" is evident in terms of the automobile—the symbol of nondurable consumption whose unit value is comparable to the investment quota needed to generate one employment in small and medium businesses in the manufacturing sector. This contrast in densities requires more profound and precise explanations than those previously mentioned and is linked to concrete differences in the respective internal markets, such as consumer credit availability and maintenance costs.

The next two indicators refer to the population density per dwelling and to the type of dwelling available in each country; both confirm the previously established ranking. In terms of population density per dwelling (disregarding dwelling surface area), the figure for Japan (1.0) is double that of the United States (0.5), and the figure for West Germany (0.7) is 40 percent greater than that for the United States. The same ranking can be applied to the ratio of dwellings with comparable sanitary facilities. With respect to energy consumption, which is related to both housing and transportation patterns, the availability of energy in the United States more than doubles that of Japan and almost doubles that of West Germany. Even in the sphere of daily caloric intake (disregarding animal or vegetable composition), there are outstanding differences.

In summary, the former comparison reveals that the consumer "vocation" of American society and its capability to materialize it is markedly higher than in Japan or West Germany. The inexhaustible nature of this comparison could be further explored using more refined indicators; the existence of a notable difference in the consumption/investment ratio in these countries is apparent, however, regardless of comparable per capita income levels.

An additional indicator linking the consumption/investment ratio to a sectoral objective emerges when contrasting the energy consumption patterns of the United States and Japan. In 1982 the distribution of energy use in the United States is more or less comparable among residential-commercial, transportation, and industry sectors; in Japan, industrial consumption tends to predominate. The dominant use in the United States is residential-commercial (35 percent), followed by transportation (34 percent) and industry (31 percent); this structure is intuitively coherent with the previous indicators of automobile density and the density and level of the housing structure. By contrast, the Japanese industrial sector absorbs more than half of the utilized energy (53 percent), followed by residential use (27 percent), and transportation (20 percent).[11] Consequently, radically distinct consumption and investment patterns reflect pronounced differences in the perspectives and deficiencies of these countries in their international insertion.

Having examined the sectorial structure of the international insertion of these countries, the configurations of their industrial sectors, their levels of international competitiveness, and the differences in their consumption pattern, we can now approach the interrelationship between what we have labelled the industrialization pattern and the achievement of the two objectives of growth and equity.

The Emergence of Different National Patterns

Contrasting the relationships existing between, growth, equity, international competitiveness of the industrial sector, and the consumption pattern reveals some interesting results. Figure 4.4 is an attempt to graphically summarize the relations among these four elements. The indicators that have been utilized for each of these dimensions are the following: for growth, the per capita product growth rate between 1965 and 1986; for equity, the ratio between the income of the 40 percent

Figure 4.4   Strategic Profiles: United States, Japan, and West Germany

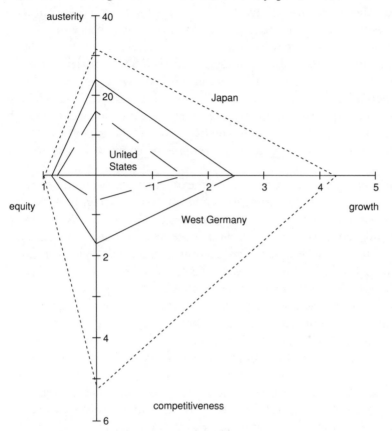

Source: Joint ECLAC / UNIDO Industry and Technology Division.

of the population with the lowest wages and that of the 10 percent with the highest wages; for competitiveness, the ratio between manufactures exports and manufactures imports for 1986; for the degree of "austerity" of the consumption pattern, the ratio of gross domestic savings as percentage of GDP for the period 1984–1986 (for consumption, the same results would obtain with automobile density).

As revealed in tables 4.3 and 4.8, the ranking in both competitiveness and consumption pattern does not vary with any of the indicators considered. This observation has been made with the purpose of limiting objections to the specific nature of the indicator. Hence, the ranking of the three countries in any of these two dimensions does not vary when using any of the other previously mentioned indicators.

Assuming the acceptance of the shared objectives of growth and equity in the three countries, the Japanese pattern is clearly "superior" to that of West Germany or the United States, and the West German pattern is "superior" to that of the United States. "Superiority" here refers to dominance in the simultaneous attainment of the objectives of growth and equity. This casts doubt on the existence of a "trade-off" between both objectives, one of the basic premises of conventional economic theory.

This convergence is associated with the observation of certain behaviors in issues pertaining to consumption and international competitiveness. The "superiority" of Japan over the other two countries in terms of growth and equity goes hand-in-hand with more austerity and international competitiveness. In line with the reasoning employed in chapter 3, the convergence of both objectives would be benefited by austerity and competitiveness. In relation to competitiveness, the absence of natural resources is associated positively with greater competitiveness in the industrial sector, which contributes to both growth and equity.

Equity sustains dynamism directly by generating a more austere consumption pattern and by freeing resources for investment, while simultaneously supporting growth to the point that a greater degree of socioeconomic articulation enhances the willingness to opt for long-term objectives that augment growth. On the other hand, growth sustains equity directly by favoring competitiveness through an acceleration in the incorporation of technological progress, which is spread productively and socially. Growth supports equity indirectly by legitimizing the sociopolitical system, and thereby making the remnants of inequity more bearable for society. Thus, stability is projected onto the process of growth, which, in turn, will be conducive to the creation of institutions that favor and solidly sustain growth and equity.

Compared with the United States, Japan has followed an industrialization pattern that has made it highly competitive internationally: it accelerates the capacity for adoption of technical progress, thereby raising that productivity associated with a frugal consumption pattern and promoted by an equitable income distribution, which in turn strengthens growth, dynamism, equity, frugality, and competitiveness. Conversely, the U.S. industrialization pattern promotes an absence of competitiveness, greater inequity in the income distribution, more affluent consumption, and, in certain aspects, a slower growth rate.

There can be spasmodic growth with inequity and an exuberance of the consumption pattern, but solid growth would seem to require competitiveness and the type of austerity that is intimately linked with relative equity. Feasibly, growth could be imagined as being the core objective and equity would naturally spring forth as a by-product (an idea prevailing in Latin American thought for decades that has not yet been confirmed empirically). This would mean omitting the impact that inequity has on the consumption pattern and, consequently, disregard eventual social tensions, on the one hand, and the later shortage of investment resources, associated with the exuberance of the consumption pattern, on the other. Although the rate of competitiveness may be high, the scheme proves to be fragile and spasmodic in terms of growth.

Sociopolitical factors and economic policy instruments involved in the three national configurations will be discussed in the final section of this chapter. West Germany constitutes an interesting equilibrium between a clear, firm opening to international trade (greater than in both Japan or the United States) and a high degree of articulation and internal social agreement accompanied by the significantly greater economic role of the State than in the other two countries.[12]

United States vs. Japan

First, a schematic contrast will be made between the extreme cases of Japan and the United States, followed by an identification of some of the policy instruments that act directly in order to materialize the differences observed in the previous figure.[13] Without intending to be original or exhaust the subject, respective "styles" in which the contrast is pronounced could be identified.

The aforementioned aspects denote the basic difference between a country that views the world from on top with a self-satisfied, complacent attitude and a country that is a mighty challenger, with a history full of traumas and a desire to make its destiny palpable. This difference arises between a continental economy whose language, monetary note, and life-style have been converted into a worldwide referent, and a small island territory whose basic asset is its population and where the internal legitimacy of its leadership is linked to the recuperation of national dignity and the conquest of international markets, particularly the penetration of the market of the most powerful country on Earth.

The strategic obsession and long-term planning that characterize Japanese leadership sectorially stimulate and orient dynamism and, simultaneously, are legitimized and receive feedback with the rapid growth rate achieved. The virtuous circle of growth—increase in productivity—international competitiveness—legitimization of internal policy management encounter their fullest expression in Japan. In the United States, the relatively slow postwar economic growth rate has been accompanied since the mid–1960s by weak productivity growth, the erosion of international competitiveness, frequent political and short-term economic policy alternation, and the absence of strategic sectorial options.

The markedly greater weight of industry in Japan as opposed to the United States (31 and 23 percent of GNP respectively) is not due to ideological differences along the lines of development, but simply reflects Japan's almost complete lack of natural resources. What the country provides the manufacturing sector is merely the intellectual added value that its population can contribute.

The loss of international competitiveness in the manufacturing sector of the United States vis-à-vis Japan is not only evident in the "low technology" sector (textiles, naval industry), but also in medium (automobiles, televisions) and high technology (computer equipment).

In terms of the educational system, U.S. self-complacence has received a jolt in recent decades by the launching of *Sputnik* in 1957 and the flood of Japanese imports in the second half of the 1970s. The notably greater preeminence of Japanese engineering is clearly reflected in the fact that the density of engineering students in Japan is double that in the United States (1982). While in the United States one out of every four hundred people is a lawyer, in Japan, the ratio equals one lawyer per every ten thousand inhabitants, a density that is 25 times less. While two-thirds of the advisers of leading Japanese companies have an engineering background, a similar ratio in the United States is occupied by executives with law and finance backgrounds. This contrast is completely coherent with regard to the respective priorities of the countries, one with an obsession for international competitiveness, the other preferring expansion by means of fusions and conglomerations. This topic, linked to "paper entrepreneuralism," will be discussed further in chapter 5.[14]

Along the lines of social integration, the concept of nation-family prevails in Japan, while social incorporation reflects "market forces" in the United States. With all the known qualifications to figures on income distribution, Japan and the Nordic countries present more equitable income levels out of the group of industrialized countries, while the United States and France are characterized by greater levels of inequity.[15] In terms of corporate labor-management relations, a considerably more harmonious relationship is observed in Japan.

Aside from the unquestionable cultural, value, and even religious differences, which could be used to explain the different features of the industrialization pattern and their incidence in growth and employment, some of the specific economic policy instruments that came into play in the results previously described merit a partial, schematic summarization. In the first place, it would be worth mentioning those policy instruments that had a direct incidence in the gestation of an austere consumption pattern and in the channeling of the resources corresponding to the investment process.

Although Japan has adopted the U.S. consumption pattern as a referent, it has done so with an eye to generating, under more favorable cost and quality conditions, the goods that the United States demands. For Japan, the U.S. consumption pattern is important primarily because its production and export strategy is targeted to it. With regard to the reproduction of that consumption pattern in the internal market, however, Japan has adopted a series of measures that allow for the slow introduction and spread of the pattern throughout the country. Thus, the basic growth requirements of the country are respected: "modernity" is reproduced, but the rate of absorption is cautiously restricted so as not to interfere with the internal strategic objectives of growth competitiveness.

The singularity of the Japanese approach is exemplified by two elements which play a key role in the U.S. consumption pattern: the automobile and residential housing. The participation of these elements in family consumption in the United States has been increasing systematically over time: the higher the income level, the greater the proportion of those items. In Japan measures are adopted that somewhat isolate the reproduction of these elements in the internal market. In fact, Japan applies a policy which systematically constrains consumption and stimulates savings for the acquisition of housing and consumer goods in general, principally durables. While the common practice in the United States is to charge taxes on interest accrued in savings accounts and to exempt interest paid on consumer loans, exactly the opposite occurs in Japan.

In the specific case of housing in the United States, interest paid on housing loans are tax exempt even though the loan may be for a second or third house. Housing loans are vigorously restricted in Japan, forcing people to make a systematic, ongoing savings effort. During the time span in which the required amount is being accumulated, the resultant available funds are steered toward investment. Additionally, the Japanese institutional mechanism for savings accounts is located in thousands of post offices situated throughout the territory, facilitating fluid access by the entire population. The higher savings trend in Japanese families is reinforced by the company payroll system, which includes semester bonuses that can equal between one-third and one-fourth of the real wage. This sporadic income in significant amounts tends to favor savings. Moreover, the pension system scheme is based on the payment of a considerable lump sum instead of periodic payments over short periods, thereby reinforcing the savings tendency. Another reinforcement is the particularly precarious and fragile social security system which induces families to save significant amounts to prepare themselves for old age or illness.[16]

These policy factors would explain the greater availability of family savings, but the mechanisms that guarantee that savings be targeted toward investment should be explored. Here the system of financial mediation intervenes directly. Since it is private, it is subject to regulation by the Bank of Japan and the Finance Ministry, which establish norms that coordinate the channeling of significant, established amounts of available funds towards those particularly capital-intensive sectors defined by the State as priority sectors. Furthermore, until recently the capital flow control system limited almost absolutely the outflow of capital overseas. Savings funds remained in the country and were routed in determined amounts to priority sectors. The generation of internal savings channeled toward priority sectors is developed within the framework of a succession of defined priority sectoral programs with the key objective of materializing this virtuous circle of growth with competitiveness.

With respect to economic policy instruments that influence the development of an industrial system with high competitiveness, it is worth mentioning those that play a determinant role in Japan and are basically absent in the United States. Without entering into detail, the following elements stand out: a series of dispositions that favor the acquisition of technology from abroad through diverse means, the merger of the efforts of distinct businesses, and the coordination of those efforts according to priority sectoral criteria defined by the Ministry of International Trade and Industry (MITI). "Reverse engineering" occupies a place of importance in this sense. This concept specifically refers to the acquisition of sophisticated technological goods with the purpose of dismantling, reconstructing, and improving them in the country, in this case, Japan.

Japan, unlike the rest of the advanced countries and Latin America, adopted an extraordinarily restrictive policy with respect to foreign investment in the industrial sector. This policy was based on the rationale that the internal market was the principal basis of learning for the national industrial sector. If that national market were ceded to foreign corporations, the possibility that the national companies would acquire knowledge and rest upon a broad, growing internal market from which they could leap into the international market would be drastically compromised. This would also be true for Japan's renowned import control policy, which systematically favored internal competition among Japanese businesses within the framework of a captive market.

Another significant aspect of differentiation refers to the sectoral component of fiscal policy. Since the Meiji era in Japan, there has been a tradition of the accountancy of public revenue spending that has enabled the preservation of macroeconomic equilibriums; in addition, since that era a series of accounts have been established specifically for sectors considered to be priorities, particularly iron and steel manufacturing, naval, railroad, mining, and silk textile industries. Since the Meiji era, the public sector has assumed with great realism the responsibility not only for protecting macroeconomic equilibriums, but also for designating specific allotments for the priority areas.[17] This tradition has been kept alive and marks the fundamental difference with the conception of macroeconomic policy prevailing in the rest of the industrialized countries. In the rest of the industrialized countries, and chiefly in the United States, the principle of intersectoral neutrality underlies the irrelevance of determining priority sectors because that is considered to be the market's job.

The clear priority that the Japanese government assigns to the industrial sector with respect to taxation is evident. Within the industrial sector, those subsectors with the greatest content of technical change and dynamism of the national and international market are prioritized. Comparing the tax-sales ratio for all economic activities for 1981, the Japanese ratio is slightly higher than the United States ratio, 1.9 percent vs. 1.1 percent. However, while in the United States the tax-sales ratio is 3.5 percent in the chemical industry and 3.3 percent in machinery (triple the global ratio), the Japanese ratio in those sectors is 1.5 percent and 1.8 percent respectively, less than the global coefficient. Inversely, the U.S. financial sector has a sales tax rate of 1.4 percent, while the Japanese rate is 2.3 percent. The global tax rate is slightly higher in Japan, but is markedly lower in high-tech industrial areas and higher in the financial sector, strictly the opposite of the situation in the United States.

Consequently, without neglecting the validity of value and religious considerations that transcend the sphere of economy, the use of concrete economic instruments explain a relevant portion of the differences between the two industrialization patterns and in their consequent capacity to contribute to the simultaneous objectives of growth and equity. (The frequent reference to Confucius in explaining the "success" of Southeast Asia is of dubious value; the same reference has been used to explain the backwardness of China.) In relation to the subject of equity, a contribution to the increase in equity in Japan came from the period of U.S. occupation, which weakened the relative weight of the existing great conglomerates and induced a redistribution of agricultural property and a partial redistribution of large urban properties.[18]

These pronounced differences at the level of specific economic policy instruments are confined to the function of the State which, observed at a given level of aggregation, seem to be similar in both countries. If the relative weight of Japanese and U.S. public spending and the role that public enterprises perform in the industrial production of both countries are compared, the result would indicate similar roles. In both cases participation is low and noticeably lower than in the European industrialized countries, particularly West Germany. This apparent institutional similarity, however, conceals fundamental differences of orientation in the use of the instruments by the public sector. Moreover, the Japanese industrialization pattern has many elements in common with that of West Germany. Nevertheless, the relative weight of the public sector in West Germany in both the gross product and the industrial sector is much higher. Hence, in order to progress in an understanding of the state role in the industrialization pattern, it would not suffice to be limited to aggregate magnitudes.

Taking this into consideration, we can only reiterate the precariousness of conventional macroeconomics that limits its attention to indicators that ignore both historical specificities and the specific use of distinct policy instruments. The almost symbiotic relationship between the state and large business groups in Japan makes the direct presence of the state in production strictly unnecessary, whereas in the United States the lack of coordination between the public and private sectors coexists with a low presence of the state.[19] In West Germany the relationship between the public sector, financial mediation, and the industrial sector is very similar to that in Japan; in this case, however, the extent of the public presence and influence is quantitatively greater.[20]

An additional quantitative indicator would be the relative size of the public deficit. Both in the United States and in Japan, the relative weight of the deficit in recent years has been approximately 5 percent of the product. The chief difference, however, resides in the fact that the U.S. deficit nearly equals the total amount of net private savings; in Japan, that percentage is only 35 percent. In other words, both the gravitation and the deficit of the public sector are similar, but the deficit has a markedly different meaning in both cases.[21]

This indicator is associated with the aforementioned differences with respect to personal savings and the most important source of savings in Japan — the companies themselves. The levels of productivity reached in that sector have a direct linkage with Japan's international insertion and guarantee the conversion of the internal market into a complementary, reciprocal support for an international market which permits direct access to international technological progress.

In sum, the schematic and unquestionably simplified contrast between the United States and Japan encounters its corresponding con-

Figure 4.5 The U.S Debate on Industrial Policy

	Industrial sector must recuperate its leadership	Transition to leadership of services is real and desirable
International competitiveness is highly eroded	A	C
Relative international competitiveness remains stable	B	D

crete projection in the scope of economic policy instruments. Next, the distinct interpretations that exist in the United States with respect to the contrast with Japan will be approached.

The U.S. Debate on Competitiveness and Services

A central theme of economic debate in the United States is the widespread concern for the erosion of productivity growth and the subsequent conclusion that favoring the development and introduction of technical progress in the productive sector in order to neutralize the previous trend should be a strict priority.[22] This consensus, however, conceals a range of varied interpretations regarding the origin of that erosion and the measures needed to neutralize it. In the first place, there is a different appreciation about the meaning of the erosion of competitiveness and the relative function of the industrial sector vis-à-vis the service sector.

The diverse positions on the subject of industrial policy can be organized around two core axes:

1.) Externally, the degree of erosion of international competitiveness of the U.S. industrial sector
2.) Internally, the relative gravitation of the industrial sector as opposed to the service sector

If these two axes are crossed, four principal categories emerge into which the positions to be contrasted in the debate can be distributed (see figure 4.5). Like every schematic organization used when dealing with a complex subject, a simplification of this type does not do full justice to certain authors located in the interface of some of the categories. As will be seen further on, considerable differences pertaining to the topics not covered by these two axes exist within each of the categories.

The proponents of the need for an industrial policy are found in quadrant "A" and maintain that "deindustrialization" is underway and an arbitrary policy of "reindustrialization" is required.[23] Quadrant "D" contains what has been the official position of the administration: no deindustrialization and, therefore, no industrial policy.[24] Those who recognize the internal and international erosion of industrial leadership but perceive it as the confirmation of a desirable transition to postindustrial society are located in quadrant "C." Consequently, not only is there no need for an industrial policy, but it is also necessary to accelerate the substitution of the "archaic" leadership of the manufacturing sector by the "revolutionary" leadership of the service sectors.[25]

Quadrant "B" contains those who recognize and lament the internal erosion of the leadership of the industrial sector, but affirm the relative stability of U.S. international industrial competitiveness. Their proposal consists of an internal recuperation of the industrial sector with little institutional modification by means of existing economic policy instruments; hence, they are skeptical about the need and institutional viability of an industrial policy in the United States.[26]

Further discussion about the services sector requires some additional clarification.

Industrial Decadence or Complementation

The perception that there is a transition underway from an era pushed by the industrial sector to one pushed by services, has been widespread. This idea is supported by two simple and, therefore, seductive observations: the increase in income generates a more than proportionate demand for services, and, consequently, the upswing in employment in the services sector is greater than that of total employment, and as a result, services activities become a source of burgeoning employment.

Based on this idea, policy recommendations in some Latin American countries have favored the relative dismantling of the industrial plant in order to accelerate the advent of a new era. However, several observations would alter the linear image of an agriculture-industry-services sequence. The rise of a high percentage of the services sector is explained by transformations experienced by the manufacturing sector as a result of the increase in income, the intensification of international competitiveness, and the expansion of the public sector. The services generated by these transformations maintain a close technical linkage with the industrial sector, wherein they enter into relations of complementation and not substitution, as might be misunderstood from the original formulation.

Some of the transformations of the industrial sector that induce the expansion of given services include:

1. The expansion of durable goods consumption — automobiles and appliances — leads to the expansion of finance, commercialization, maintenance, and publicity services, and the number of jobs generated in these activities rapidly exceed those required in the production phase.[27]

2. The plunge of the profit rate of the industrial sector that began at the end of the 1960s explains why resources were channeled to those services associated with "paper entrepreneurialism," with the consequent growth in the sectors of commercial, financial, legal advisory, and real estate mediation.[28] The recovery of the profit rate would tend to modify the proportions observed during the crisis period.[29]

3. The displacement of competition from prices to product differentiation stimulates the services of publicity and commercialization.

4. Technical progress in the industrial sector helps to reduce the work week, demanding less physical effort both in the workplace and at home. Consequently, the demand for entertainment services which incorporate the consumption of goods and industrial equipment (such as televisions, sports articles, and tourist facilities) increases.[30] U.S. leadership in the entertainment industry could be a factor of vital importance in evaluating its future insertion in the international economy.[31]

5. The intensification of competition at a national and international level stimulates the specialization of productive activities of goods and services previously incorporated into businesses and now converted into independent entrepreneurial activities — computer services, engineering firms, financial activity management, and so forth.[32]

6. The internationalization of industrial activity spurs the internationalization of related service units. This would explain why those coun-

tries having the greatest activity in services overseas — the United States and the United Kingdom — are the most enthusiastic promoters of loosening the international trade in services.[33]

7. Because it is an upshot of a complex process in which the requirements for the legitimization and accumulation of industrialization and urbanization are combined, the systematic expansion of the public sector in the industrialized economies affects the expansion of determined public services such as education and health. Additionally, attendant regulatory actions cause a business reaction that results in a broad range of consulting services that support the optimization of the state-business linkage.

Hence, there is no "magic" relationship between the increase in income and the demand for services; nevertheless, there is a socioeconomic transformation in which the industrial sector and a broad spectrum of services linked to it are simultaneously modified by means of different relations which point in the direction of complementarity.[34]

Incidence in Employment

Most of the increase in employment in the services sector is consumed by activities with a low, stationary level of productivity: retail sales, health, and education.[35] Given the slow growth in productivity in these activities, the relative price level has shot up more rapidly than in industrial activities; thus, they have become a source of considerable inflationary pressure and a factor that explains the smaller growth rate of global productivity.[36] A significant example would be the ratio between the increase in incomes and the demand for services in the health sector. The high growth rate of prices (particularly in the United States, but also in other industrialized countries) has created a growing awareness of the paramount need for introducing institutional and regulatory modifications that boost productivity and contain the rise in prices.[37]

In general terms, the initial phase of an "industrialization" in service activities of low, stationary productivity is surfacing, with the consequent presence of industrially-inspired equipment and productive processes. This is clearly evident in commercialization, health, training, and even "terciary" activities such as beauty salons and psychiatric clinics.[38]

As the "industrialization" of low productivity services with the growing collaboration of "information technology" continues, the contribution of these activities to the upswing in employment will tend to shrink. Services of high, growing productivity, such as communications, financial services, or wholesale sales, are characterized by their large degree of industrialization, with a significantly smaller employment level and a more limited growth rate than the low productivity services.[39]

Leadership of Communications

From a supply standpoint, the basic explanatory factor of the information revolution is the rapid technological advance experienced in the 1970s in the areas of microelectronics, telecommunications, and computer technology. This accounts for the significant decline in the costs of transmission, processing, storage, and reproduction of information. Technical progress operating in some branches of the industrial sector upholds the simple, seductive theory that information will replace capital and work as the basic production factor of the future. It is no accident that the communications sector is the most industrialized of all the services. In fact, if considering the indicators of the growth rate of production, employment, productivity, the productivity level, and the reduction of relative prices as attributes of leadership, communications is the only productive sector that presents more favorable levels than the economy as a whole in all five indicators.

In the manufacturing sector, those activities in which the physical component (hardware) of the information technologies reside — microelectronics, computer technology, and telecommunications — share this situation of privilege with the communications sector; consequently, this subsector experiences the greatest push. This subsector is located at the nucleus of those industrial sectors that produce information technology equipment and the activities pertaining to services that transmit, process, and spread information; based on these sectors, technical change is spread — at different rates and using distinct modalities — to all the activities geared toward the production of goods and services. The leadership of the so-called "information system" contains a symbiotic combination of physical components and logical components (software).

International Insertion and Industrial Competitiveness

The international competitiveness of countries and their perspectives on long-term insertion in the world economy is basically determined by the efficiency of the respective industrial sectors generating the technical progress that is propagated to the rest of the activities, whereby they have an incidence in their respective levels of productivity. During a recessive period, a country can solve the problem of unemployment through the expansion of services not subject to international competition, an option that is well known in Latin America. In the medium and long term, however, the problem of international insertion is determined by the competitiveness of industry and the industrialized services linked to it. Herein lies the importance of incorporating the following aspects into the medium- and long-term analysis of the new industrialization: the transformations underway in the industrial sector, the growing complementarity between the industrial and services sectors, the tendency toward the industrialization of activities previously classified as "terciary," the rise of the leadership of the information technology system with its physical and logical components integrated around the axis of communications, and the consequent importance of the competitiveness of the manufacturing sector in order to determine the extent and form of international insertion.

A primary approach to the evolution of the role performed by this displacement of employment from the industrial sector to the services sector is obtained by grouping the sectors of the productive structure according to the integration of the production of goods and services with which they are directly linked. An attempt in this direction appears in table 4.9, where the subsystems for which available information links products input, machinery, and corresponding services have been organized for the years 1972, 1977, and 1984. In this table the evolution of employment is analyzed for the subsytems of agriculture and food, clothing, housing, automobile, health, recreation, and communication.

Regardless of the methodological and information limitations and the extremely simplified nature of the exercise, the available figures yield the following information:

1. Within the production of both industrial goods and services, technical progress-intensive components and traditional components coexist.

Table 4.9 United States: Integration of Productive Systems by Goods and Services, 1972–1984

	1972		1977 Employment		1984		Employment growth rate (1977–84)	Salary per hour 1984 (US$)
	(000)	Structure	(000)	Structure	(000)	Structure		
Food System (F.S.)								
Agriculture and food	11,190	100	12,306	100	12,953	100	0.7	
Agriculture	4,373	39.1	4,170	33.9	3,389	26.2	− 2.9	
Input (fertilizers and others)[1]	180	1.6	175	1.4	143	1.1	− 2.9	12.86
Machinery[2]	137	1.2	168	1.4	114	0.9	− 5.3	10.57
Food[3]	1,835	16.4	1,742	14.1	1,692	13.0	− 0.4	8.92
Services[4]	4,665	41.7	6,051	49.2	7,615	58.8	3.3	4.09
Clothing System (Cl.S.)								
Clothing	3,530	100	3,441	100	3,202	100	− 1.0	
Clothing[5]	2,713	76.9	2,551	74.1	2,228	69.6	− 1.9	5.89
Machinery[6]	33	0.9	26	0.8	19	0.6	− 4.4	8.34
Services[7]	784	22.2	864	25.1	955	29.8	1.4	4.86
Housing System (Ho.S.)								
Housing	7,308	100	7,900	100	8,816	100	1.6	
New Construction[8]	5,279	72.2	5,612	71.0	6,200	70.3	1.4	11.90
Construction Materials[9]	493	6.7	484	6.1	484	5.5	1.0	10.29
Equipment[10]	566	7.8	547	6.9	476	5.4	− 2.0	7.57
Construction Machinery[11]	134	1.8	155	2.0	95	1.0	− 6.8	13.25
Services[12]	836	11.5	1,102	14.0	1,561	17.7	5.1	11.50
Automotive System (A.S.)								
Automobile	2,243	100	2,441	100	2,332	100	0.7	
Motor vehicles and parts[13]	1,050	46.8	1,133	46.4	971	41.7	− 2.2	13.91
Services[14]	1,193	53.2	1,308	53.6	1,361	58.3	0.6	n.a.
Health System (He.S.)								
Health	4,664	100	5,444	100	6,588	100	2.8	
Drugs[15]	242	5.2	268	4.9	298	4.5	1.5	9.17
Equipment[16]	103	2.2	145	2.7	217	3.3	6.0	8.14
Services[17]	4,319	92.6	5,031	92.4	6,073	92.2	2.7	n.a.
Recreation System (R.S.)								
Recreation	4,381	100	6,126	100	7,249	100	2.4	
Equipment and materials[18]	275	6.3	270	4.4	239	3.3	− 1.8	6.97
Services[19]	4,106	93.7	5,856	95.6	7,010	96.7	2.6	n.a.
Communication System (Co.S.)								
Communication	3,413	100	3,627	100	4,823	100	4.2	
Printing and publishing[20]	957	28.0	993	27.4	1,265	26.2	3.5	9.24
Advertising[21]	121	3.6	131	3.6	176	3.6	4.2	n.a.
Machinery and equipment[22]	1,079	31.6	1,167	32.3	1,174	35.6	5.6	9.44
Services[23]	1,256	36.8	1,336	36.8	1,668	34.6	3.2	

Source: Joint ECLAC/UNIDO Industry and Technology division, based on data from U.S. Department of Commerce, *U.S. Industrial Outlook 1985* (Washington, D.C., 1985).

[1]Includes SIC codes (Standard Industrial Classification Manual, 1972) 2873 (nitrogenous fertilizers), 2874 (phosphatic fertilizers), and 2879 (pesticides).

[2]Includes SIC codes 3523 (farm machinery and equipment) and 3551 (food product machinery).

[3]Includes SIC codes 2011 and 2013 (meat products), 2016 and 2017 (poultry and eggs), 2032 and 2035 (preserved fruits and vegetables), 2037 and 2038 (fruits and vegetables), 202 (dairy products), 2043 (cereal breakfast foods), 205 (bakery products), 2065 (confectionery products), 2082, 2084, and 2085 (malt beverages, wines, brandy, and liquor), 2086 (bottled and canned soft drinks), and 21 (tobacco manufactures).

[4]Includes SIC codes 5812/13 (eating and drinking places).

[5]Includes SIC codes 22 (textile mill products), 2823 (cellulosic manmade fibers), 2824 (noncellulosic organic fibers), 23 (apparel and other textile products), 3111 (leather tanning and finishing), 3151, 3161, 3171, 3172 and 2386 (leather gloves, luggage, handbags, clothing, and personal leather goods), 314 (footwear except rubber), and 3021 (rubber and plastic footwear).

[6]Includes SIC code 3552 (textile machinery).

[7]Includes SIC code 56 (apparel and accessory stores).

[8]Includes SIC codes 15 (residential and nonresidential building construction [private and public]), and 1629 (heavy construction).

[9]Includes SIC codes 3211 (flat glass), 3241 (cement hydraulic), 3271 (concrete block and brick), 3271 (concrete products n.e.c.), 3273 (ready-mixed concrete), and 3261 (vitreous plumbing fixtures.

[10]Includes SIC codes 251 (household furniture), 3651 (radio and TV receiving sets), and 363 (household appliances).

[11] Includes SIC code 3531 (construction machinery).

[12]Includes SIC codes 891 (engineering and architectural services), 603–12 (mutual savings banks and savings and loans associations), and 734 (services to buildings).

[13]Includes SIC codes 3711 (motor vehicles and car bodies), 3714 (motor vehicle parts and accessories), 3465 (automotive stamping), 3713 (truck and bus bodies), 3715 (truck trailers), 3011 (tires and inner tubes), and 2822 (synthetic rubber).

[14]Includes SIC codes 75 (auto repair, services, and garages), and 551 (new and used car dealers).

[15]Includes SIC codes 283 (drugs), and 284 (soap, cleaners, and toilet goods).

[16]Includes SIC codes 3693 (X-ray apparatus and tubes), 3841–42 (surgical and medical instruments, appliances, and supplies), and 3843 (dental equipment and supplies).

[17]Includes SIC code 80 (health services).

[18]Includes SIC codes 3911 (jewelry precious metals), 3961 (costume jewelry), 3914 (silverware and plated ware), 3262 (vitreous china food utensils), 3931 (musical instruments), 375 (motorcycles, bicycles, and parts), 3524 (lawn and garden equipment), and 3949 (sporting and athletic goods).

[19]Includes SIC code 79 (amusement and recreation services).

[20]Includes SIC code 27 (printing and publishing).

[21]Includes SIC code 731 (advertising).

[22]Includes SIC codes 3661 (telephone and telegraphic apparatus), 3651 (radio and TV sets), 3662 (radio and TV communication equipment), 367 (electronic computing equipment), 3555 (printing trades machinery), 3579 (office machines n.e.c.), and 3573 (electronic computing equipment).

[23]Includes SIC codes 4811–21 (telephone and telegraph communication), 4832–33 (radio and television broadcasting),
4899 (cable television), and 7374 (data processing services).

2. In some of the system studies, the decline of industrial employment is explained principally by the erosion of U.S. industrial competitiveness (clothing, automotive, and communication).

3. In several systems employment growth in services is associated with activities with a low level of qualifications and wages (food, clothing); in other cases, rapidly expanding services present high wage levels (housing, health, and communications).

4. In terms of employment, the machinery and equipment component utilized in the distinct systems is low; this should not, however, obviate its essential function as carrier of technical progress. In sectors where the United States is competitive on an international level, the highest employment growth rates observed are precisely in the machinery and equipment component, in other words, "goods" (health, communications).

5. The system with the greatest dynamism is communications, where modern goods and services converge. It embodies the transition to a technological pattern characterized by a sharp drop in the costs of information storage, processing, and transmission which favors its dissemination to the productive system.

6. This approach to the relationship between goods and services through the productive systems that integrate them seems to be fruitful and reaffirms the need for a careful reading of the industry-services relationship.

Final Reflections
on the United States

Some of the recent alternative explanations for the erosion of U.S. productivity have been quickly disregarded due to their inability to gain empirical support. For example, the high tax rate has been frequently blamed for the decline in productivity. The tax rate was conspicuously higher, however, in the 1950s and 1960s, at the very moment when productivity growth was much higher.[40] Similarly the low investment rate is periodically held responsible for the drop in productivity; what is of interest, however, is not merely the global investment rate, which is actually greater than in prior periods of rapid productivity growth, but its composition, primarily a high percentage of business equipment which has been transformed into the symbol of the incorporation of modernity into the productive sector. The significant investment increase in business equipment has not induced a surge in productivity in the corresponding activity. In recent years for example, the employment of executives and executive assistants has jumped enormously, more than total employment and a great deal more than the product and the investment in these sectors. Hence, it would seem that, regardless of high-tech content, this business equipment does not increase the productivity of the system to which it has been incorporated.

This provides further confirmation that productivity is not only related to the capital endowment available for each worker, but also to the nature of the organization into which it is inserted, interpersonal relations, and the corresponding levels of communications and motivation.[41] Productivity does not increment automatically along with the incorporation of modern equipment. Companies, institutions, countries, and societies are not more modern because they have a greater endowment of modern equipment per capita, worker, or government employee, but because of the interaction between the nature and quality of the interpersonal relations and the equipment that goes along with that institutionality.

After analyzing the erosion of productivity and the foremost need to favor technological progress, an important current of thought chiefly blames excessive governmental activism. It maintains that the fiscal deficit would give birth to a high interest rate, augment capital costs, and induce high taxes. Therefore, it proposes an expansion of the incentives for investing in technological development in order to "debureaucratize" and neutralize the protectionist pressures of other countries using compensatory measures. In sum, the fundamental responsibility for recovering technological and productivity dynamism would fall upon the public sector through the adoption of a series of actions conducive to the increase of efficiency in the private sector.[42]

With respect to this position, there are those who have stressed the considerable responsibility of the private sector itself. The strategies followed by some corporations have led to a loss of markets in sectors in which the United States was the original innovator: some have chosen the easy expedient of dealing with competition by transferring their facilities abroad, while some have systematically underestimated the decisive role played by public-sector purchasing in certain strategic categories in which U.S. industry was most competitive, such as aeronautics.[43]

Moreover, it is also argued that the entrepreneurial sector is partly responsible for the loss of management efficiency, inasmuch as it has placed its attention mainly on the potential growth through mergers — i.e., through the transfer of assets (so-called paper entrepreneurialism). In November 1986 these criticisms, which usually came from liberal economists, received unexpected support from U.S. government executives at the highest level, who stressed the enormous responsibility which the entrepreneurial sector must assume for improving its own efficiency.[44]

A third current of thought stresses the precarious coordination between the public and private sectors, and the absence of institutional mechanisms to harmonize efforts to channel funds toward priority sectors. There is a broad consensus on this subject, even though doubts exist as to the possibility of moving from the highly decentralized system to a scheme based on agreement and the subordination of private interests to national strategic interests of questionable definition.

It is important to recognize the difficulty of defining responsibilities and assigning them to certain social or institutional factors, especially if one agrees that there is a certain mimesis in the operation of society, i.e., that there are certain basic types of operation and behavior which can be well disseminated throughout the public, private, entrepreneurial, trade union, and academic sectors.

An attempt should be made to explore the possibility that part of the essential explanation for the deterioration of U.S. industrial competitiveness lies in what could be called "rent seeking from hegemony," which that nation has enjoyed for the last four decades. An expression of this situation is that its language has been converted into a universal language, its currency is universal currency, its life-style is the paradigm for the rest of the world. This situation would seem to have generated a series of "profits" that would serve as a demotivational device with regard to the most difficult of all tasks: maintaining a high level of competitiveness in the industrial sector relying on technical progress. A large, integrated, and prosperous internal market physically linked with a favorable communications infrastructure, could foster the perception that the current economic situation is more than sufficient to undertake any economic activity. Thus, it would be able to receive "royalties" for the mere fact of being on top of the world, whether that involves industrial property, product design, process design, the overseas reproduction of

U.S. life-styles and behaviors, or the conversion into an international financial center that inspires confidence due to "economic solidity" and military might even while exhibiting strong, growing foreign and fiscal deficit. At any rate, the capital of the rest of the world flows into this country in the pursuit of profits, prestige, and security. This influence would lead to the partial reproduction in the United States of the elitist opinion existing in the United Kingdom at the end of the last century. When discovering the relative, systematic erosion of that country vis-à-vis West Germany in the sectors considered to be advanced technologies at that time (chemicals and electricity), the reaction was to dismiss the problem because England definitely possessed the core role in terms of financial mediation, services, insurance, transportation, as well as a vast network of overseas investments that continued to feed the center. This was not a case of income generated by natural resources causing a certain behavior in the elite which is spread to the whole of society through the replacement of systematic effort with the enjoyment of the income provided by nature; it was a situation of rent seeking that emanated from England's position at the head of the pack. This position allowed the nation to become indebted in its own currency, to make the increase in the currency value compatible with a soaring foreign, fiscal deficit, and to provide austere economic policy recommendations to the rest of the world which did not reconcile with internal policies.

Unlike England, the United States benefits from the very important extenuating circumstance that there is no power capable of displacing it from the economic center of the world; the risk of losing leadership seems to be slim. Proposals surface that confront the problem on the basis of more simple, more seductive, but not necessarily very convincing, mechanisms. There are those who assert that, in the face of the current international market, the United States should adopt policies and behaviors similar to those of Japan, especially in regard to savings, the selection of sectorial priorities, the development of strategic public planning, intracorporate relations, the reinforcement of the deteriorated educational system, and the transformation of the Department of Commerce into an equivalent of MITI.

Another option, less arbitrary and more acceptable from the U.S. viewpoint, would be to request West Germany and Japan to abandon their austerity and competitiveness and, consequently, their dynamism and accelerate their induction into the era of exuberant consumption through the amplification of the social security system. In this manner, they would help to improve the external situation of the United States. With full awareness of their respective traumas and precariousnesses, however, neither society seems willing to adopt a life-style that not even the United States is able to finance.

A third option would take into consideration the interests of the world beyond these three great powers. First, the United States would assume that it could no longer finance its life-style and that it must take steps toward austerity and foster U.S. international competitiveness. Second, the surplus resources of Japan and West Germany, instead of being shifted to the United States for the production of commodities that would no longer be exported due to an increase in internal protectionism, would be transferred to the Third World, which, in turn, would have to carry out a series of internal transformations (to be discussed in detail in chapter 7). This would lead to the reconstruction of an international community in which the dynamization of both developed and Third World countries would become viable as a result of the channeling of the surpluses of such countries as Japan and West Germany and the internal restructuring of the United States according to its real possibilities. Undoubtedly, the success of such a proposal is no more evident than that of adapting U.S. citizens to the Japanese style or vice versa. Although it might do no more than to adjust the deficiencies of the United States and other countries to reality, the proposal would merit some degree of attention.

Aside from internal obstacles, the first proposal, the "Japanization" of the United States, confronts the no less trivial aspect of gaining access to external markets of a reasonable size. The second option, the "Americanization" of Japan and West Germany, would soon lead to the stagnation of these three countries and, consequently, to the accentuation of the recession in the rest of the world. The third possibility, which is undoubtedly the most complex and hence the least appealing, has the advantage of acknowledging, or at least trying to draw attention to, the fact that it is difficult to imagine that three-fourths of the world's population would stand by passively to watch a show which for these three protagonists might have different scripts, but which leaves them out not only of the present, but of the future as well.

5. Western Europe and the Nordic Countries: Contrasts and Similarities

In this chapter, the analytical context presented in chapter 2 and analyzed in chapter 3 for the leading industrialized countries is contrasted with the situations of a select group of Western European countries. These experiences present a series of common features that differ from the U.S. experience and constitute an important reference for subsequent reflection on Latin America:

1. All of the countries have a high opening level and are therefore vulnerable with respect to the international economy
2. The economic gravitation of the state in the economies is notoriously higher than in the United States or Japan
3. Regional integration is used to reinforce insertion in the international economy
4. In most cases (with the possible exceptions of West Germany and the United Kingdom), these European countries perceive the international economic context in terms of exogenous data to which the countries should try to adapt
5. The diversity of modalities in the emergence of capitalism in the respective precapitalist histories generates a suggestive range of national specificities and, at the interior of each one, a relatively high level of political and ideological pluralism that is not found in the United States.

In contrast to the deepness and variety of these motivations, this chapter proposes very modest objectives: to analyze the impact of natural resource availability on international insertion and on the industrial sector's specialization and competitiveness, and to explore the relationships among this competitiveness, the consumption patterns, and the growth and equity objectives. The empirical treatment is strictly similar to that conducted in chapter 4; therefore, an abbreviated and schematic presentation of the principal results is made. Attention is concentrated on the larger countries of Western Europe (West Germany, the United Kingdom, France, and Italy) and the Nordic countries (Sweden, Norway, Denmark, and Finland). Contemplating West Germany within the European context acts as a link with chapter 4, and the whole of this chapter acts as a bridge between the leading industrial countries (chapter 4) and the final comparison between Latin American countries and the "growth-with-equity industrializing countries" (GEICs) (chapter 6).

Western Europe

The Largest Countries of Western Europe: The South Is Rising in the North

This group of countries—France, Italy, the United Kingdom, and West Germany—can be subdivided according to an accentuated heterogeneity in terms of the international insertion by type of resources and productive sectors (see table 5.1). First, the basic source of international insertion in both West Germany and Italy is the manufacturing sector, which generates foreign exchange that compensates (in different degrees) for the deficit in natural resource sectors. Second, since 1975 the United Kingdom presents a profile similar to the oil countries. Paradoxically, the birthplace of the industrial revolution has arrived at a soaring deficit in the manufacturing sector, the only such case of all the countries considered. The third case is France, where a surplus in the agricultural sector coexists with a large surplus in the manufacturing sector.

West Germany and Italy rank immediately after Japan as the top three countries with a manufacturing surplus at a world level. The difference between them resides in the fact that West Germany generates a large enough surplus to be able to more than compensate for the deficit in the rest of the natural resource sectors. This has allowed West Germany to sustain a significant trade surplus for the last fifteen years, situating it alongside Japan among the countries with the greatest capacity to generate trade surpluses in the world. Italy, regardless of its spectacular performance of the manufacturing sector, has not succeeded in covering its natural resource deficit with this activity and has achieved a trade deficit comparable in size to that of France and the United Kingdom. Both West Germany and Italy absorbed the 1973 oil shock successfully by means of the generation of a manufacturing surplus which, in West Germany, more than compensated for the fuel deficit and, in Italy, covered 70 percent of it.

The United Kingdom, which in 1970 presented a surplus surpassed only by West Germany, saw the decline of its relative position with respect to France and Italy between 1970 and 1975; the situation would worsen further with the access to the oil resources of the North Sea. In one mere decade (1975–1984) the United Kingdom went from a $9 billion surplus to a $8 billion deficit. It took a $16 billion loss in the manufacturing sector that was not compensated by the additional $15 billion generated in the energy sector. This situation was reproduced in the oil countries of Latin America and, to a lesser degree, Norway. The manufacturing deficit of the United Kingdom by 1984 equalled the combined manufacturing deficit of the oil exporting countries of Latin America ($10 billion). Reinforcing a secular trend widely debated in literature, the spectacular deterioration of the manufacturing sector in England[1] suggests and reaffirms the hypothesis developed in earlier chapters. In the presence of an accessible source of foreign exchange generation that does not require the disruption of society, countries choose the easiest way, in this case, profit generated by oil.

These four countries share two important features. First, the degree of their exposure to international trade is high. When considering the sum of exports and imports in relation to GNP, the ratio exceeds 40 percent. Second, they share a high economic gravitation of the public sector. At the beginning of the 1980s, tax revenue in relation to GDP exceeded 40 percent in all the countries.[2] In relation to the weight of energy imports (with the exception of the United Kingdom), they reached a ratio as high as 6 percent of GNP at the beginning of the 1980s. The conjunction of these two characteristics is accentuated in the case of the Nordic countries and poses the following question: Can the welfare state be competitive?

Table 5.1 Western Europe: Trade Balance by Sector of Economic Activity, 1970–1987 (Millions of dollars)

Sectors	1970	1975	1981	1982
Agriculture				
France	− 741	78	2,780	1,289
West Germany	− 5,774	− 10,145	− 13,441	− 12,852
Italy	− 3,008	− 6,662	− 9,525	− 10,340
United Kingdom	− 5,498	− 9,074	− 9,415	− 9,127
Manufacturing Industry[a]				
France	2,037	9,817	9,660	4,154
West Germany	14,424	39,338	62,317	68,174
Italy	4,069	13,849	24,987	25,197
United Kingdom	5,968	9,295	6,485	650
Energy				
France	− 1,915	− 10,850	− 29,983	− 27,225
West Germany	− 1,616	− 10,286	− 32,723	− 29,867
Italy	− 1,426	− 8,227	− 26,072	− 22,252
United Kingdom	− 1,774	− 7,733	5,001	6,659
Mining				
France	− 745	− 1,432	− 1,732	− 1,609
West Germany	− 2,343	− 2,662	− 3,835	− 3,651
Italy	− 1,365	− 2,074	− 3,106	− 2,820
United Kingdom	− 1,431	− 1,640	− 2,087	− 1,620
Other sectors				
France	180	385	− 112	385
West Germany	− 318	− 431	− 176	− 712
Italy	1	11	− 2,082	− 2,568
United Kingdom	362	− 294	384	662
Total				
France	− 1,184	− 2,002	− 19,387	− 23,006
West Germany	4,375	15,814	12,142	21,092
Italy	− 1,729	− 3,103	− 15,798	− 12,783
United Kingdom	− 2,373	− 9,446	374	− 2,776

Source: Joint ECLAC/UNIDO Industry and Technology Division, based on data from UN, *Yearbook of International Trade Statistics,* various years; UN, *Commodity Trade Statistics,* various years.
[a]Manufacturing industry includes SITC sections 5 to 8 less division 68 (nonferrous metals).

1983	1984	1985	1986	1987
1,975	2,182	2,783	2,965	3,780
− 12,868	− 15,568	− 12,644	− 15,266	− 17,579
− 10,048	− 10,285	− 11,415	− 12,956	− 16,256
− 8,783	− 9,203	− 8,661	− 10,090	− 11,931
7,035	9,584	8,040	2,284	− 3,378
59,013	60,235	68,131	89,902	105,152
28,388	25,248	26,219	30,039	29,535
− 7,114	− 8,060	− 6,515	− 11,708	− 15,550
− 22,339	− 21,572	− 20,231	− 12,955	− 13,780
− 26,694	− 25,545	− 26,212	− 17,971	− 18,044
− 20,749	− 19,955	− 20,220	− 14,696	− 14,195
9,149	6,658	8,065	3,325	4,363
− 1,161	− 1,015	− 1,120	− 1,514	− 1,594
− 3,231	− 571	− 3,319	− 3,331	− 2,835
− 2,609	− 3,087	− 3,056	− 3,165	− 3,652
− 2,034	− 1,553	− 1,698	− 1,365	− 1,900
335	398	410	350	459
375	171	− 484	− 775	− 650
− 2,667	− 2,877	− 3,532	− 3,734	− 3,906
270	572	711	289	1,758
− 14,155	− 10,423	− 10,118	− 8,872	− 14,513
16,595	18,722	25,472	52,559	66,044
− 7,685	− 10,956	− 12,004	− 4,512	− 8,474
− 8,512	− 11,586	− 8,098	− 19,549	− 23,260

Specialization Trends at a National Level

Next, the configuration and competitiveness of the industrial sector will be schematically explored: in West Germany and Italy it is a basic method of compensation for the natural resource deficit; in England it has undergone a secular erosion accentuated by access to oil resources; and in France it experiences relative stagnation.

Perhaps the most relevant for Latin American discussion, Italy appears in clear contrast with the predominant pattern presented by West Germany, the United States, and Japan, where the chemical and electronics axes appear to dominate a profile of high specialization. Besides having achieved significant advances in these technological content–intensive areas, Italy is able to maintain its international insertion by raising the level of excellence in sectors that, from the viewpoints of "common sense" and academia are "losers" because of the growing competitiveness of the Asian NICs.[3] While undergoing a rapid process of deindustrialization in the rest of the industrialized countries, the textile, clothing, and shoe subsectors in Italy maintain high dynamism with higher productivity, and thereby maintain Italy's solid position in the European and U.S. markets. Additionally, non-electrical machinery and transportation equipment sectors receive as much attention in Italy as electrical equipment and areas linked to natural resources such as wood and paper.

Hence, the image of structural change within the Italian industrial sector seems remarkably different from the dominant cases observed in chapter 4. It shows a strong homogeneity in terms of dynamism, in a broad range of sectors that include labor intensive, capital intensive (iron and steel manufacturing), technology intensive (machinery and transportation equipment), and natural resources intensive (wood and paper). The only area in which deindustrialization appears at the end of the 1980s is in the area of metallic products.

An interesting aspect of the Italian case refers to small and medium industry which in quantitative terms plays a more pronounced role than in the majority of the European countries considered and, particularly, more accentuated in West Germany, England, and France. More important than the quantitative aspect is the phenomenon in the 1970s when the productivity of Italy's small and medium enterprises tended to increase and become homogenized with respect to the productivity of large businesses in a wide spectrum of sectors. The conventional image is that there are structural differences in productivity associated with scale economies and technological rigidities, at least in a relatively broad range of industrial sectors. Additionally, this surge in productivity in the small and medium industry and its ranking at levels comparable to that of large businesses enables it to perform a considerable function in the international insertion of Italy in several of the sectors under consideration — textiles, clothing, shoes, wood furniture, and certain types of machinery in which scale economies are not significant, particularly those related to machinery for specific uses such as foods. These two peculiarities — the modernization of traditional sectors condemned by academia and common sense to an inexorable disappearance and a significant upswing in productivity in small and medium enterprises in a wide range of sectors — are of particular interest for reflection on the options available to Latin America.

In France, where industrial growth in the period is comparable, although slightly inferior, to West Germany and Italy, the changes in the industrial productive profile also diverged from the classic cases of the three major countries discussed earlier. Leadership is exercised by the electrical machinery and electronics sectors. Deindustrialization is experienced in the industrial sectors of nonmetallic minerals, steel and iron, nonferrous metals, metal products, textiles, leather, and wood. There is rapid industrial growth, accentuated structural change, and specialization in the axis of electrical and electronics equipment, where the purchasing power of the public sector performs an important role (nuclear energy, aeronautics, railroad equipment, telecommunications, and armaments).[4]

Upon analysis of the specialization areas of each of these countries (see table 5.2), a comparison of participation in the world market within the group of engineering products with the degree of specialization that has been attained in specific areas reveals some interesting differences.

The three areas in which France has a high degree of specialization correspond to sectors in which the purchasing power of the public sector is determinant, a fact which is perfectly coherent with its historical process of industrialization.[5] Sectors linked to energy, telecommunications, the military, aeronautics, and railroad transportation are the areas in which France has reached levels of excellence. This is reaffirmed by the three branches identified here.

West Germany specializes in the high-tech sector of nuclear reactors (44 percent of the world market) along with equipment for processing its natural resources, paper and pulp machinery and printing machinery. These are all items in which the intellectual added value reinforces that of the corresponding natural resources.[6]

Table 5.2 Western Europe: Specialization in Engineering Products, 1984 (Percentages)

Countries	World share total engineering products	SITC Rev. 2[a]	Item	World share (each item)
France	6.0	714.4	Reaction engines	21.0
		722.1	Electrical apparatus for making, breaking protecting electrical circuits	11.5
		792	Aircraft	11.4
West Germany	14.8	718.7	Nuclear reactors	44.0
		726	Printing bookbinding machinery	33.0
		725	Paper and pulp machinery	27.0
Italy	4.4	775	Domestic equipment, electric and nonelectric	14.6
		741.4	Refrigerating equipment (nondomestic)	13.2
		722	Tractors	11.0
United Kingdom	5.6	714.4	Reaction engines	44.0
		722	Tractors	15.0
		764.3	Telecommunication transmitters and receivers	14.9

Source: Joint ECLAC/UNIDO Industry and Technology Division, based on data from UN *Bulletin on World Trade in Engineering Products,* E/F/R 88.11.E.14 (New York, 1986).
[a]UN, Standard International Trade Classification, Rev. 2, E.75.XVII.6 (New York, 1975).

What attracts attention in the case of Italy, in clear contrast with the two previous cases, is the fact that the areas of greatest specialization are those of durable appliance consumption, in which the fundamental contribution of Italy is linked to design. Moreover, Italy has also attained a high degree of specialization in the processing phase and equipment design of tractors, which form a part of the "food system."[7]

Finally, in two of the areas of greatest specialization, reaction motors and telecommunications equipment, the expansion and international competitiveness of English industry is intensely conditioned by the purchasing power of the public sector. To some extent, then, this specialization at the level of specific areas expresses the type of industrial specialization that the countries under consideration have approached in recent decades.[8]

Diverging Patterns

Our comparison involves a group of countries that share a high degree of specialization, an insertion in international trade, and a significant state participation in the economy. Within this context, some particular aspects are salient. West Germany, on one extreme, is the country with the greatest industrial significance on the whole, presents more favorable traits in terms of equity and competitiveness than all the countries considered, and belongs to the group with the greatest dynamism. This pattern locates it in an intermediate position between Japan and the United States and is characterized by a "balanced" coexistence of the four dimensions considered: dynamism, equity, competitiveness, and "austerity" (see figure 5.1).

The other extreme within the group considered is the United Kingdom, in which the high degree of equity (almost comparable to West Germany) and austerity coexist with a low level of dynamism and competitiveness. This country would appear to be a very curious combination of "Japanese" austerity, "German" equity, and "American" lack of dynamism and competitiveness.

The other three countries are located between these two polar situations. The highest levels of competitiveness in the industrial sector are found in those countries that present a systematic structural deficit in natural resources, West Germany and Italy. In terms of the consumption pattern, Western Europe shows an extremely high degree of homogeneity. The differences in the levels of the density of vehicles are minimal compared to those observed in the cases of the three great industrial powers; the greatest density is in West Germany and the least is in the United Kingdom, with a very small interval (a fractual implication of the European Common Market?).

With respect to the equity dimension, however, the results are dif-

Figure 5.1 Strategic Profiles: France, West Germany, Italy, Sweden, and the United Kingdom

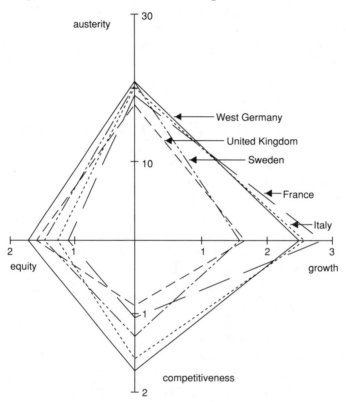

Source: Joint ECLAC / UNIDO Industry and Technology Division.

ferent. It seems possible to distinguish two groups of countries: those with a high level of equity greater than the average of the industrialized countries (the United Kingdom and West Germany) and those with low levels of equity (France and Italy) that are slightly higher than the most equitable countries of Latin America (Argentina and Uruguay). France and Italy, however, present the greatest dynamism with rates approximating 3 percent per capita annually during the last two decades. Both countries present features that pertain to two patterns of development that constitute hybrids between the U.S. consumption pattern, the U.S. income distribution pattern, and the Japanese model of dynamism and international competitiveness. As such, they would be competitive, dynamic countries with a high degree of consumption "a la Americana" and a relatively low level of equity.

In very general terms, three patterns can be distinguished. West Germany and the Scandinavian countries present a profile in which the four dimensions are balanced. The United Kingdom, with a legacy of past industrial leadership expressed in a high degree of equity and the peculiar process of modernization "from below," presents a decline in dynamism, competitiveness, and the standard of living. France and Italy—societies which in the 1950s presented a high proportion of their population in agriculture (32 and 42 percent respectively for 1950), a factor that would promote a less favorable income distribution—have experienced a high rate of growth in productivity and competitiveness.

To what extent are these characterizations compatible with the analytical scheme of reference described in the previous chapter? The cases which seem to deviate from this scheme would be those of the United Kingdom, France, and Italy. The analysis of the decline of the relative position of England has been the object of exhaustive research and the access to oil resources that accentuate the erosion of its industrial competitiveness emphasizes a "secular" decadence. In the case of France and Italy, where competitiveness and dynamism coexist with a low degree of equity and a high degree of consumption, a situation exists in which the positive effect for competitiveness with respect to equity is overlapped and neutralized by the structural characteristics of the respective modernization process (the strong weight of the agricultural sector, where the zones of less development coexist with an emerging industrial sector).[9]

This hybrid between the American consumption model and relative inequality with the Japanese component of dynamism and competitiveness would appear again in Latin America, where the most outstanding example is Brazil.

It is important to remember that within the analytical frame of reference, both objectives—dynamism and equity—are conditioned by factors other than competitiveness and the consumption pattern. While competitiveness has a positive influence over equity, the series of structural factors that influence it predominate and confirm a situation such as the one witnessed. The relationship between equity and the consumption pattern maintains that a greater level of equity must (at a level of similar income) lead to a relatively greater level of austerity; this is demonstrated by England, on the one hand, and France and Italy, on the other, but it appears to be placed in doubt by West Germany, which simultaneously presents a higher degree of equity with a higher level of consumption. In this particular case, there is a difference in the income level that would explain this apparent violation of the originally foreseen relationship—according to the World Bank, in 1986 the GDP per capita was $12,080 for West Germany, $8,550 in Italy, $8,870 in the United Kingdom, and $10,720 in France.

The Nordic Countries

Small, Open, and Democratic Countries

The four countries that comprise this category—Sweden, Norway, Finland, and Denmark—possess a population comparable to the small and medium countries of Latin America and an income level equivalent to at least five times that of the most prosperous Latin American countries. Significant common features of the Nordic countries include: particularly high exposure to the international market associated with a small internal market (exports plus imports over GDP located between 55 and 60 percent); an insertion that includes a considerable natural resource component; the keen participation of the public sector in the economy (taxes over GDP, including contributions to social security, range between 40 percent [Finland] and 60 percent [Sweden]); and, in the political sphere, a solid, long-lasting tradition of democracy, a feature that essentially differentiates them from Southeast Asian countries.

Industrial Specialization and the Realization of
Natural Resource Potential

In terms of international insertion according to type of economic activity, the Nordic countries present a sustained surplus in the agricultural sector (see table 5.3). Norway, whose international insertion is based on agriculture, energy, and mining, also presents a structural surplus in the mining sector. Between 1975 and 1981, its net revenue in foreign exchange derived from fuel amounted to almost $7 billion; this was countered, as in England, by a significant decline in the manufacturing sector, equivalent to approximately one-half the fuel surplus. Since 1981, the manufacturing deficit level has been maintained, while surpluses in the energy, mining, and agricultural sectors continue to grow. Since the beginning of the 1980s, Norway is the Nordic country that presents the most important global trade surplus of all the countries under study and, along with Sweden, is the other European country that has been able to maintain extraordinarily small unemployment rates (around 3 percent).

Norway's energy surplus represented 7 percent of GDP at the beginning of the 1980s; on the other hand, the fuel deficit in the rest of the Nordic countries reached 5 to 6 percent of GDP. The response capacity of those net oil importers at the time of the 1973 oil shock shows similar features which confirm the flexibility of their industrial sector to bounce back from this unexpected challenge. Among other factors, that response capacity is related to the particular configuration of productive specialization within the industrial sector. Industrial restructuring has been implemented without sharpening the unemployment problem; in an economy strongly inserted into the international market, restructuring assumes greater flexibility in terms of dynamism and technological content, and a mode of social functioning that stresses the maintenance of high employment levels as a priority objective.[10]

The type of product area in which these countries attain specialization at an international level is particularly revealing in terms of the capacity to add intellectual value to available natural resources. Table 5.4 indicates how, for example, Finland, whose participation in the world market is less than 1 percent, attains a presence of 7 and 6 percent in areas directly linked to its natural resource endowment: machinery for paper, pulp, and shipbuilding. Denmark has a participation that is almost five times higher than its total global participation in areas directly linked to the processing of its agricultural natural resources: industrial refrigeration equipment, food processing equipment, and agricultural machinery. In Norway, specialization areas include shipbuilding, pumps that have a direct linkage with oil exploitation, and agricultural machinery. Finally, in Sweden there is a combination of high-tech areas, such as communications equipment and nuclear reactors, and machinery for processing forest products.

Table 5.3 North European Countries: Trade Balance
by Sector of Economic Activity, 1970–1987 (Millions of dollars)

Country	1970	1975	1981	1982
Agriculture				
Denmark	664	1,958	3,228	3,322
Finland	301	152	1,612	767
Norway	18	− 26	122	176
Sweden	274	819	656	669
Manufacturing[a]				
Denmark	− 1,280	− 1,865	− 956	− 1,434
Finland	− 297	− 705	2,160	2,390
Norway	− 1,256	− 2,769	− 5,314	− 5,738
Sweden	270	1,376	4,774	3,993
Energy				
Denmark	− 337	− 1,628	− 3,714	− 3,410
Finland	− 283	− 1,424	− 3,775	− 3,139
Norway	− 231	− 19	6,785	7,111
Sweden	− 682	− 2,838	− 5,870	− 5,310
Mining				
Denmark	− 104	− 119	− 243	− 224
Finland	− 46	− 134	− 145	− 177
Norway	233	325	732	542
Sweden	− 94	− 44	− 31	− 146
Other sectors				
Denmark	− 2	− 9	− 111	− 128
Finland	− 6	—	− 36	− 97
Norway	− 9	− 9	4	21
Sweden	9	54	213	44
Total				
Denmark	− 1,099	− 1,663	− 1,796	− 1,874
Finalnd	331	− 2,111	− 184	− 256
Norway	− 1,245	− 2,498	2,329	2,112
Sweden	− 223	− 633	− 258	− 748

Source: Joint ECLAC/UNIDO Division, based on data from UN, *Yearbook of International Trade Statistics,* various years.
[a]Manufacturing includes SITC sections 5 to 8 less division 68 (nonferrous metals).

1983	1984	1985	1986	1987
3,061	2,906	3,137	3,851	4,557
944	1,147	860	835	1,181
337	263	194	47	335
1,201	1,141	808	386	536
− 931	− 1,483	− 2,153	− 4,288	− 3,507
1,746	2,417	2,230	2,313	1,567
− 4,761	− 5,057	− 5,549	− 9,578	− 10,157
4,527	5,200	4,943	6,506	5,203
− 2,395	− 2,213	− 2,208	− 1,375	− 1,267
− 2,813	− 2,365	− 2,645	− 1,954	− 2,232
8,087	8,908	8,756	6,625	7,506
− 4,256	− 3,465	− 3,916	− 2,436	− 2,347
− 221	− 203	− 200	− 259	− 267
− 144	− 93	− 85	− 126	− 208
821	918	754	874	1,255
− 41	− 20	− 53	8	28
− 88	− 56	− 93	− 99	− 156
− 70	− 41	− 62	− 64	− 117
− 5	− 2	− 12	− 39	− 65
89	130	137	249	382
− 574	− 1,049	− 1,517	− 2,170	− 640
− 337	1,065	298	1,004	191
4,479	5,030	4,143	− 2,071	− 1,126
1,340	2,986	1,919	4,713	3,802

What is interesting to emphasize is how these countries, with very small internal markets and marginal participation in the international market of engineering products, have been able to facilitate their insertion by strengthening and supporting themselves on the basis of developing the technological infrastructure, the products, processes, and equipment required to process their own natural resources. This is perhaps the most important lesson that can be taken from this group of small

Table 5.4 Northern European Countries:
Specialization in Engineering Products, 1984 (Percentages)

Countries	World share total engineering products	SITC Rev. 2[a]	Item	World share (each item)
Denmark	0.69	741.4	Refrigerating equipment non domestic	3.6
		727	Food processing machinery	3.3
		721	Agricultural machinery	3.1
Finland	0.65	725	Paper and pulp machinery	6.8
		793	Ships and boats	6.2
		711	Steam boilers	2.6
Norway	0.40	793	Ships and boats	3.8
		742	Pumps for liquids	1.3
		721	Agricultural machinery	1.0
Sweden	2.30	764.1	Electric telephone and telegraph equipment	9.5
		718.7	Nuclear reactors	8.0
		725	Paper and pulp machinery	7.0

Source: Joint ECLAC/UNIDO Industry and Technology Division, based on data from UN, *Bulletin on World Trade in Engineering Products*, E/F/R 88.11.E.14 (New York, 1986).
[a]UN, Standard International Trade Classification, Rev. 2, E.75.XV11.6 (New York, 1975).

countries open to international trade; it explains their capacity to confront the oil challenge in three of the four countries, to maintain their solid presence in the international markets, and to cautiously proceed with a high degree of social integration. In these countries, the natural resources endowment associated with the permanent incorporation of technical progress would exempt them from the "rent-seeking" condition.

Homogeneity and Convergence

In analyzing the group of strategic indicators that link growth and equity with competitiveness and the consumption pattern, the following elements exist, among others: the fact that these are societies with a very high degree of equity, and that level of equity goes hand-in-hand with a relatively high level of dynamism, which is higher in all of them than the average of the industrialized countries. But not only equity is higher, growth rates are also higher. Once again, the absence of the trade-off between equity and growth is seen (see figure 5.2).

Finland, the most equitable, is simultaneously one of the most dynamic, along with Norway; Sweden, while possessing a high degree of equity, is the lowest of the four countries and presents the smallest degree of dynamism. Equity appears directly linked to austerity. Although the consumption level in the four countries is high and similar, the most accentuated is in the country with the smallest relative degree of equity, Sweden. The country with the largest degree of equity, Finland, also has the highest level of competitiveness; in other words, competitiveness reinforces equity in this case. Sweden has the same level of competitiveness, with a development level that is higher (excluding Norway) than the rest of the Nordic countries (in 1986 the GDP per capita was $13,160 in Sweden; $12,160 in Finland; and $12,600 in Denmark).

The lowest in terms of industrial competitiveness is Norway, where the oil syndrome affects its international industrial insertion. Norway is able to cover only half of its industrial imports with its exports. Regardless, given that dynamism is a function not only of industrial competitiveness but also of the availability of external resources, and given that Norway possesses an ample natural resource endowment reinforced by the rise in oil prices, it presents the greatest level of growth and per capita income (in 1986, $15,400). Once again, given that growth depends on a series of factors, the fact that Norway presents a relatively low competitiveness does not bar it from having the highest growth rate, nearly identical to Finland.

In general terms, however, the pattern of the Nordic countries presents a basic similarity with what we could call the West Germany pattern, in which relatively comparable proportions are maintained for the four dimensions under consideration. Unlike Japan, the emphasis on dynamism, competitiveness, and austerity in the West German pattern is complemented by a high degree of prosperity. Unlike the United States, the high level of prosperity is not achieved at the cost of equity.

Behind the development and industrialization pattern of these countries is the historical process of modernization. The fundamental feature of this process is an industrialization in societies in which agriculture

Figure 5.2 Strategic Profiles: North European Countries

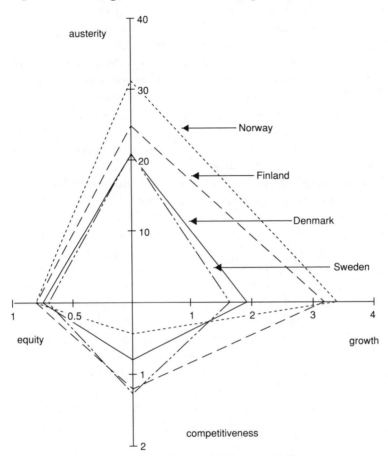

Source: Joint ECLAC / UNIDO Industry and Technology Division.

has reached a high degree of modernization associated with a relatively equitable distribution of property. The modernization of Nordic agriculture was significantly linked to access first to England's market and then to the European Common Market. What is interesting, however, is that their insertion was accomplished by consolidating the efforts of Nordic economic and social agents to increase the value of their natural resources through sustained endeavors in specialized areas to guarantee levels of excellence in quality, specification, and design, particularly in derivatives of sea products, agriculture, forestry, and metallurgy.[11]

This group of countries, which some political scientists have labelled "democratic corporatists"[12] due to past similarities in their economic profile with West Germany, has also been analyzed as an expression of their capacity to adapt to the energy crisis of the 1970s and 1980s more favorably than the rest of Europe, regardless of structural differences. A final feature of this characterization of the Nordic countries is the fact that their great insertion into international trade is "more radical" than that of the rest of the industrialized countries.[13] Their trade policies systematically oppose all impediments to international trade, and leave them extremely vulnerable with regard to that market. The situation is combined with a very high degree of internal socioeconomic integration, expressed in an income policy that has been the object of study for the rest of the world, and with a very high involvement of the state.[14] The social and political agents in these countries would seem to have arrived at the lucid conclusion that, due to their fragile size, they could not permit themselves the luxury of acute internal conflicts. The idea that efficient international insertion and the shrinking of the public function constitute necessary conditions of complementarity would take hold. In these countries a high degree of socioeconomic integration and strong state involvement in internal issues coexist with a large, unrestricted opening to the international market.

Military Supremacy and Precariousness in World Trade

The analysis of the Nordic countries would indicate that, regardless of the difference in the pattern of industrialization, there are some elements that acquire or maintain an essence within the analytical framework. In the case of the most important of the planned economy countries, the Soviet Union, the availability of natural resources in the sphere of energy, principally, and mining (respectively, $50 billion and $2 billion surplus in 1984) coexists with a growing structural deficit in both the agricultural and manufacturing sectors ($14 and $27 billion deficit in 1984). The manufacturing deficit in 1984 equalled approximately one-third of the U.S. manufacturing deficit and around three times that of

England. Thus, the generous availability of natural resources in the Soviet Union could have an impact on the precariousness of the international competitiveness of its industrial system.

As in the United States and the United Kingdom, this idea is compatible with the fact that these countries maintain a level of relative excellence by gearing resources toward high-tech military products.[15] Part of the unresolved debate over the influence of technological R&D in the military sphere on the industrial sector, this fact would reinforce the idea that these are spheres in which low levels of international competitiveness in tradeable goods can coexist with levels of excellence in the military realm. Radical differences in the challenges, procedures, time spans, and organizational forms of these activities would have an influence on this phenomenon.

In the military sphere, the idea is to define objectives and goals rather than timetables. Economic restriction performs a notably inferior role. The possibility for long-term planning in the military sphere is not reproduced in the commercial industrial sector, where flexibility and the capacity for rapid adaptation to the changing trends of international trade are essential. Moreover, the intensification of competition in the industrial trade sphere does not exist with the same intensity or within the same time periods in the military sphere. The replacement of successive generations of "products" and the "differentiation" within each generation is not determined by the test of performance. In addition, the military sphere is equipped to attract the most outstanding talent from science and technology, granting them relaxed conditions, abundant resources, the absence of demands for immediate results with peremptory deadlines, and wages that are not subject to the implacable dynamics of the market.

These facts combine to form an interesting contrast: on the one hand, those countries that have geared significant resources to the military present a substantial precariousness in international industrial competitiveness in conventional products; on the other, those countries with a high degree of industrialization which channel few resources to the military and perform the leadership function in the industrial competitiveness of those products. If the principal countries with a manufacturing surplus in 1984—Japan, West Germany, and Italy—were considered together, their combined manufacturing surplus would be approximately

$217 billion. These three countries, defeated in the Second World War, contrast their astounding surplus with that of their conquerers: the United States with a manufacturing deficit of $82 billion, the Soviet Union with a $26 billion deficit, and the United Kingdom with a $10 billion deficit, for a combined deficit total of $118 billion. In general terms, the countries that are industrial winners and military losers cater both the deficit of the military victors and the deficit of the rest of the world, primarily Third World countries.

Turning attention now to the participation of these two groups of countries in the commerce of engineering products in the last two decades, a situation exists that should not be ignored. In 1965, the "victors"—the United States, the Soviet Union, and the United Kingdom—generated approximately 35 percent of the world supply of engineering products, while the "defeated" contributed 29 percent of that supply. This situation has changed dramatically; in 1984 the countries that concentrate on military production contributed only 24 percent of the world supply, while the countries that are relatively isolated from military production efforts and concentrate on tradeable industrial goods boosted their participation to 42 percent. The population of the nonmilitary industrialized group is equivalent to 42 percent of the population of the group that concentrates their effort in military activities: 238 million in Japan, Italy, and West Germany versus 570 million in the United States, the Soviet Union, and the United Kingdom. The "victors" maintain their military hegemony by engulfing approximately 60 percent of total world resources allocated to defense, while the "defeated" allocate somewhat less than 8 percent of those same resources.

In considering the ratio between defense spending (in relation to the GDP) and the international competitiveness of the industrial sector (manufacturing surplus or deficit in relation to manufacturing product), an irrefutable inverse linkage with the Soviet Union and the United States, on the one hand (see figure 5.3), and West Germany and Japan, on the other, is visible, leaving the United Kingdom, France, Sweden, and Italy in intermediate positions. Contrary to conventional wisdom, the multiplier effect of defense spending on international industrial competitiveness would be negative.

An agreement between the United States and the Soviet Union in favor of disarmament would permit them to significantly cut back on

Figure 5.3 International Competitiveness and Defense Expenditure in Developed Countries (average 1981–83)

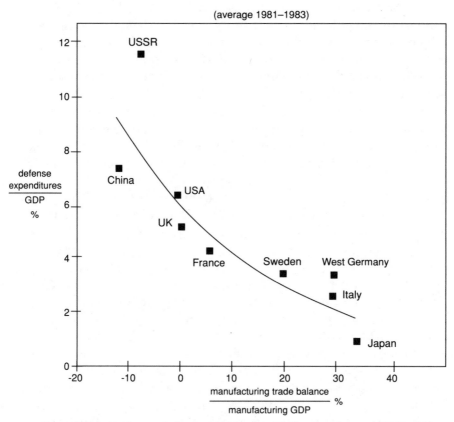

Source: Joint ECLAC / UNIDO Industry and Technology Division, based on *SIPRI Yearbook 1987: World Armaments and Disarmaments* and UNIDO DATABASE.

the resources allocated to that activity. Under the assumption that figure 5.3 describes the evolution of the performance for each country, they would be able to increase industrial competitiveness, a key factor in their respective foreign debts. They would not only contribute to enhancing the respective standards of living, but they would also favor the recovery of the equilibriums in trade and financial flows, besides the considerable impact on the currently deteriorated collective perception with respect to the future of humanity.

Final Reflections

Useful elements for reflection on Latin America encountered in this chapter would be:

1. The diversity of national models capable of facing (with different success) the challenges raised in the common external context.

2. The relevance of industrial specialization and the intellectual aggregate value associated with natural resource availability as requisites for solid international insertion.

3. The entailment between the welfare state and industrial competitiveness. Legitimacy and social cohesion combined with a solid educational infrastructure generate a frame of macroeconomic efficiency favorable to international competitivity. To this, in some measure, the microeconomic rigidity that often accompanies the welfare state is opposed.

4. The dilemma of growth versus equity is again refitted.

5. The aforementioned considerations, together with the negative effect of military expenses on international competitiveness points to the necessary formulation and implementation of new post-Keynesian policies to replace simplistic, unhistoric, "pre-Keynesian" policies of the eighteenth and nineteenth centuries.

6. Latin America Versus the "Growth-with-Equity Industrializing Countries" (GEICs)

Chapter 1 revealed that none of the countries of Latin America have been able to simultaneously fulfill the conditions necessary to achieve the objectives of growth and equity, thereby leaving an empty box. Some have shown a high degree of dynamism coupled with a strong socio-economic disintegration expressed by a particularly unequal income distribution. Others have achieved a low but relatively acceptable level of equity, while presenting the common feature of stagnation. A third group of countries simultaneously present stagnation and insufficient socioeconomic integration. The box containing countries with both dynamism and equity was empty; countries from other regions, however, with comparable levels of income or GDP have registered characteristics that would enable them to occupy that box.

Chapter 2 established a tentative trait for exploration: the fact that Latin American countries evidenced a decreasing contribution to the international economy in areas requiring greater intellectual added value. It was therefore maintained that one of the more important features to be examined was the inability of the region to absorb, innovate, develop, and incorporate technological knowledge into productive activity. The importance of this element was highlighted because it constitutes the determinant factor of a surge in productivity, which in turn favors growth, an increase in the standard of living, the development of the infrastructure, and the equitable distribution of the benefits of growth; in sum, therein lies the key to open up the "black box" of technological progress. Moreover, it was shown how the macroeconomic inspiration for current economic policies works to hinder the central theme of technical progress: macroeconomic theory is an analytical framework concerned with short-term equilibriums at an aggregate level in which the specificity of those sectors housing technological progress is ignored. This led to recognition of the need for an analytical framework that would permit the incorporation of those traits of the development and industrialization patterns that would have a positive influence on the achievement of growth and equity.

To take a step in that direction was the purpose of chapter 3 in which attention is centered on the analysis of the linkages between the availability of natural resources, the consumption and investment patterns, the configuration and competitiveness of the industrial sector, and the objectives of growth and equity. That analytical framework is then submitted to the test of empirical evidence for the United States, Japan, and West Germany (chapter 4), the West European and Nordic countries (chapter 5) and, finally, in this chapter, where the comparison between Latin America and other developing countries is undertaken.

Comparative Studies: Competitiveness or Rent-Seeking?

The comparative study of industrialization experiences in countries with distinct levels of development and socioeconomic integration conducted in earlier chapters can provide some potentially useful elements for explaining the Latin American peculiarity of the "empty box" and its inability to open the "black box" of technical progress. Growth seems to be strongly supported by high levels of industrial competitiveness in all the comparisons. Equity, in which the transformation of the agricultural sector seems to exercise a decisive influence, does not appear to be an obstacle to growth and, in a wide spectrum of situations, tends to reinforce it. There are some cases of intense dynamism and low equity which can be explained by a series of primarily historical factors associated with a lag in the agricultural modernization. The low equity in these cases has not been a hindrance for growth, and will tend to be gradually neutralized by the reciprocal support of competitiveness.

The establishment of industrial systems with strong competitiveness in both market and planned economies is clearly associated with the availability of natural resources. Apparently, the most difficult economic task that a society can undertake consists of constructing an industrial system capable of supplying, in quality and cost, the different international markets, especially those of developed countries in high-tech sectors using national enterprises. It seems that this would be a task to be approached when more comfortable alternative options do not arise, for example, the availability of revenue from natural resources or revenue furnished by benefits associated with leadership positions at an international level. That weight would permit, by means of financial services and the influence it exercises over the capital of the rest of the world, a neutralization of the gradual decline of the competitiveness of industrial systems. The United Kingdom would illustrate the latter situation, as well as the United States, to a different degree, after the first oil shock in 1973.

The strictly economic dimension does not sufficiently explain the differences observed in the distinct experiences, especially with regard to countries inserted in geopolitical contexts and in different cultural universes. This would indicate the vital need to incorporate the analysis of dimensions involving historical, social, political, and cultural processes.[1] In a strictly economic scope, however, the following linkages would provide a schematic summary of the explanation of the "successful" cases: *equity, austerity, growth*, and *competitiveness*. Competitiveness reinforces equity, legitimizes austerity, and enhances growth, thereby giving rise to the respective virtuous circles. When some of these elements are absent, they fall behind or are displaced due to the absence of transformation in the agrarian structure, excessive conspicuous consumption, or easy profit from natural resource revenue or hegemonic international positions; dynamism acquires a spasmodic nature in some cases, and a nature asynthetical to stagnation in others.

There are "Growth-with-Equity Industrializing Countries"

Let us now return to the subject of the empty box of Latin America and that region's inability to open the black box of technical progress. There are quite a few developing and semi-industrialized nations which exhibit the levels of both growth and equity represented by the empty box. These include China, Sri Lanka, Indonesia, Egypt, Thailand, Hungary, Portugal, Yugoslavia, South Korea, Israel, Hong Kong, and Spain (see table 6.1). Indeed, these countries account for a total of 73 percent of

Table 6.1 Other Developing Countries:[a] Growth and Equity (Percentages)

$$\text{Equity:} \frac{40\% \text{ lowest incomes}}{10\% \text{ highest incomes}} \text{ (since 1970)}$$

	<0.4[c]	≥ 0.4	
GDP per capita average annual growth rate (1965-1986) <2.4[b]	Kenya Zambia Philippines Ivory Coast GDP:3.5[d] Pop: 3.8[d]	Bangladesh India GDP: 17.1 Pop: 35.1	
≥ 2.4	Turkey Mauritius Malaysia GDP: 6.4 Pop: 2.7	China Sri Lanka Indonesia Egypt Thailand Hungary Portugal Yugoslavia	South Korea Israel Hong Kong Spain GDP: 73.0 Pop: 58.4

Source: Joint ECLAC/UNIDO Industry and Technology Division, based on World Bank, *World Development Report* (New York, 1987 and 1988).
[a]These countries represent 80.2% of the population and 79.5% of the GDP of the total developing countries excluding Latin America.
[b]Industrialized countries GDP per capita average annual growth rate (1965–1985).
[c]Industrialized countries half comparable relation.
[d]Percentage of GDP and population of these selected countries.

GDP and 58 percent of the population of the developing countries that were taken into consideration.[2]

This group ranges over the entire spectrum in terms of world trade orientation.[3] The same degree of diversity is observed with respect to the relative significance of the public sector.[4] The agricultural share of GDP and the level of per capita GDP is comparable in the two groups

Table 6.2 Latin America and GEICs: Strategic Profiles (Percentages)

| | | Latin America[a] | |
		Average	Standard Deviation
1. GDP Per Capita Average Annual Growth Rate.	1965–1986	1.3	1.6
2. Equity: 40% lowest income/ 10% highest income	Since 1970	0.3	0.2
3. Gross domestic savings as percentage of GDP	1984–1986	15.7	6.7
4. Manufactured exports/Manufactured imports[d]	1986	0.3	0.4

Source: Joint ECLAC/UNIDO Industry and Technology Division based on World Bank, *World Development Report, 1988* (New York: 1988).
[a]Latin America (19 countries) includes LAIA, CACM, Dominican Republic, Haiti, and Panama.
[b]Argentina, Brazil, and Mexico.

of countries. Some of these countries are similar to Latin America in that their position in international markets is based on their natural resources (Indonesia, Thailand, China and Egypt); due to a relative lack of natural resources, the rest have no alternative but to secure a place for themselves in the international market by means of industrialization (South Korea, Spain, Hungary, Israel, Portugal, and Yugoslavia).

As a first step in understanding the process of incorporating technological progress alongside agricultural change, industrialization, and international insertion, the comparative analysis which follows will not include those countries in other parts of the world in the GEIC category which have a level of industrialization under 20 percent (Egypt, Indonesia, and Sri Lanka), lack a significant agricultural sector (Hong Kong), or whose geopolitical position is highly unusual (Israel). The remaining group of countries will be referred to as "growth-with-equity industrializing countries" (GEICs).

The unsatisfactory nature of the economic performance of Latin Amer-

| ABRAMEX[b] | | GEIC[c]s | |
Average	Standard Deviation	Average	Standard Deviation
2.4	1.7	4.2	1.2
0.3	0.1	0.7	0.2
21.8	5.2	27.9	5.7
0.8	0.4	1.0	0.4

[c]Growth with equity industrializing countries (GEICs) include China, South Korea, Hungary, Portugal, Spain, Thailand, and Yugoslavia.
[d]UN, *International Trade Statistics Yearbook, 1986*, ST/ESA/STAT/SERG.G/35 (New York, 1988). Manufactured exports and imports are defined as SITC Sections 5 to 8 less Division 68 (nonferrous metals).

ica and the sharp contrast between it and that of "latecomers" in other regions of the world provide the basis for the comparative concept of GEICs. The idea of NICs, on the other hand, arose in the 1970s as a reflection of the growing concern with which OECD countries viewed the decline of their competitive position in the international market. The comparisons made below will focus on the contrast between Latin America and the GEICs and will include some specific references to the three largest countries of the region (Argentina, Brazil, and Mexico, or ABRAMEX.

Both groups of countries (Latin America and the GEICs) include a wide range of different situations. Contrasting the two groups in terms of growth and equity for the period 1965–1986 reveals a growth rate of 1.3 percent of per capita GDP and an equity ratio of 0.3 between the bottom 40 percent and the top 10 percent of the population in terms of income for Latin America versus a growth rate of 4.0 percent and an equity index of 0.62 for the GEICs (see tables 6.2 and 6.3). It is possible, however, to identify significant contrasts other than those relating to

Table 6.3 Latin America and GEICs: General Comparison (Percentages)

| | | Latin America[a] | |
		Average	Standard Deviation
1. Total external debt/GDP	1986	79.0	41.3
2. Internal direct investment/GDP[d]	1986	10.9	2.8
3. Share of manufacturing in GDP	1986	19.4	5.6
4. Share of agriculture in GDP	1986	16.7	8.4
5. Share of machinery, transport equipment and chemicals in value added[e]	1985	16.9	9.0
6. Gross output per employee (1980 = 100)	1985	98.6	45.9
7. Export coefficient (X/gross output)[e]	1985	10.0	8.5
8. Share of exports of goods and services in GDP	1986	20.8	7.4
9. Education: secondary[f]	1985	45.6	16.4
higher education[f]	1985	17.8	9.4

Source: Joint ECLAC/UNIDO Industry and Technology Division, based on World Bank, *World Development Report, 1988,* June 1988 (New York, 1988).

[a]Latin America (19 countries) includes LAIA, CACM, Dominican Republic, Haiti, and Panama.

[b]Argentina, Brazil, and Mexico.

[c]Growth with equity industrializing countries (GEICs) include China, South Korea, Hungary, Portugal, Spain, Thailand, and Yugoslavia.

[d]OECD, *Les Principales Economies en Développement et l' OCDE,* SE/M DE/2 (Paris, 1988).

[e]UNIDO DATABASE.

[f]Number enrolled in school as percentage of age groups.

ABRAMEX[b]		GEIC[c]s	
Average	Standard Deviation	Average	Standard Deviation
71.0	11.0	38.0	24.0
10.6	0.2	3.0	1.2
28.3	2.1	33.1	7.1
11.0	1.6	15.0	7.4
29.3	2.9	31.4	8.0
94.7	14.7	127.0	20.3
8.5	1.6	18.2	9.5
12.0	2.9	28.1	10.1
53.3	14.3	65.0	24.1
21.0	10.8	18.4	9.1

growth and equity. The major differences from both a theoretical and an empirical standpoint are the following:

1. Latin America exhibits a markedly lower domestic savings effort (gross domestic savings/GDP is 16 percent versus 28 percent), along with higher levels of external borrowing and direct foreign investment (debt/

GDP is 79 percent versus 38 percent, and direct investment/GDP is 10.9 percent versus 3.0 percent).

2. The population growth rate is higher in Latin America (2.5 percent versus 1.4 percent).

3. The manufacturing sector share of GDP is lower in Latin America (19.4 percent versus 33.1 percent, even though the agricultural share is similar in the two groups.

4. The relative significance of the industrial sectors which typically play an important role in technological progress (chemicals, metalmanufactures, and machinery) is considerably less in Latin America than in the GEICs (16.9 percent versus 31.4 percent, respectively).

5. The performance of the industrial sector during the 1980s has been much poorer in Latin America (if 1980 = 100, then the gross value of industrial output in 1986 yielded a coefficient of 98.6 for Latin America and 127 for the GEICs. This is particularly significant in view of the fact that this was a period during which the technological modernization of industry proceeded at a very rapid pace at the international level.

6. Latin America's coefficient of manufacturing exports was lower (10 percent versus 18 percent), as was its overall coefficient for total goods and services (21 percent versus 28 percent).

7. The level of international competitiveness, as measured by the quotient between manufacturing exports and imports was lower in Latin America (0.3 versus 1.0).

The Largest Developing Countries:
Latin America Versus Other Regions

If attention is concentrated on the objectives of growth, equity, and stability as reflected in fourteen of the largest developing countries in the world economy (see table 6.4), it is readily noticeable that the performance of the three major countries of Latin America is less favorable than any of the other countries under consideration with the exception of the Philippines. In terms of growth, the situation of Brazil is comparable to that of Mexico, Malaysia, and Thailand, better than that of Argentina, India, and the Philippines, but less favorable than the rest of the countries under consideration; in terms of equity and stability, Brazil ranks lower than the rest of the countries under consideration (in terms of stability, it is similar to Argentina and Mexico). In terms of

Table 6.4 Largest Developing Countries: Economic Performance

	Growth rate[a]	Equity[b]	Inflation[c]
Argentina	3	1	3
Brazil	2	3	3
Mexico	2	2	3
South Korea	1	1	1
Taiwan	1	1	1
Hong Kong	1	1	1
Singapore	1	1	1
China	1	1	1
India	3	1	1
Indonesia	1	1	1
Malaysia	2	2	1
Thailand	2	1	1
Philippines	3	2	2
Saudi Arabia	1	—	1

Source: Joint ECLAC/UNIDO Industry and Technology Division, based on data from World Bank, *World Development Report 1987* (New York, 1988).
[a]Corresponds to average annual growth rates of per capita GDP in the 1965–1985 period, with 1 = higher than or equal to 4.8%; 2 = higher than or equal to 2.4%; and 3 = less than 2.4%.
[b]Equity in the income distribution, as a ratio between the 40% with the smallest and the 10% with the largest incomes between 1970 and 1980: 1 = values higher than or equal to 0.4%; 2 = higher than or equal to 0.2%; and 3 = less than 0.2%.
[c]Average annual inflation rates (1965–1985): 1 = equal to or less than over 15%; 2 = equal to or less than 30%; and 3 = 30%.

economic dimensions (GNP), Brazil shares leadership with two other continent-size countries, India and China. In 1985, Brazil's GNP equalled approximately that of all the Asian NICs (Korea, Taiwan, Hong Kong, and Singapore).

From the perspective of developed nations, any evaluation of developing countries should incorporate the following four elements: market size for exports (developing countries' imports), natural resource supply source and competition in the field of manufactures (developing countries' exports), direct investment, and foreign debt. The quantitative analysis of the linkages of these four fields in table 6.5 indicates that the largest Latin American countries are in the forefront only in direct investment and foreign debt, with Brazil ranking first in both fields. Direct investment in Brazil is equal to four and seven times that in China and India, respectively, and ten times that in Korea (which has 40 percent of Brazil's GNP). By contrast, the volume of trade in both

Table 6.5 Largest Developing Countries: North's View

	I Market size imports (1985)		II Source of supply exports (1985)		III Direct investment[d]	IV Foreign debt[e]
	Total[a]	Manuf.[b]	Energy[c]	Manuf.[b]		
Argentina	3	3	—	3	2	1
Brazil	3	3	—	2	1	1
Mexico	3	3	2	3	1	1
South Korea	1	2	—	1	3	2
Taiwan	2	—	—	1	3	—
Hong Kong	2	1	—	1	2	—
Singapore	2	2	—	2	2	—
China	1	1	3	2	2	—
India	3	3	—	3	3	3
Indonesia	3	3	2	3	1	2
Malaysia	3	3	—	3	3	3
Thailand	3	3	—	3	3	3
Philippines	3	3	—	3	3	3
Saudi Arabia	2	1	1	3	3	—

Source: Joint ECLAC/UNIDO Industry and Technology Division, on the basis of World Bank, *World Development Report 1987* and OECD.

[a]The categories are: 1 = imports higher than US$30 billion; 2 = between US$20–US$30 billion; and 3 = between US$10–US$20 billion.

[b]For the imports and exports of manufactures (defined as SITC sections 5 to 8 excluding division 68) the categories are: 1 = higher than US$20 billion; 2 = between US$10–US$20 billion; and 3 = less than US$10 billion.

[c]Energy exports: 1 = higher than US$10 billion; 2 = between US$6–US$10 billion; and 3 = between US$3–US$6 billion.

[d]Direct investment: 1 = higher than US$10 billion; 2 = between US$5–US$10 billion; 3 = less than US$5 billion.

[e]The categories have been established on the basis of the total long-term foreign debt: 1 = foreign debt higher than US$40 billion; 2 = between US$30–US$40 billion; and 3 = between US$10–US$30 billion.

directions in Latin America lags markedly behind others in the group of the largest developing countries. This disturbing asymmetry between the degree of integration by way of direct investment and the foreign debt, and the relative exclusion in the sphere of international trade becomes more serious when one considers the various development strategies pursued by the GEICs: export orientation (Asian NICs), continental economies oriented toward domestic markets (China and India), Asian NICs of the new generation where the weight of agriculture

Figure 6.1   Strategic Profiles: Latin America, ABRAMEX, and GEICs

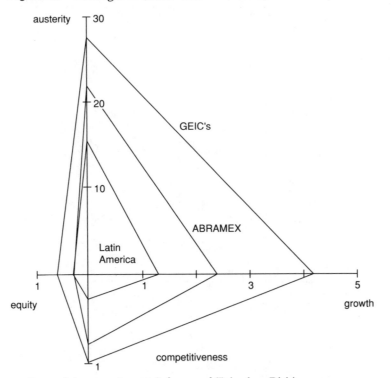

Source: Joint ECLAC / UNIDO Industry and Technology Division.

in GNP is markedly greater than in Brazil (Indonesia, Malaysia, and Thailand), and the main oil-exporting country (Saudi Arabia).

Differences in Development Patterns

In sum, compared to the GEICs, the organization of Latin America's economy promotes less equity, less financial restraint, a lower level of domestic savings, and, despite the greater contribution by external savings, less dynamism. These factors inhibit the incorporation of technological progress and international competitiveness. A graphic illustration of these four dimensions—equity, austerity, growth, and competitiveness—is given in figure 6.1.

Figure 6.2 Strategic Profiles: ABRAMEX and South Korea

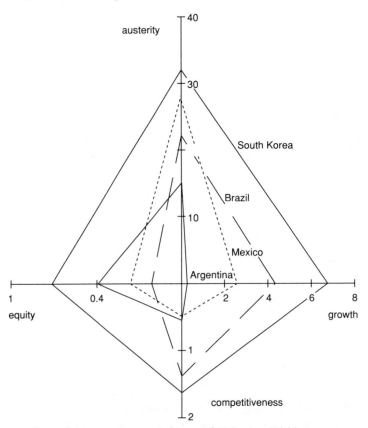

Source: Joint ECLAC / UNIDO Industry and Technology Division.

It has been observed that the GEICs exhibit greater equity, financial restraint, growth, and competitiveness than the countries of Latin America as a whole. If attention is focused on a comparison with the three largest Latin American countries—Argentina, Brazil, and Mexico (ABRAMEX)—the difference between these two groups of countries with respect to equity remains the same, while the contrasts between the two in relation to domestic savings, growth, and competitiveness are less sharp. In order to provide a clear illustration of this contrast, one of the GEICs, South Korea, was compared to the ABRAMEX countries (see figure 6.2).

The outcome of this comparison was that, regardless of the specific features of the individual Latin American countries, all of them had lower levels of equity, financial restraint, growth, and competitiveness than South Korea.

In terms of the configuration of structural change in the industrial sector three different situations exist in the ABRAMEX countries (see figure 6.3). Argentina demonstrates a profile similar to that previously observed in England: a process of deindustrialization in a broad range of industrial branches during a period of stagnation, in which the core features are a very low expansion of cheap labor-intensive sectors such as clothing, textiles, and shoes, low representation of technological progress-intensive sectors such as engineering products and plastics, and relative weight in capital-intensive sectors such as iron and steel manufacturing and basic chemicals.

Since the 1980s, the relatively dynamic case of Mexico presents a strong process of deindustrialization, a notorious integration regarding the axis of petroleum and its derivatives, the fragile presence of engineering products, a lack of dynamism in the labor-intensive sectors, and some dynamism in the iron and steel producing sector.

Brazil, the most dynamic country in the region, shows a pronounced emphasis on the chemicals sector, relative development in the nonmetallic minerals sector (linked possibly to the expansion of the physical infrastructure), intense development of electrical machinery, a certain deindustrialization in the 1980s in the area of nonelectrical machinery, and considerable dynamism in the textile and leather products sectors (partially linked to the dynamism of exports). Like Argentina and Mexico, Brazil's food industry maintains relative dynamism, determined in Brazil and Mexico by the high growth rate of the urban population and in Argentina by a particularly generous endowment of resources.

When contrasting the situation with three GEICs (South Korea, Spain, and Yugoslavia), there are important differences (see figure 6.4). First, the dynamism of South Korea more than doubles the dynamism of Brazil. There are two very clear axes: electrical equipment (the trait that marked the sectoral change in Japan), the areas of steel and nonferrous metals, and a very strong presence in terms of the dynamism of leather products, textiles, labor-intensive areas, and with a clear orientation towards exports. The feature of sectoral specialization which marks the profile of the change occurring in the last two decades in Korea is outstanding.

Figure 6.3 Industrial Structural Change: ABRAMEX, 1970–1987

Argentina

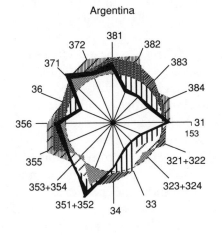

Brazil

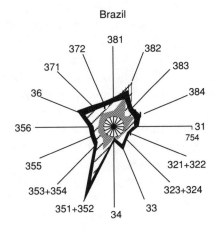

Mexico

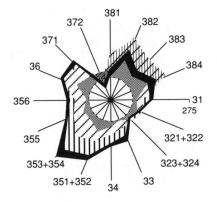

(Index of value added: 1970=100)
Key:
ISIC code (branches):
31 (Food products)
321, 322 (Textiles)
323, 324 (Leather industries)
33 (Wood and furniture)
34 (Paper and printing)
351,352 (Chemicals)
353, 354 (Petroleum and coal)
355 (Rubber products)
356 (Plastic products)
36 (Nonmetal mineral products)
371 (Iron and steel)
372 (Nonferrous metals)
381 (Metal products)
382 (Nonelectrical machinery)
383 (Electrical machinery)
384 (Transport equipment)

1970–1975
1975–1980
1980–1985
1985–1987 forecast

Source: UNIDO.

Figure 6.4 Industrial Structural Change: South Korea, Yugoslavia, and Spain, 1970–1987

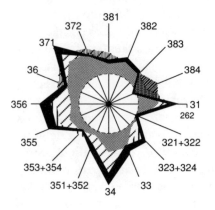

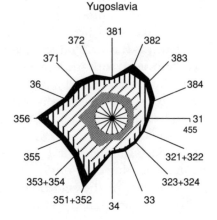

South Korea

Yugoslavia

Spain

(Index of value added: 1970=100)
Key:
ISIC code (branches):
31 (Food products)
321, 322 (Textiles)
323, 324 (Leather industries)
33 (Wood and furniture)
34 (Paper and printing)
351, 352 (Chemicals)
353, 354 (Petroleum and coal)
355 (Rubber products)
356 (Plastic products)
36 (Nonmetal mineral products)
371 (Iron and steel)
372 (Nonferrous metals)
381 (Metal products)
382 (Nonelectrical machinery)
383 (Electrical machinery)
384 (Transport equipment)

1970–1975
1975–1980
1980–1985
1985–1987 forecast

Source: UNIDO.

Spain, the country with the greatest level of development of all those considered, has a moderate growth rate. It is branded by a conscious effort toward "industrial reconversion" in which industries such as nonferrous metals, metallic products, transportation equipment, and nonmetallic minerals have lost their relative weight in the 1980s. On the other hand, areas such as leather products, paper and printing products, rubber products (associated with the location in Spain of suppliers from the European automotive sector), and plastic products have been reinforced.[7]

Yugoslavia's dynamism is comparable to that of Brazil. It exhibits a much less specialized profile with a relatively homogeneous dynamism and a broad range of sectors. Among the "classics" are plastic and chemical products, non-electrical and electrical machinery, and transportation equipment. Moreover, this country has evidenced a relative maintenance of dynamism in the traditional sectors of food, clothing, shoes, and leather products, an aspect that is comparatively similar to the case of Italy.

An analysis of the evolution of the participation of engineering products in the world market highlights the growing, sustained participation of South Korea and Spain since 1965, when both showed marginal participation, less than 0.2 percent of the world market (see figure 6.5). This was boosted to over 1 percent for Spain in 1984, while South Korea's share jumped to 2 percent, comparable to that of Sweden and the Soviet Union. The participation of Yugoslavia began to rise principally in 1980.

In Latin America, the sustained, marginal presence of a country such as Argentina (less than 0.2 percent)—which in 1987 celebrates the centennial of the *Unión Industrial Argentina* or UIA (the national entrepreneurial chamber)—is contrasted with the participation of Mexico, which, regardless of its proximity to such an enormous market for industrial imports as the United States, has maintained participation of around 0.5 percent for the last twenty years. Brazil showed a sustained growth of participation between 1970 and 1980 and relative stability during the 1980s.

Perhaps the most notable contrast is that between Argentina and South Korea, both of which possess comparable internal markets, populations, and levels of per capita GDP. These two countries started out with a share less than 0.1 percent of the world market in 1965. Since that time, they have diverged; Argentina has maintained its participation

Figure 6.5 Engineering Products: World Market Share of ABRAMEX, South Korea, Spain, and Yugoslavia, 1965–1984

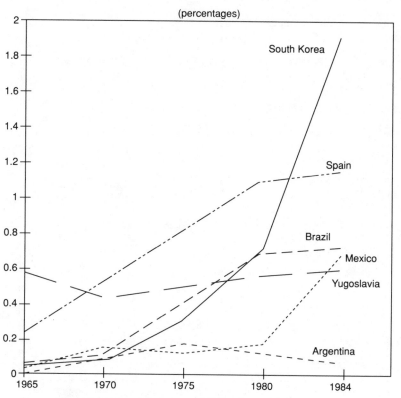

Source: Joint ECLAC / UNIDO Industry and Technology Division.

practically constant, while South Korea has increased their share to 2 percent. This sharp contrast reflects the fundamental difference between a country in which the absorption of technological progress, its distribution to industrial sectors, and the conquest of international markets in high-tech products using national enterprises are aimed at the markets of the most developed countries and a country with a comfortable existence based on a high standard of living backed chiefly by natural resource revenue.

The same situation—with differences of scale—prevails in Mexico.

Figure 6.6 Engineering Products: International Competitiveness (x/m) of ABRAMEX, South Korea, Spain, and Yugoslavia, 1965–1984

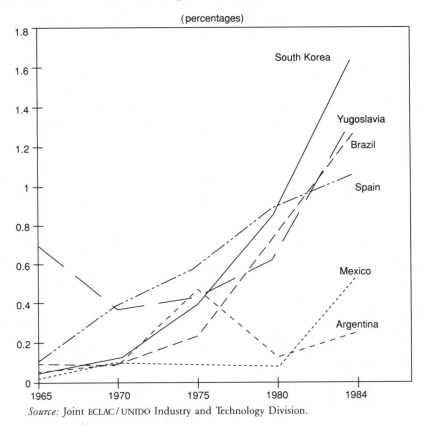

(percentages)

Source: Joint ECLAC / UNIDO Industry and Technology Division.

In the cases of Spain and Yugoslavia, it is important to consider their proximity to the rapidly expanding European Common Market (into which Spain recently became incorporated). This exposure and proximity to a market of great dynamism could explain some of the progress observed in the industrial settings of those countries; the contrast with Mexico, however, in which privileged access to the U.S. market could have induced similar changes, would indicate that proximity has a limited scope for industrial evolution.

Hence, internal factors must explain this difference in behavior, maximum when considering that the period under analysis presents basically common features for all the countries under examination. The first part of this period (1965–1975) was characterized by rapid dynamism and the second by greater intensification of international competition along with lesser dynamism. However, for countries with such a marginal participation, it presented a potentially very good opportunity anyway.

While examining the industrial competitiveness of these countries in engineering products (see figure 6.6), the trends suggested by the analysis of participation in the international market are confirmed: South Korea, Yugoslavia, and Spain present a sustained growth in competitiveness in these high-tech products since 1970. In other words, at the beginning of the period, their exports of engineering products covered 10 percent of the corresponding imports; during the course of two decades, that figure was boosted to almost 80 percent of imports. This was a period in which all three countries absorbed technological knowledge, incorporated it into national businesses, and projected it toward the international market (especially South Korea).

These trends reveal the evolution of the productivity of those countries and their ability to diffuse that productivity throughout industrial productive activity as a whole. In Latin America, situations like those of Argentina and Mexico surface, in which, between 1965 and 1980, the levels of competitiveness remained stationary, except during 1970–1975 in Argentina, when a process of rapid "industrial enlightenment" began, that later, due to widely documented internal events, regressed to a previous state.[8]

In terms of the recent evolution of competitiveness, such as appears in the figure, for Argentina, Brazil, and Mexico, the 80s has meant a period in which growth is significantly eroded and imports of those goods have been drastically reduced. Specifically in the cases of Argentina and Brazil between 1980 and 1985, the imports of those areas were trimmed to practically a third, and in the case of Mexico, to 60 percent, while exports of those areas remained nearly constant, except in the case of Mexico in which they were increased significantly during that period. The surge of competitiveness in Argentina, Brazil, and to a lesser extent, Mexico, in the initial phase of the 80s, largely came from a drop in imports than from a substantial rise of competitiveness in those areas (see table 6.6).

Between 1980 and 1984, South Korean imports of capital goods nearly doubled. In Spain, both imports and exports remained relatively con-

Table 6.6 Selected Countries: Imports, Exports, and Trade Balance in Capital Goods[a] (Millions of dollars)

	1980	1981	1982	1983	1984	1985
Argentina						
Imports	3,157	2,948	1,464	1,146	1,017	954
Exports	413	366	469	212	306	398
Balance	− 2,744	− 2,582	− 995	− 934	− 711	− 556
Brazil						
Imports	4,630	4,240	3,708	2,550	1,827	2,074
Exports	2,276	2,685	2,297	2,085	2,232	2,538
Balance	− 2,354	− 1,555	− 1,419	− 467	405	464
Mexico						
Imports	6,315	9,195	4,752	3,090	3,605	4,464
Exports	355	492	554	1,000	1,238	2,192
Balance	− 5,960	− 8,703	− 4,198	− 2,090	− 2,367	− 2,272
South Korea						
Imports	4,072	5,003	5,076	6,069	7,930	8,799
Exports	1,915	2,901	3,897	5,436	6,850	7,370
Balance	− 2,102	− 2,102	− 1,179	− 633	− 1,080	− 1,429
Spain[b]						
Imports	4,353	3,900	3,958	3,718	3,691	4,807
Exports	3,400	3,142	3,099	2,469	3,227	3,068
Balance	− 953	− 758	− 859	− 1,249	− 464	− 17,39
Yugoslavia						
Imports	4,171	3,941	3,512	2,620	2,459	2,625
Exports	2,213	2,479	2,697	2,450	2,585	2,802
Balance	− 1,958	− 1,462	− 815	− 180	126	177

Source: Joint ECLAC / UNIDO Industry and Technology Division, based on data from UN, *Commodity Trade Statistics* for years 1980–1985.

[a]Defined as : SITC Rev. 2, section 7 less automobiles, household appliances and other noncapital goods, and plus (SITC Rev. 2, 874) measuring and controlling instruments.

[b]Provisional data, 1985.

stant. Yugoslavia, where the effect of the crisis was also noticeable, imports were curtailed and exports were kept constant, whereby the index of the surge in competitiveness for that country during that period is relatively deceiving.

A basic distinctive feature between the countries of Latin America — principally Argentina and Mexico — and the cases of South Korea and Spain is the fact that the latter countries have sought the absorption of technological progress through the physical transplantation of information in the appropriate sectors and its incorporation into products geared toward both internal and international markets. Both cases exhibit a strong percentage of exports destined for the markets of industrialized countries. Brazil presents comparable traits to South Korea and Spain in terms of competitiveness in high-tech sectors, but it deviates from those cases in the core element of the distribution of the benefits of technological progress to the whole of society.

A Summary of the Hypotheses Concerning the Specific Characteristics of Latin America

In the following presentation, the hypotheses previously discussed in chapter 3 are outlined in a simplified form; additional theoretical and empirical research will clearly have to be carried out with respect to these hypotheses. The main thrust of this analysis is to demonstrate the need to link the subject of technological change with the complex process of economic and social change in which these sources, institutions, and policies are closely interrelated.

Eighty-nine percent of the GDP of Latin America is accounted for by countries whose level of equity is less than half that prevailing in developed countries. Various studies conducted at the international level and the experience of Latin America support the hypothesis that there is a clear cause-and-effect relationship between the structural transformation of agriculture and an improvement in income distribution. As will be indicated later in this discussion, income distribution plays an important role in shaping the system of production and, consequently, in determining an economy's ability to absorb and generate technological progress and its position in the international market. As is also the case with mean income levels, equity (along with what it represents in terms of social articulation) tends to give rise to a relatively more restrained consumption pattern than that which is usually found in situations of high income concentration inasmuch as it hinders the higher-income sectors from engaging in an exaggerated imitation of the consumption patterns associated with the more advanced societies.

In addition to the fact that a more restrained consumption pattern makes more resources available for investment, the hypothesis could be advanced (although it would be very difficult to corroborate empirically) that a relationship may exist between the lavishness of a given consumption pattern and the capital/product ratio. On the basis of such a hypothesis it might be supposed that the productivity of investment would be higher in societies whose consumption pattern is relatively more restrained in the sense that it involves a lower proportion of consumer durables and less use of energy and foreign exchange.

In such countries the capital/product ratio would tend to be lower than in those where an attempt is made to maintain a consumption pattern characterized by a high proportion of consumer durables, heavy consumption of energy, and a physical communications and transport infrastructure capable of supporting such a pattern in a large and sparsely populated country having an abundant supply of capital.

Growth enables the incorporation of new generations of equipment and products, thereby raising productivity and reinforcing a country's international competitive position. An initial broadening of the domestic market through the introduction of a growing variety of goods and services associated with growth and promoted by equity and financial restraint is the only feasible basis for the industrial/technological learning process necessary to expand a country's share in the international market. The virtuous circle between growth and competitiveness (in which the need for equity, financial restraint, and the accumulation of technological knowledge are often overlooked) is one of the pivotal elements in successful cases of industrialization.

Precisely because of its shortcomings with respect to equity, financial restraint, and protectionism, growth and competitiveness in Latin America have increased by fits and starts which do not correspond to the cyclical growth trends of the industrialized societies. In the latter case these variations follow a generally upward trend in the incorporation of technological progress, whereas in Latin America they reflect the consequences of "weak links in the chain," links that are necessary in order for this type of virtuous circle to function.

Given a social context in which a certain minimum threshold of equity (agrarian transformation) has been reached, an internationally competitive industrial system may tend to promote equity by means of the following phenomena:

1. A relatively broader distribution of ownership associated with the creation of small and medium-scale enterprises

2. A wide range of manpower skills

3. A more rapid increase in employment associated with the dynamism of the international markets

4. A rise in productivity and wages

5. The operation of the educational system on a broader and more integrated social basis as a precondition for the maintenance of a competitive position in the international markets

6. The formal and informal dissemination of an industrial logic to society as a whole, which will make it more receptive to technological progress. This factor will contribute to an increase in productivity and, by the same token, to the redistribution of the benefits of technical progress on a more equitable basis in the society as a whole.

Such phenomena do not necessarily occur in cases where competitiveness is achieved at the expense of wages paid to labor and where generated resources are used for consumption or exported rather than being channelled via investment towards the incorporation of technological progress. This is a spurious and ephemeral type of competitiveness which should not be confused at either a theoretical or historical level with the type of competitiveness discussed earlier. Equity, then, is directly conducive to growth through the promotion of a consumption pattern in keeping with a higher rate and more efficient form of investment, and indirectly conducive to the creation of a social environment that is compatible with an effort to "build the future," inasmuch as such an effort requires that both elite groups and the system have a rightful claim to legitimacy so that society as a whole will be willing to take the types of actions and decisions that will lead to growth.

Growth, in its turn, tends to help society function more flexibly and, by the same token, to soften any lags in distribution in situations of economic stagnation. This does not mean that growth per se results in equity (something which has been disproved time and again in Latin America and in other regions); what it does mean, however, is that if the growth process is proceeding on the basis of a competitive industrial pattern, delays in achieving equity will not necessarily result in social conflicts insofar as there is a general feeling of hope for the future.

A competitive industrial sector confronted with a faster growing demand than that of the rest of the productive sectors will make a positive contribution to growth. Experience shows that international trade in manufactures is expanding at a faster pace than world trade as a whole, and this difference is even greater in the case of the product lines representing a greater degree of technological innovation (during the past four decades, most of these product lines have corresponded to the metal-manufactures, machinery, and chemical industries).

At a more disaggregated level, the leading product lines in terms of international trade and technological progress are continually changing. Consequently, the ability of countries to gain a solid foothold in international markets is heavily influenced by their ability to keep up with international technological trends and their opportunities for doing so. As this aptitude is developed, a greater feedback effect on growth is produced via modifications in relative prices, a rise in productivity, and the expansion of the domestic market. While it is true that competitiveness reinforces growth, its contribution is much greater when productivity is high in product lines having a greater technological content and when business enterprises and their technological support infrastructure make a part of these resources available to the country in question.

This does not mean that a contribution may not be made by product lines having little technological content or by those developed by foreign enterprises. What it does is to stress the importance of the relationship between *production sectors, business enterprises*, and *types of markets*; a more in-depth analysis of this relationship is essential if we are to gain a better understanding of the process of technological innovation. The fact that conventional macroeconomic theory sidesteps this linkage (sectors–enterprises–markets) hinders its ability to grasp the core elements of the dynamics of technological progress.

The presence of an abundant natural resource base generally gives rise to a heavy concentration of property in either the private or public sector; consequently, the business leadership in such societies tends to rely on the use of profits from these natural resources, and there may be a tendency for rent-seeking societies and wealth-oriented states to form. Given the existence of a certain tendency for the values expressed by leaders to spread and be imitated throughout society, this rent-seeking world view could penetrate into and spread through various spheres of the public sector, the private sector, and a wide range of institutions that help them to function—political parties, the armed forces, trade and labor unions, professional associations, and the bureaucracy. Specific manifestations of this dissemination of rent-seeking values would include parochialism, an emphasis on the short term, an aversion to risk and technological innovation, and a certain stress on the usefulness to the individual of given activities rather than on institutional roles. A detailed examination of this phenomenon falls outside the scope of this paper; nonetheless, this is a subject which warrants further investigation, particularly in Latin America, where this type of situation appears to be of greater significance than had previously been thought. The process of urbanization, industrialization, and institutional modernization may have caused its significance to be underestimated.

The presence of a national entrepreneurial base is undoubtedly a very important factor in determining the possibilities of building and maintaining an internationally competitive industrial system. This is not a prime requirement for supplying the domestic market; indeed, the leadership of the most dynamic sectors may shift to transnational corporations which can easily adapt their behavior to suit these market conditions. A foothold in international markets, however, requires the incorporation of technological progress and innovation (i.e., adding intellectual value to natural resources or to available unskilled manpower). Obviously, the existence of a national entrepreneurial base with possibilities for linkage with foreign investment will be a crucial factor.

It is futile to ignore the existence of the consumption pattern which has captured the collective imagination of the regional population, including the inhabitants of rural zones; a wide variety of examples corroborating this may be found at the national and even the continental level. Acknowledging this reality does not, however, free us from the obligation to try to make the absorption of this "modernity" as expressed in access to goods and services compatible with the domestic needs for growth and socioeconomic integration.

The differences found from one country to another are not due to the adoption of different consumption patterns, but rather to differences in the speed and means by which this single consumption pattern is internalized in each of these societies. In Latin America, the imitation and absorption of this universal "modern" consumption pattern appears to have taken place without even a basic minimum of consideration being given to internal needs for socioeconomic integration and for the creation of the conditions necessary for the maintenance of a solid position in the international market. Moreover, the pattern seems to have been adopted at a time when the mean income levels of Latin American countries were far lower than those prevailing at the time of their adoption in the societies where the model originated.

Final Reflections on "Les Treinte Glorieuses"

It is quite clear to historians that in order to understand a region like Latin America it is absolutely essential to know about regions other than Latin America. While this may seem fairly obvious, it has sometimes been ignored by the methodological approaches to the subject of development in the region.

Acknowledgment of this shortcoming associated with what we have called the empty box is entirely compatible with a recognition of the sweeping changes that have taken place in the Latin American economy and society during the past thirty years (1950–1981). This period is what Hirschman has referred to as "*les treinte glorieuses*" of Latin America.[9] During this period GNP grew fivefold, the population grew from 155 million to nearly 400 million, and a very rapid urbanization process took place. As a result of this process, a number of the countries in the region which had more than half of their population in agriculture in 1950 saw this proportion drop to between one-fourth and one-third. In these same countries, education and health services improved significantly, and institutions were created which helped to promote the economic, social, political, and cultural integration of the region; furthermore, the foundations were laid for technological development in major areas linked to agriculture, public works, and energy, and the life expectancy rose significantly in all the countries of the region.

Since the end of the Second World War, the world has grown and changed in economic, social, political and cultural terms at a pace without precedent in human history. Many of these changes have taken place in Latin America as well. An awareness of the positive changes which have occurred in the region should not, however, be seen as a cause for the complacency often displayed by countries which have played a leadership role at the international level for a number of decades.

7. Final Reflections

General Characteristics

Considering what has been expressed in previous chapters, on the one hand emanate the general conclusions on directions and actions, in Latin America and in the North, that could contribute to confront what, in the first chapter, was defined as the challenge of Latin America, that is, to approach the until now empty box wherein growth converges with equity. On the other hand, it is possible to formulate some orientations on strategic criteria, institutional framework and necessary policies to promote industrial restructuring in Latin America in the 1990s. The following are the most salient lessons of a general characteristic that would seem to emanate from this exploratory exercise.

1. The solidity of international insertion is firmly linked to the capacity of the countries to add intellectual value to their resource endowment. It would be illusory to imagine a solid insertion in international markets without the incorporation of technological progress into those resources. Possession of natural resources does not imply that a country must relinquish the revenue that they can produce, but it is vital that that revenue be utilized to transform and modernize the agricultural sector and strengthen the development of an industrial sector with a growing level of exposure and competitiveness in international markets.

2. The widespread idea of a necessary trade-off between growth and equity is not supported by the empirical evidence of a broad range of national situations. Within Latin America it is true that these two objectives have not converged; countries with greater equity suffer stagna-

tion while countries with greater dynamism do not manifest equity. This parochial view of the relationship between both objectives is overcome, however, when the Latin American pattern is contrasted with patterns prevailing in other regions with different socioeconomic systems and different levels of development. Nonstop growth, unlike spasmodic growth, requires an internally integrated and equitable society, and generates conditions which enhance a sustained effort toward incorporating technological progress, a surge in productivity, and, consequently, growth.

3. Latin American leaders concentrate on the modest reproduction of the standard of living of the developed countries in the top part of the income pyramid while ignoring the fact that the pattern is barely financeable even in the country of origin, the United States. Furthermore, these same leaders disseminate this pattern to the rest of society in the guise of a collective aspiration, concurrently advancing the structural configuration of a particular use of space, fuel, transportation, and communications. This behavior could lead to an evolution from the situation of the empty box to an immensely more dramatic situation with unpredictable consequences, in which the most widely occupied box would be that of stagnation with socioeconomic disintegration.

4. The opening of the black box of technological progress is a task that transcends the industrial and business world, and forms part of a social attitude vis-à-vis the incorporation of technological progress. This new attitude of social appreciation of creativity—that is, the pursuit of formulas that respond to internal deficiencies and potentialities—assumes a modification of the leadership from which flow the values and orientations diffused through society as a whole. It is difficult to imagine the linkage between a leadership influenced by a rent-seeking mentality and a society-wide diffusion of values in which the internal deficiencies and potentialities are converted into a conductor axis for socioeconomic transformation.

The growing diffusion of modern objects in Latin America does not modify the precarious character of the traditional social relations in which those objects are inserted. The modernity of a society has less to do with the objects that are diffused than with the modernity of the institutions and relations where the design, acquisition, selection, and evaluation of the relevance of those objects takes place.

5. A major difficulty in the monumental task of transforming the economic structure(s) of Latin America is the equally monumental but necessary task of transforming the perceptions of the distinct strata of society with respect to the economic challenges of growth and equity. It is hard to envision favorable economic change in Latin America without the implementation of a profound process of democratization which would incorporate the contribution and active, ongoing participation of those segments of society who have not benefited from the current consumption pattern and the experience and recent frustration of some of those sectors inserted in the pattern. It is important to realize, however, that neither the capacity for the economic legitimization of democracy in this context nor its ability to respond rapidly to the deficiencies existing today are guaranteed. In part, democratization in some countries of the region has been the result of the inability of authoritarian regimes to confront these same problems. It would be naive to conclude, however, that the symbolic goods that democratization diffuses could replace concrete answers to the most urgent problems. Consequently, the long- and medium-term potential associated with the democratization process enters into short-term conflict with the need for forms of legitimacy in other fundamental areas.

6. The subject of democracy leads to reflection on the possibility of gaining access to resources from developed countries to support this recovery. Until now, the foremost importance of internal transformations has been stressed, and it is obvious that the recovery of the levels of external financial support that would simply prolong the preceding development pattern would not be satisfactory. Nonetheless, though the center of gravity is internal effort, the economic, social, political, and cultural transformation required in Latin America requires complementary external economic backing. With some exceptions, those nations with a trade surplus and hence the ability to channel resources beyond their borders—chiefly Japan and West Germany—ignore the challenge represented by the situation of the less developed countries; instead they continue to concentrate on the resolution of imbalances among themselves

in relation to the external fiscal deficit situation and consumption pattern of the United States. It may very well be that they discover some formula for civilized coexistence among themselves, but by ignoring the growing imbalances spreading throughout the southern hemisphere, they help to promote and perpetuate those imbalances.

Hence, certain requirements seem evident. In the first place, the principal debtor nation, the United States, should adopt necessary measures to adapt its life-style to its reality. Second, instead of channeling resources in order to facilitate the maintenance of the U.S. consumption pattern, surplus nations should gear resources precisely toward the countries of the South. Third, socioeconomic transformations in the developing countries should be generated endogenously and should permit the absorption of those resources to innovate in the direction of the development pattern. Finally, resources directed to the South should promote a pattern in which transformations generated in the direction of the empty box are compatible with short-term requirements associated with the current crisis.

7. The sequence which seems to emerge from the study is the following: *equity, austerity, growth* and *competitiveness*. Thus, the reality is different from the theory, which starts with competitiveness and does not stress the technological content of exported goods in the view that growth will follow from the dynamic effect of the international market as it gradually incorporates the previously excluded population. Both experience and external political and economic considerations show that in Latin America it will be increasingly difficult to avoid dealing with the issue of equity, even though this will mean bringing up unpleasant issues from the past which seem to have been overtaken by modern developments.

8. An important factor in the generation of resources in the North and the modalities of their utilization in the South is the cutback in military spending. There is a clear inverse relationship in the North between industrial competitiveness and the military effort which suggests that a reduction of the latter would favor the much desired recovery of international trade and financial equilibriums. To this can be added the still more important impact on the world political climate and its in-

evitable beneficial effects on social peace, democratic modernization, and the consolidation of the vital processes of regional integration in the South, particularly in Latin America.

Imperative Industrial Restructuring in Latin America

Overcoming the empty box syndrome will require more than redressing the severe macroeconomic imbalances. Latin America urgently requires an industrial restructuring that would bring about an increase in labor productivity, maintain "real" international competitiveness through the incorporation of technological progress, strengthen and expand the regional entrepreneurial base, improve the level of labor skills, and establish constructive cooperative relations between government, the business sector, and labor based on strategic agreements that give permanence to economic policies.

The ideas outlined for industrial restructuring presuppose that inflation and severe fiscal imbalances would have been brought under control. The nature of the adjustment process through which these objectives are achieved, however, is central to the subsequent evolution of the productive sector. Where the adjustment process calls into question the existence of the productive agents required to bring about the industrial restructuring—enterprises with a high technology content, research institutes, the exodus of professionals and skilled labor, the shutdown of engineering firms or engineering departments in the large public and private enterprises—the process will take longer and the economic and social costs will be greater. The analysis which follows presupposes that an adjustment has been undertaken which reconciles reasonable levels of stability and fiscal discipline with the (possibly weakened) maintenance of the protagonists of industrial restructuring.

The role of the state in promoting this transformation of the productive structure is different from that in which it promoted the industrialization of the preceding phase. The principal task of the state in the preceding phase of industrialization was to create the physical support infrastructure for an industrialization aimed primarily at the domestic market. The methods employed included the transfer of resources to the private sector (particularly to the sectors of durable and nondurable consumer goods) and the establishment of public enterprises in some sectors of widely used inputs. Resources in foreign exchange were obtained primarily from the export of natural resources and from external credit. Encouragement was given to the formation of national industrial groups through extensive and indiscriminate protection and through the demand created by investment and public consumption; this led to the well-known complementarity between public and private investment. An educational base was developed which placed emphasis on university professions and produced a government and private sector elite instead of the mass upgrading of labor skills and the training of intermediate-level cadres. Development and technological support institutions were established in the areas of energy, public works, and agriculture. While a start was made in the systematic development of natural resources, these resources remained institutionally and operationally separate from manufacturing activity. Relations between the government and the business sector were characterized by tactical complicity accompanied by mutual distrust and a lack of transparency. Relations between the business sector and labor were generally characterized by inequality and confrontation, and were resolved in terms that were relatively more favorable to labor in capital-intensive sectors and sectors dominated by trade unions. These sectors contained the large private enterprises which received most of the financial transfers from public development agencies and major state enterprises. With a visible leadership in the automobile sector, branches of transnational enterprises pursued incentive policies in keeping with the context in which they operated, and geared their production mainly towards the domestic market.

Together with the rise of orthodox thinking, the limited results of industrialization obtained in Latin America in the 1970s led to widespread questioning of the role of industrialization and the leadership function of the public sector. The proposal for industrial restructuring outlined below includes suggestions regarding the modifications which should be made to the model followed in the previous phase. The adoption of these "corrections" leads to a schema which differs markedly from the approach to industrialization implicit in the "orthodox eighties," and whose application is linked to the servicing of the Latin American external debt. While the well-known national peculiarities of Latin America are an obstacle to the formulation of simple and homogenous proposals for the region as a whole, it is possible to identify, at a given level of abstraction, a set of strategic institutional and policy approaches which delineate the outline of the urgent industrial restructuring.

The reality of the national cases is undoubtedly more complex than the formal characterization presented here; not only are elements of the preceding period of industrialization combined with efforts towards industrial restructuring and orthodox experiments in specific areas, but there is also a process of learning and evaluating the feasibility of the various proposed changes. This same complexity can be seen in the analyses and activities of the international organizations and the academic milieu which provide the intellectual support for this discussion. To this must be added the fact that these proposals are made in the context of realities characterized by "interests" and "passions" in which the scope of the recommendations are amplified or neutralized.

The general thrust of the proposed industrial restructuring is as follows:

1. Displace "nonrenewable income" earned from the exploitation of natural resources with "renewable income" that could be obtained by incorporating technological progress into the productive sector

2. Shift priority from the manufacturing sector as a whole to those specific subsectors that contribute to incorporating and disseminating technological progress to the productive sector as a whole

3. Promote insertion into the international economy by enhancing productivity and competitiveness in specific sectors

4. Introduce changes into public institutions and policies with the aim of fostering policies in the private sector that are consonant with the first three steps

5. Create an institutional climate that promotes strategic cooperation between the government, business, and labor sectors.

While industrial development may be promoted in a protected market despite the passivity of public agencies, the strengthening of international competitiveness requires public institutions that display initiative and possess the capacity and dynamism to coordinate the different productive, educational, research, financing, and marketing agents. In the previous phase, attempts were made to promote investment without regard to the international competitiveness of the industry. Today such competitiveness is clearly a central requirement. In addition, the institutional requirements associated with the management of a system of extensive, indiscriminate and permanent protection are obviously fewer and qualitatively different than those associated with a system that is both sectorally and temporarily selective and geared towards promoting technological apprenticeship and international competitiveness.

Industry in the preceding phase had few links with the natural resource sectors and required limited support from the specialized services linked to business management; therefore the need for the continuous upgrading of human resources was rhetorical. In three respects this situation has changed radically. Cooperation between enterprises and with specialized public agencies is now a recognized requirement for survival which presupposes continuous communication and mutual confidence, ingredients that were absent from the previous phase. Inefficiencies in plant, transport, marketing, or communications infrastructure were previously passed on to captive consumers; there is a present awareness of the urgent need to overcome these inefficiencies. In addition, systematically adversarial relations between the business and labor sectors cannot contribute to an increase in productivity or to a solid insertion into the international economy; such relations may be maintained in captive markets but usually result in increased prices, irregular supplies, and a decline in quality. In short, the innovation required by the state in its links to business and labor transcends the short-term and necessarily casuistic context of the privatization of public enterprises.

The insertion of Latin America into the international economy has been based principally on natural resource income and industrial growth has been fueled by income obtained through indiscriminate and prolonged protection. Both sources of growth, which are clearly interrelated, have been dwindling. Industrial restructuring should make it possible to progress towards the only source of income that is renewable, that based on technological innovation in the processing of natural resources, on manufactured goods that are not based on natural resources, and on technology-intensive services.

Clearly, international experience teaches very clearly the lesson of institutional pluralism: the most varied configurations of economic agents are to be observed in market economies. Successes in terms of growth and equity share two common features: the incorporation of technological progress and the enhancement of productivity. Consequently, rigid institutional prescriptions regarding the role of the state, public enterprises, and the private sector are necessarily fragile, but the failure to incorporate technological progress carries very serious consequences. Curiously, in the Latin America of the 1980s one hears frequent recommendations on how countries should organize their institutions while, at the same time, less attention is paid to institutions and policies geared towards promoting the incorporation of technological progress into the productive sector.

Notes

Introduction

1. W. Suzigan, *Industria Brasileira: Origem e Desenvolvimento* (Sao Paulo: Brasiliense, 1986).
2. CEPAL, *Estudio Económico de América Latina,* 1949 (Santiago, 1949); R. Prebisch, *Problemas teóricos y prácticos del crecimiento económico* (Mexico: CEPAL, 1951); A. Gerschenkron, *Economic Backwardness in Historical Perspective* (Cambridge: Harvard University Press, 1965).
3. F. Fajnzylber, *La industrialización trunca* (Mexico: Nueva Imagen, 1983; Buenos Aires: Grupo Latinoamericano, 1985). See also "Democratization, Endogenous Modernization, and Integration: Strategic Choices for Latin America" in *The United States in the 80s,* ed. K. Middlebrook and C. Rico (Pittsburgh: Pittsburgh University Press, 1986).

1. The Empty Box in Latin America

1. World Bank, *World Development Report* 1986 (New York: Oxford University Press, 1987); J. Lecaillon et al., eds., *Income Distribution and Economic Development: An Analytical Survey* (Geneva: ILO, 1984).
2. A. Hirschman, "The Political Economy of Latin American Development: Seven Exercises in Retrospection," presented at the International Congress of the Latin American Studies Association, Boston, October 1986.
3. A. Barros de Castro and E. Peres de Souza, *Economia Brasileira em Marcha Forzada* (Rio de Janeiro: Paz e Terra, 1985).
4. World Bank, *Price Prospects for Major Primary Commodities*, Washington, D.C., 1986.
5. ECLAC, *Preliminary Overview of the Latin American Economy during* 1986, LC/13/G, 1383 (Santiago, 1986); ECLAC/UNDP, *América Latina: Sistema monetario internacional y financiamiento externo* (Santiago, 1986).
6. Understood as biological energy (or commercial energy) required by per capita consumption unit of foodstuff calorie.
7. J. Steihart and C. Steihart, "Energy in the United States Food System," cited by A. Schejtman, "Sistemas Alimentarios y Opciones de Estrategia," *Pensamiento Iberoamericano* 8 (July-Dec. 1985): 53.

8. Ibid.
9. F. Fajnzylber, "The United States and Japan as Models of Industrialization for the Latin American and East Asian NICs," in *Development Strategies in Latin America and East Asia*, ed. G. Gereffi and D. L. Wyman (forthcoming).
10. Joint ECLAC/UNIDO Industry and Technology Division, "Ciencia y tecnología en la OCDE y posición relativa de América Latina," in *Industrialización y Desarrollo Tecnológico*, No. 1 (Santiago, Sept. 1985).
11. "Asian Development Review," *Asian Development Bank* 2, no. 2 (1984): 5–6.
12. Fajnzylber, *La industrialización trunca*.
13. ECLAC, *Multilateralismo y Bilateralismo en la ALADI*, LC/R.564 (Santiago, 1987).
14. UNIDO, *World Industry: A Statistical Review*, UNIDO/15.590 (Vienna, 1985).
15. Barros de Castro and Peres de Souza, *Economia Brasileira*.
16. F. Sagasti and C. Cook, *Tiempos difíciles: Ciencia y tecnología en América Latina durante el decenio de 1980* (Lima: GRADE, 1985).

2. The Black Box of Technical Progress

1. UNIDO, *Industry and Development Global Report 1986* (Vienna, 1987). The diagram of industrial structural change is based on the value added in 1980 constant prices. For each branch an index number for the periods 1975, 1980, and 1987 is calculated from the base year 1970. The index number determines the distance from the origin of the star diagram. For each year the index numbers are connected by a line which reflects the typical "shape" of expansion for the specific country. Since this size is different for each country (absolute values of the index numbers), a different scale is used in each diagram.
2. R. Gordon, "Postwar Macroeconomics: The Evolution of Events and Ideas," in *The American Economy in Transition*, ed. M. Feldstein (Chicago: University of Chicago Press, 1980), 113.
3. N. Rosenberg, "The Impact of Technological Innovation: A Historical View," in *The Positive Sum Strategy*, ed. R. Landau and N. Rosenberg (Washington, D.C.: National Academy Press, 1986), 20.
4. P. Samuelson, *Economics*, 11th ed. (New York: McGraw-Hill, 1980), 693.
5. The linkage between technical progress and economic and social development is one of the notions of structural strength of ECLAC. See CEPAL, *Estudio Económico 1949*, "Concentración del progreso técnico y de sus frutos en el desarrollo latinoamericano"; A. Pinto, "La CEPAL y el problema del progreso técnico," *El Trimestre Económico* (Jan.–Mar. 1965); A. Pinto, "Cinco etapas de mi pensamiento sobre el desarrollo," *El Trimestre Económico* (Apr.–June 1976); R. Prebisch, "Crisis y desarrollo: Presente y futuro de America Latina y el Caribe: Obstaculos requerimientos y opciones," *El Trimestre Economico*, no. 198 (Apr.–JUNE 1983).
6. D. Jorgensen, "Microeconomics and productivity," in *Positive Sum Strategy*, Landau and Rosenberg, 69.
7. The relevance of the sectoral separation has recently been reiterated in several studies included in R. Landau and N. Rosenberg, eds., *The Positive Sum Strategy* (Washington, D.C.: National Academy Press, 1986): M. Boskin, "Macroeconomics, Technology, and Economic Growth: An Introduction to Some Important Issues,"

55; Jorgensen, "Microeconomics and Productivity," 65–67; A. Friedlaender, "Macroeconomics and Microeconomics of Innovation: The Role of the Technological Innovation," 327.

8. M. Piore and C. Sabel, *The Second Industrial Divide: Possibilities for Prosperity* (Washington, D.C.: National Bureau of Economic Research, 1984), chapters 2 and 3.

9. Centre d'Etudes Prospectives et d'Informations Internationales, *Economie mondiale: La montée des tensions: Rapport du CEPII* (Paris, 1983); D. Heath, ed., *America in Perspective* (Boston: Houghton Mifflin, 1986), part 3, chapter 8.

10. J. Zysman and L. Tyson, eds., *American Industry in International Competition: Government Policies and Corporate Strategies* (Ithaca, N.Y., and London: Cornell University Press, 1983).

11. Text of the Economic Declaration published at the end of the Tokyo Summit Conference, May 6, 1986.

12. OECD, *OECD Science and Technology Indicators: Resources Devoted to R&D* (Paris, 1984); E. Denison, *Trends in American Economic Growth* 1929–1982 (Washington, D.C.: Brookings Institute, 1985); Jorgenson, "Microeconomics and Productivity," 77–88; C. Reeder, "The Effect of Recent Macroeconomic Policies on Innovation and Productivity," in *Positive Sum Strategy*, Landau and Rosenberg, 88–91.

13. OECD, *Productivity in Industry: Prospects and Policies* (Paris, 1986).

14. P. Drucker, "The Changed World Economy," *Foreign Affairs* (Spring 1986).

15. S. Cohen and J. Zysman, *Manufacturing Matters: The Myth of the Post-Industrial Economy* (New York: Basic Books, 1987).

16. L. Thurow, "Tomorrow, U.S. in the Back," *International Herald Tribune*, 24 Apr. 1987; R. Dornbusch, "Heading Toward 100 Yen: Why the Dollar Must Fall Another 30%," *New York Times*, 10 May 1987; P. Drucker, "From the World Trade to World Investment," *Wall Street Journal*, 26 May 1987; J. Jeffrey, "Product Liability vs. Competitiveness," *Washington Times*, 20 May 1987; J. Norman, "Can America Compete? Its Options Are a Surge in Productivity or a Lasting Decline," *Business Week*, 27 Apr. 1987; M. Elliot, "U.S. Manufacturers Should Try Making Good-Looking Products," *Washington Post* (National Weekly Edition), 12 Mar. 1987; R. Samuelson, "Glimmers on Manufacturing Revival," *Washington Post*, 12 Nov. 1986; H. Rowen, "Remedial Acts Urged to Cut Trade Deficit," *Washington Post*, 14 Nov. 1986; R. Ellsworth, "U.S. Business Should Take On More Debt," *Wall Street Journal*, 1 Dec. 1986; R. Samuelson, "U.S. Steel Industry's Grand Illusions," *Washington Post*, 29 Oct. 1986; J. Baler, "Competitiveness Vital to Banking," *Journal of Commerce*, 24 Feb. 1987; E. Goodman, "The Craze to Be Competitive," *Washington Post*, 10 Jan. 1987; S. Chira, "Soaring Yen Stirs Concern," *New York Times*, 19 Jan. 1987; J. Markham, "Bonn Uneasy On Exports" and "Japan and Germany Fear Falling Dollar," *New York Times*, 19 Jan. 1987; K. Gilpin, "What the Dollar Falls Means," in *New York Times*, 15 Jan. 1987; H. Rowen, "Why the Dollar Declines But the Trade Deficit Doesn't," *Washington Post*, 23 Nov. 1986; O. Kenicho, "Rising Yen But No Falling Trade Gap," *Wall Street Journal*, 1 July 1986; A. Meltzer, "How to Reduce the Trade Deficit," *Journal of Commerce*, 6 Mar. 1987; R. Hershey, Jr., "When Business Asks the Government to Meddle," *New York Times*, 5 Mar. 1987; S. Richman, "Trade Deficit or Delusion?," *Washington Times*, 3 Mar. 1987; D. Sease, "Japanese Firms Export U.S.-Made Goods," *Wall Street Journal*, 3 Mar. 1987; H. Stein, "Leave the Trade Deficit Alone," *Wall Street Journal*, 11 Mar. 1987.

17. OECD, *Politique de l'Innovation: Tendences et perspectives (Paris,* 1982).
18. It is worth mentioning that despite the great variety of national situations concerning the origin and use of the debt, institutional modalities, its negotiation, economic role, international insertion, and even political regime, the countries of the region have converged in the decision of transferring abroad a net amount of resources during the period 1982–1986, since there are only previous histories linked to military defeats (France 1872–1875 and Germany 1925–1932). See R. Devlin, "Socioeconomic restructuring in Latin America in the Face of Foreign Debt and a Transfer Problem," ECLAC draft, February 1987.

3. The Analytical Framework: From Black Box to Empty Box

1. R. D. Tallison, "Rent Seeking: A Survey," *Kyksos* 35 (1982).
2. Gerschenkron, *Economic Backwardness.*
3. B. Johnston and P. Kilby, *Agriculture & Structural Transformation: Economic Strategies in Late-Developing Countries* (New York: Oxford University Press, 1979), 34–75 and 182–298; Y. Hayami and V. Ruttan, *Agricultural Development: An International Perspective* (Baltimore: Johns Hopkins University Press, 1985), 11–41; B. Moore, *Social Origins of Dictatorship and Democracy* (Boston: Beacon Press, 1970).
4. Hayami and Ruttan, *Agricultural Development,* 358–62; UN Dept. of Economic Affairs, *Land Reform: Defects in Agrarian Structures as Obstacles to Economic Development* (New York, 1951); Lecaillon et al., *Income Distribution and Economic Development,* 53–74.
5. Hayami and Ruttan, *Agricultural Development,* 396.
6. See chapter 6.
7. Hypothesis suggested by J. Casar and J. Ross, from ILET, Mexico.
8. Gerschenkron, *Economic Backwardness.*
9. See the introduction to chapter 4.
10. This is also the case of countries which have resources other than natural resources, for instance, the "rent" coming from the international leadership at political, economic, and military levels, an issue which will be discussed in the next chapter.
11. Gerschenkron, *Economic Backwardness;* Johnston and Kilby, *Agriculture and Structural Transformation,* 34–75 and 182–298; Hayami and Ruttan, *Agricultural Development,* 11–41.
12. J. Medina, *Aspectos sociales del desarrollo económico en América Latina,* SS.65/V.13a/s (Paris: UNESCO, 1963).
13. Hayami and Ruttan, *Agricultural Development,* 398.
14. Schejtman, "Sistema Alimentario," 37–40.
15. FAO, "El minifundio en América Latina," Round Table on Small Scale Agriculture and VI Interagency Consultation on Follow-up of the World Conference on Agrarian Reform and Rural Development, Santiago, 22–29 April 1987, 15.
16. Gerschenkron, *Economic Backwardness;* Johnston and Kilby, *Agriculture and Structural Transformation,* 34–75 and 182–298; Hayami and Ruttan, *Agricultural Development,* 11–41.
17. FAO, "El minifundio," 15.
18. Ibid.

19. Hirschman, "Political Economy."
20. Schejtman, "Sistema Alimentario," 37–40.
21. A. Schejtman, "Proyecto de investigación articulación agricultura-industria," mimeo, División Agrícola Conjunta (Santiago: CEPAL/FAO, 1986), 2.
22. ECLAC, *El desarrollo de América Latina y el Caribe: Escollos, requisitos y opciones*, LC/G 1440 Conf. 79/3 (Santiago, 1986), 66.
23. T. Mizoguchi, "Economic Development Policy and Income Distribution: The Experience in East and Southeast Asia," *The Developing Economies* 23, no. 4 (Dec. 1985). See also A. Pinto and A. Di Filippo, "Desarrollo y pobreza en la América Latina: Un enfoque histórico estructural," *El Trimestre Económico*, no. 183 (July-Sept. 1979); M. Selowsky, "Distribución del ingreso, necesidades básicas y trade-offs con crecimiento: El caso de los países latinoamericanos semiindustrializados," *Cuadernos de Economía*, no. 56 (Apr. 1982): 37–68; R. Cortázar, "Desempleo, pobreza y distribución: Chile 1970–1981," in *Apuntes CIEPLAN*, no. 84, (Santiago: cieplan, 1982); O. Altimir, "Extent of Poverty in Latin America," World Bank Staff Working Paper No. 522, Washington, D.C., IBRD, 1982; S. Trejo, "Distribución del ingreso, empleo y precios relativos," *Comercio Exterior* 32, no. 10 (Oct. 1982); J. Wells and A. Drobny, "Distribuição da renda e o salario minimo no Brasil: Uma revisão critica da literatura existente," *Pesquisa e Planejamento Econômico* 12, no. 3 (Dec. 1982): 893–914; O. Altimir and S. Piñera, "Análisis de descomposición de las desigualdades de ingreso en la América Latina," *El Trimestre Económico* 49, no. 196, (Oct.-Dec. 1982): 813–60; M. Syrquin and S. Teitel, eds., *Trade, Stability, Technology, and Equity in Latin America* (New York: Academic Press, 1982); R. Bonelli and P. Cunha, "Distribução de renda e padroes de crescimento: Um modelo dinamico da economia brasileira," *Pesquisa e Planejamento Econômico* 13, no. 1 (Apr. 1983): 91–154; W. Leontief, "Technological Advance, Economic Growth, and the Distribution of Income," *Population and Development Review* 9, no. 3 (Sept. 1983): 403–10; R. Prebisch, "Desigualdad y acumulación de capital en el capitalismo periférico," lecture, La Jolla, Nov. 1984. A. Di Filippo. "Uso social del excedente, acumulación, distribución y empleo," *Revista de la CEPAL*, no. 24 (Dec. 1984): 117–35; R. Rati, "Role of Real Income Level and Income Distribution in Fulfillment of Basic Needs," *World Development* 13, no. 5 (May 1985): 539–95; UN, Office of Statistics, *National Accounts Statistics: Compendium of Income Distribution Statistics* (New York, 1985); O. Altimir, "Estimaciones de la distribución del ingreso en la Argentina, 1953–1980," *Desarrollo Económico* 25, no. 100 (Jan.-Mar. 1986): 521–66; J. Ramos, *Capital Inmobility and the Distribution of Income* (South Bend, Ind.: University of Notre Dame Press, 1986); ECLAC, Statistics and Quantitative Analysis Division, *Antecedentes estadísticos de la distribución del ingreso: Brasil 1960–1983* (Santiago, 1986); G. Papanek and O. Kyn, "Effect on Income Distribution of Development, the Growth Rate, and Economic Strategy," *Journal of Development Economics* 23, no. 1 (Sept. 1986): 55–56.
24. Schejtman, "Proyecto de investigacion."
25. Hirschman, "Political Economy"; Barros de Castro and Peres de Souza, *Economia Brasileira*; Fajnzylber, "United States and Japan; ECLAC / UNIDO, "Ciencia y tecnologiá,
26. OECD, *OECD Science and Technology Indicators*; Fajnzylber, *La industrialización trunca.*
27. E. Faletto, *Burocracia y Estado en América Latina* (Santiago: FLACSO, 1981).

28. "A Report by the World Resources Institute and the International Institute for Environment and Development, *1986," in World Resources 1986: An Assessment of the Resource Base That Supports the Global Econmy* (New York: Basic Books, 1987); L. Brown et al., *State of the World 1986: A Worldwatch Institute Report on Progress Toward a Sustainable Society* (New York: Norton, 1986); S. Ciriacy-Wantrup, *Conservación de los recursos: Economía y politica* (Mexico: Fondo de Cultura Económica, 1957; N. Gligo, "El manejo integrado de recursos naturales agrícolas: un desafío ambiental en América Latina," in *Revista SIAP*, 86–109; O. Sunkel and N. Gligo, *Estilos de desarrollo y medio ambiente en América Latina* (Mexico: Fondo de Cultura Económica, 1983).

29. Despite the fact that this issue was emphasized in the sixties, it has been covered only systematically since the early eighties. Brazil is, perhaps, the case in which attention has mainly focused. See F. Cardoso and E. Faletto, "Dependencia e Desenvolvimento na America Latina" (hypothesis for a sociological interpretation, Santiago, ILPES, 1965); L. Martins, *Industrialização, burguesia nacional e desenvolvimento* (Rio de Janeiro: Saga, 1968); F. Cardoso, *Hegemonia burguesa e independencia econômica: Raizes estruturais da crise politica Brasileira* (Rio de Janeiro: Paz e Terra, 1977); idem., *Empresario industrial e desenvolvimento economico* (Sao Paulo: Difusao Europeia do Livro, 1964); idem., *Ideologias de la burguesia industrial en sociedades dependientes (/Argentina y Brazil)* (Mexico: Siglo Veintiuno, 1971); L. C. Bresser Pereira, *Estado de subdesenvolvimento industrializado* (Sao Paulo: Brasiliense, 1977); idem., "Notas introdutorias ao modo tecnoburocratico ou estatal de produção," *Estudios CEBRAP*, no. 20 (Apr.-June 1977); idem., "Seis interpretacoes sobre o Brasil: Bourgeoisie brésilienne en Question," *Amérique Latine*, no. 5 (Spring 1981); P. Evans, *Dependent Development: The Alliance of Multinational, State, and Local Capital in Brazil* (Princeton, N.J.: Princeton University Press, 1979); R. Newfarmer and W. Mueller, "Multinational Corporations in Brazil and Mexico: Structured Sources of Economic and Non-economic Power," in *Modernização autoritaria: O empresariado e a intervenção do estado na economia* (Brasilia, 1986). For other countries, see L. Gomez Izquierdo and Karl-Heinz Stanzick, eds., *Contribución del empresario nacional al desarrollo socioeconómico de América Latina* (San José: ILDIS, 1974); O. Muñóz, "Industrialización y Grupos de Interés," in *Apuntes CIEPLAN*, no. 7 (Santiago: CIEPLAN); N. Leff, "Industrial Organization and Entrepreneurship in the Developing Countries: The Economic Groups," *Economic Development and Cultural Change* 26, no. 4 (July 1987): 661–75; N. Leff, "Entrepreneurship and Economic Development: The Problem Revisited," *Journal of Economic Literature* 17, no. 1 (Mar. 1979); G. Grossman, "International Trade, Foreign Investment, and the Formation of the Entrepreneurial Class," *American Economic Review* 47, no. 4 (Sept. 1984): 605–14; O. Muñóz, "Papel de los empresarios en el desarrollo: Enfoques, problemas y experiencias," *Colección Estudios CIEPLAN*, no. 20 (Dec. 1986): 95–120; P. Ramos, "Empresarios en el poder: La nueva política económica de Bolivia," *Nueva Sociedad*, no. 88 (Mar.-Apr. 1987): 178–91; A. Touraine, *Actores sociales y sistemas políticos en América Latina* (Santiago: PREALC/OIT 1987); I. Medina Echavarria and B. Higgins, eds., *Aspectos sociales del desarrollo económico de América Latina* (Paris: UNESCO, 1963).

30. R. Ffrench-Davis, "Intercambio y Desarrollo," *El Trimestre Económico*, no. 38 (1981); R. Ffrench-Davis, *Economía internacional, teorías y políticas para el desarrollo* (Mex-

ico: Fondo de Cultura Económica, 1979); F. Fajnzylber, *Industrialización e internacionalización en América Latina* (Mexico, Fondo de Cultura Económica, 1981); UN Center for Transnational Corporations, *Caracteristicas y tendencias destacadas de las inversiones extranjeras directas* (New York, 1983); idem., *Empresas transnacionales en el desarrollo mundial, tercer estudio* (New York, 1983); R. Ffrench-Davis, "Estrategia de apertura externa selectiva," in CIEPLAN, *Reconstrucción económica para la democracia* (Santiago: Aconcagua, 1983); C. Kindleberger, *Multinational Corporations in the* 1980s (Cambridge, Mass.: MIT Press, 1983); Group of Thirty, *Foreign Direct Investment 1973–1987: A Survey of International Companies* (New York: The Group, 1984); G. Grossman, "International Trade, Foreign Investment, and the Formation of the Entrepreneurial Class," in *American Economic Review* 47, no. 4 (Sept. 1984): 605–14; R. Wade and G. White, "Development States in East Asia: Capitalist and Socialist," *Bulletin-IDS* 15, no. 2 (Apr. 1984); C. Oman, *New Forms of International Investment in Developing Countries* (Paris: OECD, 1984); J. Sourrouille, F. Gatto, and B. Kosacoff, *Inversiones extranjeras en América Latina: Política económica, decisiones de inversión y comportamiento económico de las filiales* (Buenos Aires, 1984); C. Correa, "Características y tendencias de la regulación de las inversiones extranjeras en América Latina y el Caribe," *Integración Latinoamericana* 9, no. 97 (Dec. 1984): 20–31; K. Yojima and T. Ozawa, "Micro and Macro-economic Models of Direct Foreign Investment: Toward a Synthesis," *Hitosubashi Journal of Economics* 25, no. 1 (June 1984): 1–20; D. Goldsborough, "Finance Direct Investment in Developing Countries: Trends, Policy Issues, and Prospects," *Finance and Development* 22, no. 1 (Mar. 1984); E. Lahera, "Empresas transnacionales y el comercio internacional de América Latina," *Revista de la CEPAL*, no. 25 (Apr. 1985): 45–65; S. Bitar, "Inversión norteamericana en el Grupo Andino," *El Trimestre Económico* 52, no. 206 (Apr.–June 1985): 313–26; F. Schneider and B. Frey, "Economic and Political Determinants of Foreign Direct Investment," *World Development* 13, no. 2 (Feb. 1985): 161–75; OECD, *International Investment and Multinational Enterprises: National Treatment for Foreign-Controlled Enterprises* (Paris, 1985); J. Rothgeb, "Contribution of Foreign Investment to Growth in Third World States," *Studies in comparative international development* 19, no. 4 (Winter 1985): 3–37; UN Center for Transnational Corporations, *Trends and Issues in Foreign Direct Investment and Related Flows: A Technical Paper* (New York, 1985); R. Newfarmer, ed., *Profits, Progress and Progress: Case Studies of International Industries in Latin America* (South Bend, Ind.: University of Notre Dame Press, 1985); R. Vernon, *Exploring the Global Economy: Emerging Issues in Trade and Investment* (Cambridge, Mass.: Harvard University Center for International Affairs, 1985; Lanham, Md.: University Press of America, 1985); Joint ECLAC/CET on Transnationals, *Banco de datos sobre inversión extranjera directa en América Latina y el Caribe* (Santiago, 1986); R. Ffrench-Davis and R. Feinberg, eds., *Más allá de la crisis de la deuda: Bases para un nuevo enfoque* (Santiago: CIEPLAN-Diálogo Interamericano, 1986).

31. Ffrench-Davis and Feinberg, *La crisis de la deuda*; A. Foxley, *El problema de la deuda externa visto desde América Latina* (Santiago: CIEPLAN-Diálogo Interamericano, 1985); C. Massad, *External Financing in Latin America: Developments, Problems, and Options* (Washington, D.C.: Woodrow Wilson International Center for Scholars, 1984); C. Massad, ed., "The Debt Problem: Acute and Chronic Aspects,"

Journal of Development Planning, no. 16 (1985); R. Devlin, "Socioeconomic Restructuring in Latin America in the Face of Foreign Debt and a Transfer Problem," ECLAC Draft, Feb. 1987.

32. R. Prebisch, *Un aporte al estudio de su pensamiento: Las cinco etapas de su pensamiento sobre el desarrollo* (Santiago: ECLAC, 1987).

4. The United States, Japan, and West Germany: Winners of Losers?

1. W. Branson and P. Peterseon, "Trends in United States International Trade and Investment since World War II," in *The American Economy in Transition*, ed. Martin Feldstein (Chicago: University of Chicago Press, 1980), 183–274; G. Lodge, *The New American Ideology* (New York: New York University Press, 1986); Zysman and Tyson, *American Industry in International Competition*; Heath, *America in Perspective*; G. Lodge and E. Vogel, eds., *Ideology and National Competitiveness: An Analysis of Nine Countries* (Boston: Harvard Business School Press, 1987).

2. For a debate on impact under competitiveness as well as on the notion and its measurement, see F. Quesnais, "Science, Technology and Competitiveness," in *STI Review*, no. 1 (Autumn 1986): 85; President's Commission on Industrial Competitiveness, *Global Competition: The New Reality*, Vols. 1 and 2 (Washington, D.C.: U.S. Government Printing Office, 1985); S. Cohen et al., "Competitiveness," Berkeley Round Table on International Economy (BRIE), working document, Berkeley, California, November 1984; G. Lodge, "Introduction: Ideology and Country Analysis," in Lodge and Vogel, *Ideology and National Competitiveness*, 1–28; G. Lodge, "The United States: The Costs of Ambivalence," in Lodge and Vogel, *Ideology and National Competitiveness*, 103–39; B. Hannay, "Technology and Trade: A Study of U.S. Competitiveness in Seven Industries," in Landau and Rosenberg, *Positive Sum Strategy*, 479–99; J. Young, "Global Competition—The New Reality: Results of the President's Commission on Industrial Competitiveness," in Landau and Rosenberg, *Positive Sum Strategy*, 501–9; G. Eads, "Dangers in U.S. Efforts to Promote International Competitiveness," in Zysman and Tyson, *American Industry in International Competition*.

3. E. Vogel, "Japan: Adaptative Communitarianism," in Lodge and Vogel, *Ideology and National Competitiveness*, 147–72; J. Zysman, *Governments, Markets, and Growth: Financial Systems and the Politics of Industrial Change* (Ithaca, N.Y.: Cornell University Press, 1983), 233–84. See also three articles in Landau and Rosenberg, *Positive Sum Strategy*: O. Okimoto, "The Japanese Challenge in High Technology," 541; A. Masahiko, "The Macroeconomic Background for High-Tech," 569; R. Landau and G. Hatsopoulos, "Capital Formation in the United States and Japan," 583.

4. OECD, *OECD Science and Technology Indicators*; R. Landau and N. Rosenberg, "Macroeconomics, Technology, and Economic Growth: An Introduction to Some Microeconomics of Innovation," in *Positive Sum Strategy*, 327–32.

5. Ships, sewing machines, and boilers, items which in 1977 were 49 percent, 33 per-

cent, and 31 percent of the world offer of Japanese exports. See Fajnzylber, *La industrialización trunca*, 52–53.

6. Apart from the publications mentioned in note 2, see Piore and Sabel, *Second Industrial Divide*; Cohen and Zysman, *Manufacturing Matters*, 79–202; Heath, *America in Perspective*, 204.

7. W. Finan, P. Quick, and K. Sandberg, *The U.S. Trade Position in High Technology: 1980–1986*, Report prepared for the Joint Economic Committee of the U.S. Congress (Washington, Oct. 1986).

8. A. Malabre Jr., *Beyond Our Means* (New York: Random House, 1987); "Excerpts from Final Draft of Bishop's Letter on the Economy," *New York Times*, 14 Nov. 1986; P. Kennedy, "A Historian of Imperial Decline Looks at America," *The Guardian*, 14 Nov. 1982; L. Silk, "A Dependence on Foreigners," *New York Times*, 6 May 1987; P. Magnusson, "As U.S. Loses Grip on World Markets Jobs, Standard of Living Are at Stake," *Journal of Commerce*, 27 Apr. 1987; L. Silk, "Reconstructing World System," *New York Times*, 8 May 1987.

9. Piore and Sabel, *Second Industrial Divide*, 19, 73.

10. U.S. Department of Commerce, *U.S. Industrial Outlook 1986* (Washington, D.C., 1986), chapter 36.

11. Thomas K. McGraw, ed., *America Versus Japan: A Comparative Study* (Cambridge, Mass.: Harvard Business School Press, 1986), 195.

12. Zysman, *Governments, Markets and Growth*, 251; Piore and Sabel, *Second Industrial Divide*, 142–51 and 229–34; C. Allen, "Germany: Competing Communitarianis," in Lodge and Vogel, *Ideology and National Competitiveness*.

13. McGraw, *America Versus Japan*; Piore and Sabel, *Second Industrial Divide*, 41–48 and 240–50 (U.S.), and 152–56 and 226–29 (Japan); Malabre, *Beyond Our Means*.

14. Lee Iacocca's autobiography shows an anecdotic perspective of the priority of marketing in relation to production.

15. For a strict analysis of methodological problems linked to the measurement of income distribution in the United States, see A. Blinder, I. Kristol, and W. Cohen, "The Level and Distribution of Economic Well-Being," in Feldstein, *The American Economy in Transition*, 415.

16. McGraw, *America Versus Japan*, 14.

17. Ibid., 311.

18. Ibid., 20; T. Mizoguchi, "Economic Development Policy and Income Distribution: The Experience in East and Southeast Asia," *The Developing Economies* 23, no. 4 (Dec. 1985).

19. Lodge and Vogel, *Ideology and National Competitiveness*; McGraw, *America Versus Japan*, 311.

20. Zysman, *Governments, Markets, and Growth*.

21. McGraw, *America Versus Japan*, 324.

22. Attention has been centered on these two issues because of their relevance for designing industrial strategies. The most complete, recent, and clear expression can be found in Landau and Rosenberg, *Positive Sum Strategy*. For a critical comment, see L. Thurow, "Comment on The Positive Sum Strategy," *Scientific American* 225 (1986).

23. L. Tyson, "Creating Advantage: An Industrial Policy Perspective," Economics Department Round Table on International Economy, University of California, Berkeley,

October 1986; R. J. Alexander, "Is the United States Substituting a Speculative Economy for a Productive One?," *Journal of Economic Issues* 20, no. 2 (June 1986); R. Brinkman, "The Genesis of a New Industrial Policy: Equity and Efficiency," *Journal of Economic Issues* 20, no. 2 (June 1986); R. D. Norton, "Industrial Policy and American Renewal," *Journal of Economic Literature* 24 (Mar. 1986): 1–40; S. Cohen and J. Zysman, "The Myth of a Post-Industrial Economy," *Technology Review* (Feb.-Mar. 1987); R. Reich, *The Next American Frontier: A Provocative Programme for Economic Renewal* (New York: Times Books, 1983); B. Scott, "National Strategy for Stronger U.S. Competitiveness," *Harvard Business Review*, no. 62 (1984): 77–91; Thurow, "Comment."

24. U.S. Government, *Economic Report to the President 1984* (Washington, D.C.: U.S. Government Printing Office, 1984).

25. D. Bell, "Communications Technology—For Better or For Worse," *Harvard University Review*, no. 57 (1979): 20–45; D. Birch, "Who Creates Jobs?," *The Public Interest*, no. 65 (1981): 14–35; B. Bartlett, "Is U.S. Industry Collapsing All Around Us?," *Wall Street Journal*, 8 May 1987.

26. J. Badarocco and D. Yoffie, "Industrial Policy: It Cannot Happen Here," *Harvard Business Review*, no. 61 (1983): 96–105.

27. Cohen and Zysman, *Manufacturing Matters*, part 1.

28. R. Reich, *The Next American Frontier*.

29. Information on the rentability recovery on developed countries can be found in *OECD Economic Outlook* (June 1985): 35–49.

30. Annual working hours per capita were estimated at 140,000 at the beginning of this century, but it is probable that they have diminished to 72,000 hours per year. See S. Tsuru, "Marche's technologies: Nouvelles relations internationales," in *Economica* (Paris: CEPII, 1983), 101.

31. "Print Culture and Video Culture," *Daedalus* (Autumn 1982).

32. OECD, *Industry in Transition: Experience of the 70s and Prospects for the 80s* (Paris 1983), 25.

33. Cohen and Zysman, *Manufacturing Matters*, 28–48.

34. T. Stanbaek et al., *The Service Economy: Conservation of Human Resources* (New York: Columbia University Press, Series 20, 1982), 40.

35. R. Reich, *The Next American Frontier*, chapter 10; U.S. Department of Commerce, *U.S. Industrial Outlook 1985* and *U.S. Industrial Outlook 1986* (Washington, D.C.: U.S. Government Printing Office, 1985, 1986).

36. Stanbaek, *Service Economy*.

37. U.S. Department of Commerce, *U.S. Industrial Outlook 1986* (Washington, 1986).

38. P. Drucker, "Our Entrepreneurial Economy," *Harvard Business Review* (Jan.-Feb. 1984): 62–64; R. Egdhal, "Should We Shrink the Health-Care System?," *Harvard Business Review* (Jan.-Feb. 1984).

39. U.S. Department of Commerce, *U.S. Industrial Outlook 1985* (Washington, D.C., 1985), n. 37, table 1.

40. Jorgensen, "Microeconomics and Productivity," 57, table 3.

41. Thurow, "Comment."

42. R. Landau and N. Rosenberg, "Editors Overview," in Landau and Rosenberg, *Positive Sum Strategy*, 1–16.

43. H. Brooks, "National Science Policy and Technological Innovation," in Landau and Rosenberg, *Positive Sum Strategy*, 119–67.
44. M. Green and J. Berry, "Takeovers: A Symptom of 'Corporacy,'" *New York Times*, 3 Dec. 1986; H. Rowen, "Darman Hits 'Corporacy' in U.S. Again," *Washington Post*, 25 Nov. 1986; P. Blustein, "Top Treasury Aide's Criticism of Firms May Trigger Debate on U.S. Productivity," *Wall Street Journal*, 10 Nov. 1986; S. Auerbach, "Baldridge Joins Attack on U.S. Firms," *Washington Post*, 13 Nov. 1986; M. Sesit, "Paul Volcker Says Business Must Do More to Compete," *Wall Street Journal*, 17 Nov. 1986; Thurow, "Comment."

5. Western Europe and the Nordic Countries: Contrasts and Similarities

1. T. Barker and V. Brailovsky, eds., "Oil or Industry," in *Academic Press Geology Series: Mineral Depletion and Global Tectonic Settings*, 191; A. Singh, "U.K. Industry and the World Economy: A Case of De-industrialization?," *Cambridge Journal of Economics* 1 (1977): 113–36; idem., "North Sea Oil and the Reconstruction of U.K. Industry," in Frank Blackaby, ed., *De-industrialisation* (London: Heinemann, 1979), 202–24; T. Barker, "Depletion Policy and the De-industrialisation of the U.K. Economy," *Energy Economics* 3 (1981): 71–82.
2. OECD, *Economic Survey* (Paris), different publications. France, July 1985; Italy, July 1986; United Kingdom, Jan. 1986; Sweden, May 1985; Denmark, Feb. 1986; Finland, June 1986; Norway, Jan. 1985.
3. World Bank, *World Development Report* 1987, 83.
4. World Bank, *World Development Report* 1988, 51; R. Hemming and A. Mansoor, "Is Privatization the Answer?," *Finance and Development* (Sept. 1988).
5. OECD, *Economic Survey: France* (Paris, July 1985).
6. Zysman, *Governments, Markets, and Growth*, 233–84; Piore and Savel, *Second Industrial Divide*, 142–51 and 229–334; Allen, "Germany: Competing Communitarianisms," 79–102; C. Herzog, "L'Allemagne entre son excédent industriel et son déficit d'invisibles," *Economie Prospective Internationale*, no. 23 (Sept.-Dec. 1985): 87–95.
7. World Bank, *World Bank Development Report* 1987.
8. Barker and Brailovsky, *Academic Press Geology Series*; Singh, "U.K. Industry and the World Economy"; idem., "North Sea Oil"; Barker, "Depletion Policy."
9. See chapter 4.
10. Barker and Brailovsky, *Academic Press Geology Series*; Singh, "U.K. Industry and the World Economy"; idem., "North Sea Oil"; Barker, "Depletion Policy."
11. Emmerij, *Development Policies*.
12. P. Katzenstein, *Small States in World Markets: Industrial Policy in Europe* (Ithaca, N.Y.: Cornell University Press, 1985); G. Garrett and P. Lange, "Performance in a Hostile World: Economic Growth in Capitalist Democracies 1974–1980," *World Politics* 38, no. 4 (July 1986): 517–45.
13. Barker and Brailovsky, *Academic Press Geology Series*; Singh, "U.K. Industry and the World Economy"; idem., "North Sea Oil"; Barker, "Depletion Policy."

14. Zysman, *Governments, Markets, and Growth*, 11–98; G. Therborn, *Why Some Peoples Are More Unemployed Than Others: The Strange Paradox of Growth and Unemployment* (London: Verso, 1986); Katzenstein, *Small States in World Markets*.

15. SIPRI, *World armaments and disarmament, Yearbook* 1985 (Stockholm: Almquist and Wiksell; New York: Humanities Press, 1985); UN, *Reducción de los presupuestos militares: Elaboración de índices de precios y paridades de poder adquisitivo para la comparación de gastos militares*, UN Document A/CONF.130/PC/INF/4, *Relación entre desarme y desarrollo*, Series no. 15 (New York, 1–11 Apr. 1986); O. Palme et al., "Military Spending: The Economic and Social Consequences," *Challenge* (Sept.-Oct. 1982); L. Klein, "Disarmament and Socioeconomic Development," *Disarmament* 9, no. 1 (Spring 1986); P. Lewis, "Military Spending Questioned," *New York Times*, 11 Nov. 1986; A. Varas, "Economic Impact of Military Spending," *Disarmament* 9, no. 13 (Autumn 1986).

6. Latin America Versus the Growth-with-Equity Industrializing Countries

1. R. Dore, "Reflection on Culture and Social Change in Latin America and East Asia," and G. Gereffi, "Development Strategies in Latin America and East Asia: Toward an Explanatory Framework," both in G. Gereffi and D. Wyman, eds., *Development Strategies in Latin America and East Asia* (forthcoming).

2. Countries under consideration are those for which the World Bank gives information on growth and income distribution. The GNP and the population of that group reaches 80 percent of the total of developing countries (Latin American countries excluded). Taiwan accomplished both aims, but it is not included in the World Bank figures. China—for which the World Bank gives no information on income distribution—is included because (as indicated in other sources) distribution would be at least more favorable than that of India. See, L. Emmerij, ed., *Development Policies and the Crisis of the 1980s* (Paris: OECD, 1987), part 4.

3. World Bank, *World Development Report* 1987, 83.

4. World Bank, *World Development Report* 1988, 51; Hemming and Mansoor, "Is Privatization the Answer?"

5. The hypothesis that the two samples are similar has been rejected for almost all variables with a probability higher than 95 percent, with the exclusion of the difference in the export coefficient (the lower limit is 75 percent). For agriculture share in GDP and GDP per capita the two samples are similar (T Test). See R. Steel and J. Torrie, *Principles and Procedures of Statistics*, 2nd. ed. (New York: McGraw-Hill, 1980).

6. Countries selected and criteria used are based on OECD's current works. Philippines has been added to include all countries in ASEAN.

7. J. Braña, M. Buesa, and J. Molero, *El estado y el cambio tecnológico en la industrialización tardía: Un análisis del caso español* (Mexico: Fondo de Cultura Económica, 1984); J. M. Isac, *Estrategias de desarrollo tecnológico: El caso de España*, Ministry of Industry and Energy Seminar on Technological Policies and Industrial Restructuring, Banco de la Provincia de Buenos Aires, World Bank, July 1986; Joint

ECLAC/UNIDO Industry and Technology Division, "Nota sobre el proceso de reconversión industrial en España," in *Industrialización y Desarrollo Tecnológico*, no. 3 (Santiago, 1986).
8. V. Tokman, "Monetarismo global y destrucción industrial," *Revista de la CEPAL*, no. 23 (1984).
9. A. Hirschman, "Political Economy."

Index

Agrarian structure, transformation of, 56–57, 63, 70–71, 74–75, 79
American life-style, 15, 77, 129–30
Austerity, 109, 139
Automotive system, 124–26

Black box, 5, 41, 154, 155, 183

Capital goods, 96–100
Communications, 122; system, 124–26
Competitiveness, 139; industrial, 128–56; international, 12–15, 45–46, 49–53, 62–64, 68, 79, 95, 109, 112
Conglomerates, 17, 52
Consumption: cosmic, 68–69, 74–87; pattern, 56–62, 77, 106, 113; problem, 53, 61
Corporations: national private, 18; state, 18; transnational, 18, 66. *See also* Conglomerates; Enterprises

Daily intake 14, 107. *See also* Diet
Defense: expenditure, 152; spending, 151
Degree of specialization, 98–99, 137
Development: levels, 183; pattern, 4, 156, 165; process, 4; strategies, 164

Diet, 13, 23
Dynamic sector, 30
Dynamism, 1, 15, 110, 139, 147; criterion for, 1; dividing line for, 1; erosion of, 29, 45. *See also* Growth; Growth rate

Economic levels, macroeconomic contrast of, 42
Empty box, 1, 3, 44, 154–55, 156, 182. *See also* Growth-with-equity box
Endogenous nucleus of technological dynamization (ENTD), 21
Engineering products, 35, 40, 93–99; commerce in, 151; export/import ratio of, 96, 100, 148; specialization of, 137–39, 143, 171. *See also* Industrial specialization
Enterprises, 10, 67
Entrepreneurial agents, 81
Entrepreneurial base, 57, 66–67, 77
Entrepreneurial capacity, 67–74
Entrepreneurial class, 17, 56–57, 66–67
Entrepreneurial function, 5, 16
Equity, 1, 15, 54, 64, 139; dividing line for, 1
Export coefficient, 10, 68
Export promotion policies, 9
Exports of manufactures, 87, 93, 164. *See also* Manufactured exports

Fernando Fajnzylber, a Chilean national, is a senior
United Nations expert on industrial development, a
university professor, an adviser to various Latin American governments, and the author of various books on
the subject.

Library of Congress Cataloging-in-Publication Data

Fajnzylber, Fernando.
  Unavoidable industrial restructuring in Latin America / Fernando Fajnzylber.
    p. cm.
  Includes bibliographical references and index.
  ISBN (invalid) 0–8223–1055–5. — ISBN 0–8223–1095–3 (pbk.)
    1. Latin America—Industries. 2. Industry and state—Latin
America. 3. Latin America—Economic policy. 4. Europe—Industries.
5. Industrialization. I. Title.
HC 125.F343 1991
338.98—dc20   90–36418
                                                              CIP